D0833148

How to Survive and Prosper After a Financial Misfortune:

A Complete Guide to Your Legal Rights After Bankruptcy, Foreclosure, Repossession, and Eviction

Presented By:

With F...

HOW TO SURVIVE AND PROSPER AFTER A FINANCIAL MISFORTUNE:
A COMPLETE GUIDE TO YOUR LEGAL RIGHTS AFTER BANKRUPTCY,
FORECLOSURE, REPOSSESSION, AND EVICTION

Copyright © 2011 Atlantic Publishing Group, Inc.
1405 SW 6th Avenue • Ocala, Florida 34471 • Phone 800-814-1132 • Fax 352-622-1875
Web site: www.atlantic-pub.com • E-mail: sales@atlantic-pub.com
SAN Number: 268-1250

Library of Congress Cataloging-in-Publication Data

Carr, Tracy Alexandra.
 How to survive and prosper after a financial misfortune : a complete guide to your legal rights
after bankruptcy, foreclosure, repossession, and eviction / by Tracy Alexandra Carr.
   p. cm.
Includes bibliographical references and index.
ISBN-13: 978-1-60138-298-6 (alk. paper)
ISBN-10: 1-60138-298-7 (alk. paper)
1. Bankruptcy--United States--Popular works. 2. Finance, Personal--United States. I. Title.
KF1524.85.M38 2008
346.7307'8--dc22
                         2008038687

PROJECT MANAGER: Nicole Orr • PEER REVIEWER: Marilee Griffin
INTERIOR DESIGN: Samantha Martin
COVER DESIGN: Jackie Miller • millerjackiej@gmail.com

Printed on Recycled Paper

Printed in the United States

We recently lost our beloved pet "Bear," who was not only our best and dearest friend but also the "Vice President of Sunshine" here at Atlantic Publishing. He did not receive a salary but worked tirelessly 24 hours a day to please his parents. Bear was a rescue dog that turned around and showered myself, my wife, Sherri, his grandparents  Jean, Bob, and Nancy, and every person and animal he met (maybe not rabbits) with friendship and love. He made a lot of people smile every day.

We wanted you to know that a portion of the profits of this book will be donated to The Humane Society of the United States. *–Douglas & Sherri Brown*

The human-animal bond is as old as human history. We cherish our animal companions for their unconditional affection and acceptance. We feel a thrill when we glimpse wild creatures in their natural habitat or in our own backyard.

Unfortunately, the human-animal bond has at times been weakened. Humans have exploited some animal species to the point of extinction.

The Humane Society of the United States makes a difference in the lives of animals here at home and worldwide. The HSUS is dedicated to creating a world where our relationship with animals is guided by compassion. We seek a truly humane society in which animals are respected for their intrinsic value, and where the human-animal bond is strong.

Want to help animals? We have plenty of suggestions. Adopt a pet from a local shelter, join The Humane Society and be a part of our work to help companion animals and wildlife. You will be funding our educational, legislative, investigative and outreach projects in the U.S. and across the globe.

Or perhaps you'd like to make a memorial donation in honor of a pet, friend or relative? You can through our Kindred Spirits program. And if you'd like to contribute in a more structured way, our Planned Giving Office has suggestions about estate planning, annuities, and even gifts of stock that avoid capital gains taxes.

Maybe you have land that you would like to preserve as a lasting habitat for wildlife. Our Wildlife Land Trust can help you. Perhaps the land you want to share is a backyard— that's enough. Our Urban Wildlife Sanctuary Program will show you how to create a habitat for your wild neighbors.

So you see, it's easy to help animals. And The HSUS is here to help.

THE HUMANE SOCIETY
OF THE UNITED STATES®

2100 L Street NW • Washington, DC 20037 • 202-452-1100
www.hsus.org

Dedication

This book is dedicated to all of the individuals who have gone through the turmoil of financial misfortune and have struggled to find a way out. Rest assured, there is a way to turn your life around and get back on track.

Table of Contents

Chapter 3: The Fundamentals of Foreclosure 113

Chapter 4: Your Housing Options   133

Chapter 5: The Real Facts on Repossession   155

Chapter 6: Overcoming Eviction   167

Chapter 7: How to Rebuild Your Credit — 181

Chapter 8: How to Take Control of Your Debt — 199

Chapter 9: How to Overcome the Social Stigma of Financial Misfortune   239

Chapter 10: Striding Toward the Future   247

Conclusion: Onward and Upward   271

Appendix A: Financial Freedom Checklist   275

Appendix B: Bankruptcy Court Fee Schedule   279

Appendix C: Foreclosure Assessment Form   285

Foreword

Moving Past Crippled Debt

Financial disaster can strike anyone at any time. It most often takes the form of a medical emergency, job loss, or divorce, but the severity of the impact of a financial crisis varies widely.

Families with a savings cushion and no credit card debt can typically weather a short-term storm with few lasting effects. But for families living on the edge financially, job loss or a severe illness can push high credit card balances past their limits, leaving them unable to meet even basic financial commitments.

I suspect you are reading this book because you fall in the latter category. At this point, the damage is likely done, and you are weighing which option is best for you and your family. Whether it is credit counseling, debt settlement, or even bankruptcy, it is important to not only focus on your options for getting out from under your debt, but also to gather the tools that will help you build a healthy financial future after your debt has been resolved.

Before embarking upon any "debt reduction" effort, it is important to understand the options available and whom they are best suited for. There are three basic ways to alleviate debt — each very different, and each with its own impact on your credit score and total debt. If you have yet to file for bankruptcy or become involved with a particular debt relief alternative, weigh each of these options and determine which is the right fit for your unique situation:

Credit counseling

Credit counseling does not reduce principal balance — only interest and fees. This option is best for consumers not completely overwhelmed by debt and who are looking for a way to better manage their finances. Credit counseling typically includes a financial education and budgeting component in addition to the actual debt management plan.

Debt settlement

Debt settlement is more aggressive than credit counseling and involves a third party negotiating with your creditor to reduce the principal amount owed. This is a great option for consumers interested in avoiding bankruptcy at all costs. To learn more about debt settlement and get a list of accredited debt settlement companies, visit **www.usoba.org**.

Bankruptcy

Bankruptcy is the option best suited for people with the most severe and unmanageable amounts of debt. While bankruptcy might feel like a quick fix, it carries the most long-lasting impact to your credit score and financial reputation. *You can read more about bankruptcy and your filing options in Chapter 2 of this book.*

Bankruptcy, while scary, is sometimes the only choice a consumer has to get out of debt. Consumers should not let fear keep them from doing what is best for their financial situation.

What is most important to remember is that there is no easy or quick fix. Any program that is designed to help you get out from under crippling debt is typically going to be a long process, and one that involves sacrifices on your part. Conduct research and make comparisons before making any decisions so you know exactly what you are signing up for, how long it will take, and exactly how it works.

The good news is that in most cases, once your debt is paid off, settled, or "forgiven" via bankruptcy, you have a fresh start. You will need to begin rebuilding your credit to demonstrate to banks, apartment landlords, creditors, and even potential employers that you can be trusted to meet your financial commitments. Chapter 7 provides excellent tips and tools for rebuilding your credit score, but the main idea is to start with a secured line of credit, pay on time and as agreed, and demonstrate your new financial responsibility. Following is one such story of rebuilding financial security:

My name is Penny. My husband had severe health issues that resulted in us having to close our family business. Due to the business debt, a great deal of which was in our personal name, we had to declare bankruptcy.

My husband was unable to work, so I had to return to the job market, and we had to use our credit cards for many necessities in life (e.g., doctors and hospital bills, medicines, and vehicle expenses). The debt kept climbing, and our income was stagnant.

When I heard about debt settlement, for the first time I thought that maybe there was light at the end of the tunnel. After a personal consultation and review of my financial situation, I was told I qualified for the program. I told my account specialist I wanted to get this settled as quickly as possible, so we set it up for an 18- to 24-month program.

I stuck to the program, and when the first debt was settled — what a wonderful feeling. Once I was able to tell the creditors that I was in a debt management program, the harassing telephone calls stopped, the threatening letters began to come less and less, and my husband and I could begin to see a brighter future. The monthly calls from my account specialist were a comfort — she always encouraged me to stick with the program and kept me apprised of the progress being made with my debt.

I am happy to say I graduated early despite some months in which I was not able to make my payment due to family emergencies. We are able to live within our means and have credit cards, which we kept only for rare emergencies and paid off immediately.

All thanks to our debt settlement program, the quality of our life has been greatly enhanced by the fact that we are at last debt free. I would highly recommend the program to anyone who is in what appears to be a hopeless financial situation. It was a lifesaver to us.

Staying out of debt is simple in theory — do not spend more than you have. But we all know it is much harder in reality. It will take practice and a continued focus on your financial goals. Without the cloud of credit card debt looming, you can do things you were never able to do before: save for family vacations, prepare for retirement, and put money toward your children's college educations. What begins as a long and painful process ends with great feelings of liberation and relief.

Best wishes in your journey!

Jenna Keehnen

Jenna Keehnen is the executive director of the U.S. Organizations for Bankruptcy Alternatives (USOBA). USOBA is dedicated to providing its member companies with important, industry-related information, including compliance requirements, as well as advocating on behalf of its membership for fair and appropriate industry regulation that maintains the utmost in consumer protection. USOBA members are provided a USOBA State Law Summary guide, the only one of its kind in the industry, to better ensure and promote national compliance. This guide contains the laws and regulations, state by state, and has been reviewed by regulators and legislators. For further information, visit ***www.usoba.org.***

 # Introduction

You are reading this book because you have found yourself in a financial dilemma. Maybe you lost your job due to a recession. Maybe you were hit with extraordinary medical bills. Maybe you were the victim of a lawsuit. Or maybe you tried to help someone else out financially and the person never paid you back. Whatever the reason, you are not alone. Take a look at the headlines in any major newspaper across the country: from "Economic Troubles Plague Families" to "Foreclosures at Record Rates" to "Bankruptcies on the Rise," you can see the state of the economy affects everyone, everywhere. The ups and downs of the economy impacts millions of working people and their families. Jobs disappear. Mortgage rates increase. Prices go up. For some families, there is little that could have been done to prevent these financial crises. For others, a little financial planning and discipline would have prevented a detrimental outcome. No matter what got you into this mess, you can rest assured that there is a way out. This book is the first step.

Throughout these chapters, this book will go into detail on the top personal financial disasters:

- **Illness**: Whether it is an accident or a long-term illness that threatens to keep you out of work, becoming sick or injured can be a real financial disaster for you and your family. However, with an adequate health insurance plan and disability coverage, you can overcome this financial threat.

- **Job loss**: In an uncertain economy, job loss becomes a reality for thousands of workers, and more and more families find one or both spouses out of work. If you have lost your job, you will need to rely on severance, unemployment benefits, and savings to keep your head above water.

- **Divorce**: Divorce is a devastating financial disaster to millions of men, women, and children. It takes a massive toll on a family's household finances — essentially fracturing it and disrupting the income(s) that supported the family's home and lifestyle. The key to coming out on top financially is making sure you have a good lawyer who can help you get, or keep, what you deserve.

- **Unexpected death**: There is no more tragic and emotionally devastating personal event than the unexpected death of a loved one. The shock and power of grief can be overwhelming and debilitating. There may be significant medical bills that accumulated quickly. There are arrangements to be made. To ensure that a loved one's unexpected death does not leave you on rocky financial ground, take steps now to make sure wills, living trusts, and life insurance plans are in order.

- **Judgment against you**: A momentary lapse of judgment, an act done in anger, something that may not have been your fault, or simple carelessness may produce a court judgment against you that can tie up your assets. The key to getting out of this situation financially unscathed is to be up-front; attempt to negotiate a settlement and pay what you can. Good faith with creditors may be your best bet.

- **Civil calamity**: The most traumatic result of hurricanes, tornadoes, wildfires, floods, earthquakes, and other natural disasters is the feeling of helplessness that engulfs those who have lost their homes and possessions. Your pre-disaster solution? Insurance. Insurance. Insurance.

- **Bankruptcy**: If you have lost your job and can no longer pay your bills, you may be a candidate for bankruptcy. If you find yourself in this situation, know your circumstances. Be aware of how much money you owe and what your monthly payments are, individually and as a whole. It is also essential to communicate with your lenders and make them aware of any changes in your circumstances. Whatever you do, do not ignore letters or phone calls. It will not help the situation go away, and will actually make it worse.

- **Foreclosure**: If you are facing foreclosure because you cannot make your mortgage payment, communicate with your lender and offer a plan to keep your home. If your financial crisis is temporary, explain how you will become current on your loan. If there is no hope of becoming current, become proactive in the foreclosure process by learning your state's laws and your rights under those laws.

- **Repossession**: Repossession is an action to seize property that was used as collateral in a debt. The most common cause of repossession is the inability to pay the monthly obligation. Before you agree to purchase or lease a vehicle, know the terms of the agreement you are signing and whether you can make the payment without causing your personal budget to collapse.

- **Eviction**: Eviction is a form of repossession or foreclosure. Your landlord is taking back the property by forcing you to move out. Know the terms of your lease or rental agreement and avoid verbal agreements, details of which can fade over time and result in misunderstandings and hard feelings.

Once you have a sense of the most common ways that people get into financial distress, this book will encourage you to accept your problem, however overwhelming and frightening it may be. It will inspire you to not just accept, but to embrace your solution. Your success will depend on your dedication to solving this financial problem. This book will help you to set goals for what you want to achieve, where you want to go, and provide valuable checkpoints along the way to unburden you and help you move forward. It will explain the process of bankruptcy and your options, should you determine that it is your best, or only, alternative. It will explain foreclosures and how the process works, as well as the housing options available to you after undergo foreclosure. This book will even discuss eviction and repossession, and offer you strategies to overcome these financial burdens. Overall, this book addresses the steps you can take to rebuild your credit score and outlines ways to change your attitude about credit and spending so that you can get out — and stay out — of debt.

Most importantly, this book will arm you with the tools necessary to make the best financial decisions for rebuilding your life. You can recover from even the worst financial crisis and move on with your life. It may not be quick or easy, but it is possible, and you can live a prosperous, financially stable life.

It is time to begin transforming your financial future. Welcome to the first day of the rest of your life.

Chapter 1

Common Types of Financial Misfortune

Overcoming the Debts Associated with Illness

Studies have shown that about half of all Americans who seek protection under bankruptcy laws cite medical problems as a primary reason they are in financial crisis.

Surveys of those who have filed bankruptcy petitions show that illness or accidents can create an avalanche of debt and financial misery, particularly if the family does not have health insurance or other benefits to help pay medical expenses. One study showed that the average person filing for bankruptcy because of medical bills was a middle-aged woman who had children, owned a home, and had a job.

The effects of illness on your family are:

- Loss of income from medical expenses.
- Loss of jobs if the ill family member is unable to work — or a healthy family member must quit his or her job to become the caretaker.
- Stress from being ill — or from being the caretaker.

Take Jackie, for example: She suffered from acute arthritis that hindered her from completing her data-entry job. During the two years prior to filing for bankruptcy protection, she lost her telephone service, missed doctor and dentist appointments, failed to fill one or more prescriptions, and may have gone without food — all because of the financial disaster that was produced by her health problems. In order to help pay the bills, Jackie was forced to take out a second mortgage on her home, and she had piled up credit card debt. By the time Jackie went to bankruptcy court, she was emotionally and financially drained. She worried that the illness that had produced this financial calamity would create more bills in the future and that health insurance coverage would be denied — or that state or local benefits would also be denied.

> The financial implications of debts associated with illness are the inability to pay bills and the potential for bankruptcy, foreclosure, and repossession.

Serious illness or injury can devastate the financial picture of solid, middle-class, hard-working people who have a history of paying their bills on time and handling their money responsibly. The tidal wave of bills and expenses can overwhelm family savings, threaten home ownership, and produce serious hardships on the entire family.

As you can imagine, health insurance is the single most important resource to handle this type of catastrophe. Millions of people have no insurance at all and wake up each morning hoping that they will not become ill or injured. Others have limited coverage, which is not nearly enough to cover major medical expenses. Both types of people often put off doctor's visits or filling prescriptions, like Jackie, for fear of spending unnecessary money. Some people, however, have excellent coverage that will pay most, if not all, of their medical bills should they need hospitalization and doctor care.

If your employer offers medical insurance, sign up for it. You may balk at the cost, which could be several hundred dollars or more each month, but ask yourself what would happen to you and your family if a medical crisis were to strike. It is essential for you to explore your options and obtain the best coverage available.

If your employer does not offer medical insurance, look into individual plans. They will be expensive, particularly if you have a history of medical problems. If there is a serious, pre-existing condition, you may be turned down for individual family health insurance. If that is the case, look into government benefits packages that may be available to you. Web sites like **www.usa.gov/Citizen/Topics/Health/HealthInsurance.shtml** are a good place to begin in your search for this information. However, you may be able to find an individual plan that can be customized to include the services you need, excluding the services you do not need.

Medicaid, a government health program, may also be an option. Qualifications vary by state but generally are limited to people who have very low incomes and few assets. Medicaid provides inpatient hospital services, outpatient care, vaccinations for children, laboratory services, and other medical coverage.

If you find that you do not qualify for Medicaid and cannot afford a comprehensive medical plan, consider a plan with a high deductible that will provide coverage for catastrophic health issues, such as cancer or other serious illness. These policies typically have a yearly deductible of thousands of dollars, meaning you will be required to pay out-of-pocket for most routine health care, but you will have coverage in the event of a serious medical event.

Think about Jackie again. To protect herself in case of a serious illness, she can purchase a catastrophic health insurance policy. This type of policy will allow her a low premium (a periodic payment to continue her policy), but a higher deductible (the payment made toward a claim before insurance pays), generally beginning at $500 when compared to other health plans. These plans are common for younger people — for example, people in their 20s, or older people between ages 50 and 65. It is important to note that if Jackie needs hospitalization, she may end up paying more due to her high deductible — therefore, she must be certain she has enough money to cover that deductible in the case of serious emergency. These types of health insurance plans generally have a cap between $1 million and $3 million. Therefore, if Jackie spends $1 million on medical care, comparable services would likely be covered under her policy, which could help her overcome the financial implications of an illness.

Tips to prevent or overcome the debts associated with illness:

- Purchase an adequate health insurance plan.
- Apply for government health programs, like Medicaid, if you cannot afford an individual plan and have a low income.
- Contact the health insurance company to try to work out a payment plan or reduction in the total fee due.
- Look into government and state assistance programs that may be able to help you pay medical bills — and purchase a low-cost insurance plan.
- Consider bankruptcy as a final option. *This book will go into more detail on the different types of bankruptcy in Chapter 2.*

Remember that health insurance is your best bet to prevent future medical bills from getting out of control. If Jackie had adequate health insurance and had been able to get treatment for her acute arthritis, she may have never missed work and would have not fallen into the financial situation that she did. But rest assured, you can get out of the debt associated with your medical bills by following the previous recommendations.

Taking Charge of Job Loss

Being laid off, fired, downsized, or outsourced is one of the most stressful experiences in life — especially given the circumstances of the 2008 economic crisis. In November 2009, unemployment in the U.S. had reached an all-time high of 10.2 percent. In fact, the U.S. Department of Labor has monitored employment trends and found:

- People hold about ten jobs in their lifetimes (though this estimate is based on limited studies).

- People experience unemployment almost five times during their working years.

- The better educated people are, the fewer times they are unemployed.

- The agency projects that in 2016, many older persons (age 55 or older) will be employed.

- Service-related jobs will continue to be important areas of employment.

If you lost your job due to economic hardships, you are not alone; thousands of Americans struggled as jobs were cut left and right. Losing your job is right up there with a death in the family or a divorce as a major cause of emotional pain. Once you get past the emotional pain, there are the obvious financial hardships to take care of. Having a rainy day fund — also known as an emergency fund — can protect you and your family financially in the case of job loss, and it can take some of the stress out of the situation. However, it is important to have a game plan when faced with job loss.

The effects of job loss on your family are:

- Loss of income.
- Draining of family savings.
- Loss of professional self-esteem.
- Stress.

Losing your job means loss of income, health insurance, social status and, in many cases, self-esteem. Your first reaction may be shock or anger. Then you may experience fear and embarrassment. If you are being downsized or offered some kind of early retirement or severance package, you may feel pressure to agree to what is being offered out of fear that you will have less, or even nothing at all, if you ask for time to think about the offer. Once you sign an agreement to terminate your employment, you are committed to it, as it is a legal contract.

Avoid making hasty decisions — and whatever you do, do not quickly sign any agreement that is put in front of you. Ask for at least one day to consider the offer and take a copy with you. If you have a personal or family lawyer, make an emergency appointment to discuss your severance or early retirement package to ensure that it meets applicable regulations and agreements. If you are a union member, take the agreement or offer to your shop steward, or other union official, to make sure it meets the terms of the contract.

There are many reasons for employment terminations. The worst, of course, is being fired "for cause," such as chronic tardiness, not showing up at all, showing up drunk, or abusing customers. Some firings are due to personality conflicts between the worker and the management. Poor performance reviews or failing to meet sales goals can result in job loss. Another common cause of termination is for economic reasons. The company may have determined that it cannot afford to keep an employee on the payroll, either because business is bad, or a decision has been made to move the job to another state or country.

> The financial implications of job loss are the inability to pay bills; the possibility of going into credit card debt; and the potential for bankruptcy, foreclosure, and repossession.

Whatever the reason, the financial consequences of being laid off can be devastating. Millions of Americans live paycheck to paycheck, and the impact of a job loss is immediate, even assuming there is some kind of severance package or buyout. Losing a job can be a moment when everything changes, leaving you reeling and unable to grasp your next move.

If you are working with a financial planner or another professional who gives you financial advice, contact him or her as soon as possible to explain your situation. If not, find a trusted friend or family member. Do not hide the situation from your spouse. The more knowledge you have at the beginning, the more control you will have over your resources. Once you have settled things with your now-former employer, take a close look at everything that is available to you, including gaining unemployment benefits, continuing your health insurance, and accessing any other public or private resources at hand. This will allow you to put down hard numbers to know how to budget your money and how to prioritize your bills and obligations.

This is where your rainy day fund will be important. Gather your budget figures together and start cutting out all unnecessary items, such as vacations, new cars, new appliances, and so on. During the transition from one job to the next, you must spend your available cash wisely to stretch it out. These are the circumstances under which you may cancel your cable television service and high-speed Internet. You are trying to save your home, so small sacrifices like these will help you with your financial situation.

The hardest part of this experience may be to pick up the pieces and start looking for another job. This can be tough, as it forces you to tell everyone you know that you have lost your job. However, this is an important part of moving on because it spreads your network to a wider area. This type of networking will prove to be the single most important way for you to land new work. The people you network with will be likely to recommend you for jobs that they know of, so do not be shy about sharing your new situation with friends and acquaintances.

Unemployment benefits

Contact your state's unemployment office and sign up for all benefits for which you are entitled. While every state has different laws, most states require that you are entitled to benefits such as unemployment, health insurance through COBRA, and even job assistance.

There are a number of ways to qualify for unemployment payments:

- If you have been laid off.

- If you were part of a business closing or bankruptcy.

- If you lost your job because you were fired without cause. Your case will probably be reviewed to determine whether you became unemployed through no fault of your own.

You may not qualify for unemployment benefits:

- If you quit your job.
- If you were fired with cause.

Whether or not you believe you will qualify, you should apply for benefits. As the unemployment situation changes, eligibility rules also change. And you certainly will not be eligible if you do not apply.

Unfortunately, if you were employed as one of the following, you are likely not covered by unemployment insurance in most states:

- Farm workers

- Those working on 100 percent sales commission

- Casual domestic workers and babysitters

- Newspaper carriers under the age of 18

- Those employed by family, such as a child working for a parent or an adult employed by a spouse or adult child

- Employees of religious organizations

- Some corporate officers

- Elected officials

Filing for unemployment benefits may be an embarrassing moment for someone who has held gainful employment for many years while working in a cubicle or small workstation. You now find yourself standing in a long line of others who may or may not share your professional qualifications. You also must face a bureaucrat who spends each day facing anxious people like you, and who will most likely be unable to distinguish your situation from another person's. Many states, however, allow you to file discreetly from the comfort of your home via the Internet or telephone. But it is important to discuss your situation with the unemployment specialist and ask what benefits are available to you and your family.

Also, get information on additional income you can earn while collecting unemployment. Every little bit helps, and many states allow you to earn a certain amount per week in addition to your unemployment benefit. For example, Steve, a graphic artist, was awarded $500 per week from unemployment and was allowed to generate up to $300 extra per week as a contractor. You may be able to keep your company's health benefits for some period of time at a subsidized rate — which essentially means that your employer will still provide partial financial support as when you were an employee — or, if you are fortunate, at 100 percent of your former company's expense.

State employment agencies often have lists of job openings, which may be a good source of leads for you. If you have been downsized, it may be time for you to look at a new career or think about retraining in another field. The state employment services office may have classes or tuition assistance available for those who qualify. Ask about it and take advantage of any opportunity to increase your skills and marketability. Losing your job may ultimately be a chance to upgrade your skills, leading you to a better job at which you make more money.

If you are negotiating with your former employer, attempt to determine how much leverage you have — you may have more than you think. If you do not already have an exit interview with human resources, make sure you set one up and then ask about your options. Do you have vacation time in the bank? Ask to be paid for it. What about sick days? You may be eligible to earn a payout on those as well. Find out if you have compensatory time for any job-related travel. If so, are you owed money for them? You can write down a list of possible benefits and payments due to employees who are terminated or downsized. Some companies will offer different benefits packages to employees who are being bought out or given early retirement than they do to those employees who are being let go for performance reasons. Learn your status. If it is negative and falls into the "poor performance" category, ask to see the justification. It may be that you have been given that designation to save the company from complying with the benefits of someone who is in the "downsize" category.

Negotiation does not automatically mean confrontation and hard feelings. It is simply a process of asking questions and offering solutions and ideas. Your former employer may be willing to offer you extended benefits, or even part-time work if you are willing to take it. Your company may also have firm policies concerning buyouts or layoffs and offer you a standard plan. Either way, it is beneficial to inquire about this before you leave. Avoid signing the first agreement placed in front of you; ask for at least one day to look it over. It may be that the first agreement deprives you of benefits you would otherwise be entitled to, such as stock options and pension plans.

If there are no hard feelings, ask for reference. It will be something you can take to prospective employers. If the reference letter explains that competitive or financial pressures forced your former employer to downsize you, the new employer may see you as a potentially valuable addition to the team, and not as someone who was ejected from his or her last job for performance reasons. At this point, you are looking for any advantage available to you in your search for a new job.

Severance pay

Many companies provide severance pay for employees involved in a layoff, restructuring, or business closing. For those who receive severance packages, the actual payout can vary widely, depending on the company, the employee's position, and the length of service. A common rule of thumb is to give two weeks' pay for every year of employment. You may also receive payment for unused vacation leave. All these payments will have taxes withheld, just like a regular paycheck.

Career support

In addition to unemployment insurance offices, most states also have JobLink or Career One-Stop Centers designed specifically to help the unemployed find work. Rapid response teams generally go on-site to assist a company and its employees in the case of a mass layoff or plant closing. The Rapid Response program partners with the Career One-Stop Center program. These offices provide a wide range of employment-related services, including:

- Access to computers, phones, and other office equipment
- Job placement and career counseling services
- Education and training services
- Counseling for coping with the stress and financial strain of unemployment

There are more than 2,000 centers across the country. Find a local Career One-Stop Center online at **www.servicelocator.org** or by phone at 1-877-US2-JOBS (1-877-872-5627).

Some states have additional laws, regulations, or ordinances that apply in the event of a plant closing. Your Rapid Response office can provide information. In addition, some states offer supplementary assistance beyond that required in the WARN Act. For example, some states mandate that employers provide laid-off workers with severance payments and/or other benefits.

How to prevent or overcome the financial implications of job loss:

- Establish a rainy day fund.
- Preserve and tightly budget whatever money you have.
- Find out if you qualify for unemployment benefits — and start collecting them immediately.
- Rely on severance money to give you a cushion — the best-case scenario is that you find a new job before you use all of your severance money (meaning you would come out ahead, financially).
- Apply for health insurance coverage through COBRA.
- Network with other professionals immediately to help ensure you land work quickly.

One thing to note: Now is not the time to turn to credit cards as a way to supplement your income. Many families go this route only to find themselves in high-interest-rate credit card debt months later. Look into minimizing costs on utilities, such as cutting out cable TV and cell phones, and cut back on extras to make sure you are living within your means.

Remember, if you find yourself going through a job loss, you are not alone. Many people find themselves in this situation at one point in their careers. Just be sure to take these steps immediately to ensure that you are on the right path to protecting yourself financially.

Conquering the Costs of Divorce

It is often said that 40 to 50 percent of American marriages will end in divorce. Whether it is due to irreconcilable differences or another reason, divorce can be costly. According to U.S. Census Bureau reports, women and children suffer the most dramatic lifestyle deterioration due to divorce.

This is because in a two-income household, salaries or other sources of cash are combined to pay mortgage or rent, car payments, utilities, and everything else. After a divorce, the income is broken up, and each person experiences a lower standard of life. The income distribution can be uneven, with the mother and the children usually suffering a dramatic loss of financial resources — even if the father provides child support payments.

The effects of divorce on your family are:

- Breakdown of family unit.
- Loss of income.
- Draining of family savings.
- The need for increased childcare.

What happens in a divorce? The financial fabric of the family tears, and there is a loss of what in business is called "economics of scale" — the savings that are the result of the combined of resources. The word "resources," in this instance, refers to more than just income. There is also childcare, house cleaning, and the sharing of insurance benefits to consider. Loss of these other benefits produces unintended financial strains. You now need to hire a babysitter more often, or for a longer period of time, and you have to foot the grocery bill on your own.

State laws determine the distribution of assets in a divorce settlement. Some states have community property laws, meaning everything acquired, whether earned or inherited during a marriage, belongs to both parties equally. Other states distribute property according to which party acquired it. Under this system, the husband and the wife each keep what they acquired while they were married, whether earned or inherited. In what used to be considered a traditional marriage — where the wife stays home to raise the kids and forgoes her own career — the wife may be penalized because she has no significant property or other assets that were acquired during the marriage. In this case, a judge will determine the support the spouse will have to pay, whether it is alimony, child support, or both.

If one party has the financial power to hire an expensive lawyer and the other does not, there is potential for the party with the money — and thus the expensive lawyer — to come out ahead, if for no reason other than that he or she has more legal power. Likewise, if both parties do not have money and the couple is already living paycheck-to-paycheck, the likelihood of poverty following divorce is much greater, given that the already limited financial resources will become even more scarce when separated by husband and wife.

> The financial implications of divorce are the inability to pay bills; the potential for bankruptcy, foreclosure and repossession; the need for members of the family to move into a new house that is smaller and more crowded; the potential loss of health insurance benefits; and legal bills for both sides.

The first impact is the cost of the divorce in terms of dollars. Legal fees add up quickly. There may also be a need to move into a new home, which costs money. Loss of income can produce foreclosure or eviction, repossession of the family car, and so on. The divorce may have meant the loss of health insurance, which means illness or injury without such medical coverage can produce an even greater financial disaster.

As difficult as it may be, treat the divorce as a business matter, not as a personal and emotional disaster. Know your rights under state law and protect yourself (and your children) with the laws that apply. Married couples accumulate more than assets; they also accumulate liabilities, such as debt and other financial obligations. These may be in the form of car loans, home mortgages, shared credit cards, and furniture payments.

To avoid a worst-case divorce settlement, equal distribution of marital assets and obligations should leave each party with half of everything, including the good and the bad. Special consideration will be given to the financial, and other, needs of children.

If a decision to dissolve the marriage has been made, consider your options. Evaluate your assets and sit down with an advisor to examine your needs and those of your children, and others, who will rely on you for support following the divorce. Talk to someone who has no emotional or financial stake in the outcome. Divorce proceedings can become so emotional and bitter that huge sums are spent on legal fees to fight over relatively insignificant items. But it is essential to put away as much money as possible so that you are financially sound after the divorce; therefore, do not waste it on legal fees for trivial arguments.

Also, consider that you may be entitled to a portion of your spouse's social security or other government benefits, and that your children may be entitled to support as well. If you have been out of the workforce or have refrained from updating your marketable skills, consider enrolling in training programs to increase your earnings potential. Many community colleges offer reasonably priced training programs for office or technical workers, and the demand for such workers remains strong, even in economic downturns.

Many community colleges offer free advisory services to help you match your interests and aptitude to available training programs. You may be eligible for training and education grants that will reduce or eliminate your school expenses. Education has been shown to be the key to future earnings. By increasing your skills and knowledge, you will dramatically alter your potential for financial security. It is possible to recover from the negative financial effects of divorce. Protect yourself and your children during the process, then move on to secure your future.

The cost of custody

The No. 1 legal ramification of divorce that most fathers care about is not how much they pay in alimony, but how much time they will get to spend with their children. There are some surprising statistics from the Center for Children's Justice related to custody and divorced fathers in the United States:

- Roughly 37.9 percent of all fathers have no access or visitation rights to their children.

- For non-custodial parents, child support from fathers is estimated to be awarded to less than one-half of single mothers.

- More than one-third — 40 percent — of mothers have reported that they interfered with the visitation rights of the father on at least one occasion in attempts to punish their ex-partner.

- More than half of all divorced mothers do not see the value of the father having contact with the children.

- An estimated 30 percent of mothers stop visiting their children at least yearly after a divorce, compared to 47 percent of fathers.

- Slightly more than 10 percent of mothers want the opinion of their ex-partners when dealing with issues relating to parenting.

- For fathers, 70 percent feel they have too little time with their children on a regular basis.

The biggest financial mistakes made during a divorce

The seeds for financial stress following a divorce are created before the divorce is ever completed. On average, a divorce is going to cost you $20,000, which can put a lot of financial stress on you. Obviously, the faster you make decisions and come to a resolution in the divorce, the more money you are going to save, especially when it comes to attorney fees. Thus, if you take the time to make good decisions during the divorce, you will be able to protect your finances, at least partly. If you are going through a divorce, keep in mind the main reasons for financial stress — both during and after the divorce:

1. **Not being aware of your living expenses:** Many people fall into this trap, where they leave all the financial decisions to their spouse. When a divorce happens, it can be natural for you to underestimate your expenses, which can lead to severe debt. One way to prevent this is to budget and pay attention to what you pay. It is common that when you start thinking about your expenses, you think about your bills and mortgage, but there are many other expenses, including clothing, transportation, entertainment, school costs, insurance, food, and more.

2. **Making assumptions about who gets the house:** There is a common assumption that the custodial parent gets the house, but this is not always the case. Even if it is, you may not able to afford the mortgage payments anymore, and that will result in selling the house, forcing you to move somewhere cheaper.

3. **Believing that splitting equally is fair:** When you split everything in a 50/50 manner, you may think that it is fair, and that both you and your ex will get enough of an income from the assets. However, this does not always work out in a fair manner. Who gets the expensive car and who gets the cheap car? Who gets the expensive electronics and who gets furniture? Who gets the stock portfolio and who gets the savings account? Often, disagreements over who gets what can cause divorce costs to rise, which can eat into any savings you may have had by going 50/50.

4. **Underestimating alimony and child support:** Probably the biggest mistake you can make is to underestimate how much you may be paying out in support. It can end up costing a lot of money, and if you do not plan for it, you will get a big surprise when you suddenly find yourself paying out 25 percent of your income to your ex-spouse and kids.

5. **Not thinking about outstanding debt:** When you go through a divorce, the debt is not always equally split. If you have joint credit cards with your ex-spouse, you still have to pay those off, even if he or she racks up a large bill. Credit card companies make both of you responsible for the unsecured debt, so by not paying the credit card of your ex, he or she can damage both your credit scores. Even if the judge decreed that your spouse is responsible for paying it off, if it is under both your names, then the credit card company sees it as a shared debt that affects both of your credit scores.

6. **Failure to plan:** The biggest mistake people make in their lives is a failure to plan. If you do not plan for your future, you will get a rude wake-up call. Divorce happens in about half of all marriages, so it may be a good idea to get a financial advisor who can look at your new finances and expenses and help you determine how to plan best if this does happen.

7. **Failure to understand the effect of divorce on finances:** This is part of planning for the future because you need to know how to survive the financial hit of divorce before it happens, not after. If you think your finances will not change after the divorce, you are wrong. Once the divorce is done, there is no going back, and you need to wake up and start planning for your new financial life.

How to prevent or overcome the financial implications of divorce:

- Evaluate your assets — make a list of what is yours and what you are entitled to keep.
- Strive for equal distribution of marital assets and obligations.
- Meet with an advisor to examine your financial needs and those of others who will rely on you for support following the divorce.
- Reduce your debt obligation so you have extra money saved.
- Make sure you and your dependents have continued health insurance coverage.
- Consider making a career move to put yourself on more secure financial footing.
- Do not turn to credit cards for supplemental income.

If you are currently going through a divorce, try to keep the situation as amicable with your spouse as possible. The result will be a better end for both parties so that you are able to successfully move on — both emotionally and financially.

Enduring the Financial Implications of Unexpected Death

Although your income and financial well-being are probably the last thing on your mind after an unexpected death of a loved one, there are financial implications associated with death, and it is important that you take the necessary steps to ensure you are protected financially. The following information will assist you in surviving this situation — and will take you through the steps of preparing yourself for facing this financial crisis.

If the loved one was your spouse, you should expect your income to change drastically — especially if your spouse was the main source of the family's income. The first major difference you will see is the source of your income. Although you previously relied on your spouse's salary to pay the bills, you may now have to rely on social security benefits, which will likely be much less than you are used to. Sometimes, life insurance payments or investment income can help financially.

The effects of unexpected death on your family are:

- Loss of a loved one.
- Loss of income.
- Draining of family savings.
- Need for increased childcare.

How to Ensure You Remain Financially Secure

If something has happened to your spouse or close family member, one of the biggest questions you may have is, "How will I survive financially?" One major life insurance company surveyed 1,000 people who had lost a spouse within the previous five years of the survey, and more than half of them said the life insurance benefits they received were inadequate and forced them to make serious negative changes in their lifestyles. They reported that it took them about five years to recover financially.

> The financial implications of unexpected death are the inability to pay bills; the potential for bankruptcy, foreclosure, and repossession; the need for members of the family to move into a new house that is smaller and more crowded; and the potential loss of health insurance benefits.

Social security benefits

Once called "widow's benefits," the U.S. Social Security Administration offers a portion of the deceased's Social Security benefits in the form of survivor benefits to the spouses and minor children of those who would have qualified for a monthly retirement check. Under certain circumstances, even a deceased's elderly parents may collect benefits — but only if the deceased supported them financially.

There are two types of social security benefits offered by the federal government:

1. A one-time lump sum of $255 to help pay for funeral costs.

2. A monthly survivor benefit that is calculated by the retirement benefits the deceased would have qualified for at retirement age. This benefit runs between 70 and 100 percent of the projected retirement benefit, depending on who qualifies. Of course, there are maximums allowed by law. Most American workers receive an annual review of their benefits from the social security office that clearly states the death benefits allowed by the worker's family in the event of his or her death. Finding a copy

of this benefit sheet will tell you right away what your monthly benefits check will be. Otherwise, you will have to wait for the Social Security Administration office (**www.ssa.gov**) to calculate the benefit for you.

To qualify for either of these benefits, you will have to make a formal request and prove that you meet the qualifying standards. This includes making sure that the deceased spouse was indeed "insured" by the government. To qualify for benefits, a worker must be insured or must have worked enough hours during his or her adult life to rack up enough "credits" for retirement savings. The younger you are, the fewer credits you need to be "insurable." Those individuals who did not earn enough credits may leave their survivors with no benefits at all.

The second qualifier is for the surviving family members themselves. To qualify for social security benefits, a survivor must:

- Have been married to the deceased for at least nine months prior to the death (unless is the death was caused by an accident or military duty).

- Be a divorced spouse whose marriage lasted at least ten years.

- Be the parent (or legal guardian) of the deceased's minor child.

- Be at least 60 years of age, disabled, or caring for the deceased's child under the age of 16.

- Be the natural, adopted, or stepchild (who was at least 50 percent dependent on the deceased's support), or a dependent grandchild, who is either under the age of 18, or who may have been disabled before the age of 22 and requires ongoing care.

- Be 62 years of age or older and the parent of the deceased, if you relied on at least 50 percent of your monthly support from the deceased.

To learn more about the qualifying standards for collecting social security benefits for you and your children, call 1-800-772-1213 and request the "Social Security Survivor Benefits booklet" (publication #05-10084). Or, you can download it at **www.ssa.gov/pubs/10084.html**.

Collecting social security benefits

The amount of money you will receive following your spouse's death depends largely on how much the person contributed during his or her working years. The more money contributed, the larger the death benefit.

With any type of government bureaucracy, filing for social security benefits can take time and tax your patience, so it is important to begin the process as soon as possible after an unexpected death of your spouse. When filing for benefits, you will need to gather plenty of information. Here is a run-down of the type of information and documents you may be required to present during the application and interview process:

- Social security numbers: You must submit the social security numbers of all involved individuals (the deceased, yourself, and any minor children applying for benefits).

- Your name and your spouse's name at birth (if different).

- Birth certificates: This legal documentation will be required for survivors as well as the deceased.

- Death certificate.

- The deceased's last address.

- Whether the deceased had already filed (or was receiving) any social security or Medicare benefits.

- Whether the survivors have become disabled or unable to work during the last 14 months — and why.

- Whether the deceased was unable to work during the last 14 months due to illness or injury — and why.

- Military service reports: It is important to notify the Social Security Administration if the deceased was an active serviceperson before 1968, as this could affect your benefits and pension monies owed. Discharge records may be required.

- Employment history: Certain industries pay an additional annuity or pension. Be sure to list any work done by either you or the deceased in the railroad industry. Another thing to consider is social security benefits paid to other countries during work aboard. This may entitle you to benefits from that country also.

- Marriage certificates: You will be required to produce not only your own marriage certificate, but the marriage certificates and divorce decrees from any marriages your deceased spouse may have had in the past.

- Income and earnings: The amount of your spouse's earnings and your own during the three years preceding his or her death.

- The names and social security numbers of any parents who may have relied on your spouse for support.

- A date on which you would like your benefits to begin.

If you are unsure whether your spouse had life insurance, there are several places for you to look to see whether a policy exists:

- **The carrier that handles your other insurance needs.**

- **Your mortgage company:** Many mortgage lenders offer inexpensive mortgage insurance policies that pay off your mortgage in the event of the mortgage holder's death.

- **Your spouse's employer:** Check with the human resources department at your spouse's place of employment. Many employers offer small policies ranging anywhere from $10,000 to twice the employee's salary as an added work benefit. The higher your spouse's position in the company, the better the chance that the company holds a policy on him or her for you. Depending on the types of jobs your spouse has had in the past, it may be a good idea to check with previous employers also, especially if he or she worked for someone else for a long period of time.

- **The military:** Depending on the type of military service offered, you may qualify for extra insurance or pension payments. Low-cost plans are also available starting at $28 a year.

- **Any organizations in which your spouse was an active member:** Many social, professional, and union organizations offer group life insurance plans for their members. Be sure to see whether such a policy exists for your spouse.

- **Your spouse's credit card accounts:** Many banks and credit card companies these days offer accidental death coverage in the event of a cardholder's death. Because the premium is relatively small, many people opt for this limited coverage, with little thought to recording it in their important papers.

Once you figure out what kind of life insurance policy or policies are held on your spouse, you will need to research how the death benefits will ultimately be paid. The most common forms are:

1. **Lump-sum payments:** This gives the beneficiary the entire benefit amount at one time.

2. **Specific income provision**: This type of policy allows the life insurance carrier to distribute benefits in accordance to a predetermined (and agreed upon) schedule.

3. **Life income option:** This gives the policyholder's survivor a monthly stipend until the person's own death. The amount is dependent on the policy's benefits and the survivor's age.

4. **Interest income option:** With this type of policy, the insurance company will pay the beneficiary the interest earned on the policy on an annual basis. Upon the death of the survivor, the actual death benefit will be paid to your children or other secondary beneficiary.

Making a social security claim

When making a claim for life insurance benefits, you will be required to contact the agent, group, or insurance carrier for the proper forms. Group policies, such as those held by organizations and employers, are handled in-house. You will be able to obtain the necessary forms directly from them.

Filing a claim for a privately held policy may take more work, and paper-work, on your part. Contact the agent or company whose name appears on the policy. You will need a copy of the policy or the policy number to begin the claim process. In the event that you cannot locate a copy of the policy, or do not know which agent was used, you can contact the policy search division at The American Council of Life Insurers (**www.acli. com**) in Washington, D.C., for assistance. If there is a policy listed in the deceased's name (regardless of the carrier), they will find it and give you the information you need to submit your claim. This is a free service offered by the federal government.

Once you have the policy number in hand, contact the life insurance car-rier and request a claim packet, which will describe the entire process and provide you with the forms necessary to file your claim.

Some important documents to begin gathering before your claims packet arrives include:

- Certified copy of your spouse's death certificate
- Insurance policy number
- Policy's face value
- Deceased's occupation on his or her last day of work
- Deceased's birth certificate, as well as your own
- Attending physician's statement
- Coroner's report, if applicable
- Police report, if applicable
- Beneficiary's legal name, address, and social security number

Employee benefits

One thing many survivors fail to realize is they may be eligible for additional benefits from their loved one's current — or even past — employers. Some of the benefits you may find yourself qualified to receive include:

- Any unpaid salary
- Any unpaid sick days or vacation time
- Workers' compensation
- Disability payments
- Pensions
- 401(k) contributions
- Accrued bonus monies
- Flex benefits

Retirement savings

The rules for disbursing retirement savings differ depending on the type of the account, the type of beneficiary you are (e.g., spouse, non-spouse, entity, or trust), and the age or ages of all beneficiaries. Check with a certified public accountant or financial planner for guidelines. Most IRAs and 401(k) plans require beneficiaries to begin taking required minimum distributions (RMD) from inherited IRAs at some point.

Veteran's benefits

The Department of Veterans Affairs (VA — their Web site can be visited at **www.va.gov**) offers a variety of death benefits to the survivors of our country's veterans. Although benefits vary depending on the type of service (wartime veterans are eligible for more), the amount of time served, and other variables, all veterans' survivors are eligible for some help.

For instance, the families of most veterans qualify for up to $2,000 in reimbursement for burial costs, a free headstone or marker, a burial flag and, in some cases, burial in one of the VA National Cemeteries. You can also be buried at sea. Some may also qualify for a veteran's pension and, in some cases, may even qualify for help obtaining or paying for medical services for the surviving spouse and dependents.

There is no time limit in requesting these benefits, so if you were not aware of them at the time of your spouse's death, you can apply years later and receive the benefits due to you. To find out more about these and other benefits offered by the VA, call 1-800- 827-1000 or visit your local office today.

Now that you have a clearer understanding of the income you can expect after your spouse has died, look at some other changes you are likely to experience.

How to Overcome the Financial Implications of Unexpected Death

A will ensures that the wishes of your loved one are carried out when he or she passes away. Estate laws vary by state. Some state laws automatically pass property to spouses unless the deceased has left legal instructions to pass the property to someone else. There is also probate court, which is a specialized court that handles the administering of a deceased person's estate. In probate, estate issues can be tied up for months, if not years. Because the will essentially clears the path to the orderly distribution of your loved one's assets following their death, as well what their wishes are for burial and funeral arrangements, it is the first place to begin.

Other legal documents to explore:

- **Living will**: These documents let family members know what their loved one wanted if he or she becomes incapable of making medical decisions. It is an important way to ensure that their wishes regarding their health are known — saving you and the rest of your family from unnecessary legal and emotional stress. Key things to include in a living will are personal wishes for artificial life support, cardiac resuscitation, pain management, and more. For more information on creating a living will, Web sites like **www.alllaw.com** and **www.legalzoom.com** are great places to start. A living will can be done with a lawyer or by using online planning Web sites like **www.doyourownwill.com**.

- **Living trust**: A living trust lets your loved one distribute and manage their assets while they are alive — and then controls the distribution of those assets after he or she dies. At this time, a designated trustee will pay off any debts and distribute assets according to the wishes of the deceased. This can all be done without court supervision. Creating a living trust is an important way to ensure that property in the trust does not go through probate court. Information to put in a living trust includes your decisions on which items of property go to certain individuals whom you want to handle your trust after your death (your trustee). For more information on creating a living trust, Web sites like **www.nolo.com** are great resources, and can be created with online planning Web sites like this one, or by a lawyer.

- **Durable power of attorney**: This allows your loved one to appoint someone to make financial decisions for him or her in the event that he or she is unable to do it. The durable power of attorney expires when the person dies, and it does not replace the living trust. There are two types of power of attorney — a general one that is unlimited in type and length of time, and a specific one that places limitations on the named individual. For more information on a durable power of attorney, visit **www. expertlaw.com**. A durable power of attorney can be done with a lawyer or online at Web sites like **www.legalhelpmate.com**.

Steps to take to keep your finances intact after an unexpected death

When a spouse dies, not only are you stricken with grief, but you are faced with a slew of choices that need to be made. While your spouse may have taken care of things like life insurance and established a will prior to his or her death, there are important steps you need to take to reorganize your finances in the even of an unexpected death. Use the following list to ensure the proper transfer of your spouse's funds:

- Consolidate multiple bank accounts into one or two, but be sure that no single account contains more than $100,000. This amount is all the Federal Reserve will guarantee should the bank suddenly close its doors. Another aspect to consider: Consolidate accounts with multiple institutions into accounts with just one bank or credit union to make it easier to keep track of what accounts (and money) you have.

- Consolidate brokerage accounts.

- Put all jointly held accounts in the surviving spouse's name. This will eliminate the need to have your accounts placed in the person's estate and liquidated from there.

- Transfer vehicle and property ownership into the survivor's (or beneficiaries') name to avoid prolonged legal proceedings and paying inheritance taxes.

Why life insurance is so essential

The purpose of life insurance is to replace the income that is lost in the event of death. It is an important way to protect family members in the event of death. There are two types of life insurance: whole and term. If your loved one had a life insurance policy, find out if it was whole or term. Whole life insurance combines a death benefit with some kind of investment vehicle that, over time, develops a cash value. Term insurance provides no investment or savings mechanism and offers a cash payout to your beneficiaries when you die. *We will go into more detail on life insurance later in Chapter 10.* It is a must-have in helping to protect yourself against this type of financial disaster.

Rising Above Judgment: Another Source of Financial Disaster

If you have missed payments or walked away from a financial obligation for whatever reason, you may be subject to a lawsuit and a court judgment. It may involve a traffic accident or some other act that you were at fault for. Or, it may be nothing more than a disagreement with a lender or a medical provider. There are many avenues to the court. The outcome may be a judgment and a lien being placed against the property you own. A judgment is a ruling by the court that you are liable or at fault and must pay a sum of money. A lien is a claim upon your property to satisfy the judgment.

Obviously, the amount of the lien is critical. If you have a judgment against you for hundreds of thousands of dollars, and you make $40,000 per year, you are not in a position to satisfy the judgment. If the judgment is for $4,000, you may want to pay it off as soon as you can, especially because this judgment is smaller.

The process of going to court, obtaining the judgment, and collecting the damages can be long and expensive. That is why many companies or businesses that are owed money are reluctant to begin the process unless the amount owed is considerably greater than the cost of going to court. For example, if you owe $5,000 to a utility company, but it would cost them $10,000 in legal fees to settle the debt, it may not be worth it for the company to pursue the debt in court.

The effects of judgment on your family are:

- Loss of income.
- Draining of family savings.
- Embarrassment due to social stigma.

State laws vary. Each state has specific statutes that must be met during the process of obtaining a judgment and lien, and many states allow for liens to expire after, for example, 10 or 15 years. Some states' laws wipe out judgments and liens during the bankruptcy process. Others have provisions for certain types of liens to survive bankruptcy, meaning you will still owe the money even after your bankruptcy petition has been approved.

On a practical level, whomever you owe money to will not move from a single late payment to the court without first attempting to get you to pay what you owe. Many businesses will not bother to sue someone who has no practical ability to pay. It is easier for them to take the loss as a tax deduction. Therefore, they may be willing to be more flexible with you and may let you come to some sort of agreement — such as a payment plan.

> The financial implications of rising above judgment are potential loss of job; inability to pay bills; potential for bankruptcy, foreclosure, and repossession.

If you own a home, however, the business or lender may determine that if they go to court and win a judgment, they can then file a lien against your home. That does not mean you will lose your home. It means that should you choose to refinance or sell your home, the lien must be satisfied before closing. If the amount of the judgment is substantial, it could wipe out any profit you will make from the sale of the property. State laws may protect property that is defined as your primary residence. You should consult an attorney who specializes in such matters before you make any final decisions regarding the disposition of property against which a lien is held.

On the other hand, tax liens — which is the way that a lender can regain their property if the debts are not paid — are more difficult to remove because tax issues survive bankruptcy. All judgments and liens will appear on your credit report with a notation about the status of the judgment or lien and whether it has been satisfied, challenged, or is still unresolved. This type of judgment occurs when someone has walked away from a debt and the lender has gone to court to order the debtor to pay.

There is another type of judgment, however, that can result due to damage caused by an action of one party against another. For example, if you are at fault in a traffic accident and have no insurance, you may find yourself being sued for damage by the individual who was in the car that you hit.

Or, if your child throws a baseball through a neighbor's window, breaking not only the glass but damaging a valuable collection of crystal figurines, your neighbor may sue you and win a judgment.

Some consumers assume that a debt of a few hundred dollars may just go away because the business or person the money is owed to might think it is not worth it to spend money going to court. But the business or company in question may assume opposite — that not going after you will send the wrong message to other consumers.

A business or other entity that has obtained a monetary judgment against you may also have a legal right to seize some of your assets, and even garnish your wages. State law will outline each party's legal rights.

One myth about this topic is that no one brings lawsuits against people who appear to have no assets. It is no secret that there are those who are irresponsible, or even dishonest, in their dealings with others, as they try to obtain credit through fraud or misrepresentation and have no intention of paying back the loan. These people either then hide their assets — or simply have nothing of value and assume that they are not worth suing. Businesses will occasionally go after these people to create a legal record of their activities to prevent consumers from repeating the process in the future. If the business owner is angry enough, he or she may pursue seizure of property or garnishment of wages.

If you find yourself unable to pay a debt, communicate with the business and explain your situation. Such communication will, in many cases, avoid the court option. As stated earlier in this book, do not ignore the people you owe money to.

Small claims court

If you disagree with a claim, challenge it. If the amount meets the requirements for your state's small claims court, use the small claims process as a way to fight the case. Many states allow small claims actions if the amount is under $2,000. You will not need an attorney and will be given a chance to present your side of the story. This is a good process for claims made against you by a business that has not, by your standards, delivered the goods and services promised, but it is demanding payment anyway. For larger claims, however, your case will go to another court, and legal representation will be required. Costs can be significant; depending upon the complexity of the case; a full civil suit may even go before a jury.

When considering whether you have a good case, evaluate:

- **Evidence**: In court, it does not matter what truly happened. It is only significant what you can *prove* happened. Witnesses are crucial. When witnesses from both sides agree on critical issues, your case is sound. If the critical issues are points of disagreement, your case may not be strong; therefore, you should consider any compromises that are on the table.

- **Legal proof**: If you go to court with a particular type of issue, you must know the key points that the law requires you to prove before you can win a favorable verdict. In an injury-by-automobile case, for example, if the defendant claims the cause was bad brakes, be sure you have sued both the driver and the company responsible for the brakes failing to work on the defendant's car. This way, if the judge rules in assigning fault, you will be the beneficiary of the judgment.

- **Adversary's story**: One of the advantageous aspects of a demand letter is that it elicits from your opponent his or her side of the story. As with previous demand letters, response letters are rare, and you may face going to trial with no knowledge of the opponent's defense strategy.

- **"Damage control" defense**: When you sue for a wrongful act, such as malicious or wrongful termination of a job or employer discrimination, be prepared for a positive defense. As a defendant, the employer likely will plead that there were mitigating circumstances or perhaps misconduct for similar acts that initiated the cause for termination or penalty given to the offending employee. When possible, have other later cases of the wrongful act exposed by your witnesses. You should argue that after-the-fact changes are not a defense for wrongful conduct you received.

- **Malpractice coverage**: Some professionals, such as doctors, may carry insurance coverage against the malfeasance on which you are basing your suit. Subpoena, in advance, documentation of this coverage so that you can add the insurance company's name to your list of parties being sued. If your medical insurance covered all or part of your medical costs, subpoena the records to see what specialties the doctor is said to be capable of practicing. If you find the listed specialties do not match the doctor's credentials, add your carrier as a named defendant. The carrier is liable for his or her certification of ability.

- **Frivolous lawsuit**: The Federal Rules of Civil Procedure advise potential plaintiffs that they must have evidentiary support for the claims of their case. A case where the defendant claims he has been bitten many times by a neighbor's dog, without any pictures of the bites, scars, or records of treatment by a professional, might be classified as a "malicious prosecution." If you sue that defendant for the same cause at different points in time without winning a case, this may be considered an "abuse of process," and the case may result in damage being awarded to the defendant.

How to prevent or overcome judgment:

- If unable to pay a debt, communicate with the lender to explain your situation.
- Challenge any claims that you disagree with.
- Collect accurate records of all contracts, agreements, correspondence, e-mails, telephone calls, and personal meetings.
- Attempt to negotiate a settlement and pay what you can.

As with all other serious financial issues, these are best dealt with before they explode into a full-blown lawsuit. Communication is your best strategy. Genuine disagreements occur during business transactions. Keep accurate records of everything, and attempt to find common ground to resolve disputes — that will go a long way in overcoming this situation.

Making Sense of Civil Calamity

When Hurricane Katrina swept through New Orleans in 2005, it left a dramatic reminder that community-wide disasters occur, forcing those communities to pick through the rubble and rebuild, sometimes even from the ground up. Earthquakes in California, tornadoes in the Midwest, and wildfires in Texas are just a few more examples of how nature can take its toll on a community. Recovery from such disasters is left to civil authorities and individuals. In a time of distress and disaster, it is important to have something to fall back on, even if it is just knowledge of how such a calamity can affect your life.

The effects of natural disasters on your family are:

- Loss of income.
- Loss of job.
- Loss of home.
- Elimination of health and other insurance.

Nature is powerful; no one has the power to stop or prevent its force. There are, however, ways to prepare and protect yourself. The first is by getting insurance. If you live in an area with a high probability of hurricanes, like a beach on the east coast of Florida, you should know the details of your homeowner's or renter's policy and obtain the necessary insurance. Many of the victims of Hurricane Katrina discovered that they did not have adequate flood insurance after the fact and were devastated to learn that insurance companies would not pay claims because their homes were damaged by water, not wind.

Flooding

Many home insurance policyholders are not aware that flood coverage is excluded on nearly all homeowner policies. Flood insurance must be purchased separately; it carries a separate premium charge.

The National Flood Insurance Program (NFIP) is a federal program that enables you to purchase flood insurance on your home, if your home is located in a designated flood zone. Although it is a federal program and is not offered by your insurance company, your agent can help you secure flood insurance and can answer questions about the details of this coverage. If your home is in a flood zone, it is critical you contact your agent to inquire about securing flood coverage on your home.

A flood occurs when an excessive amount of water or mud covers land that is normally dry. A flood can occur when water rises above the normal level because of heavy rain or because of water runoff from a heavy snowfall. Floods can also be caused by hurricanes. Although hurricane coverage is almost unheard of, a flood policy can provide coverage for water damage caused by a hurricane, while your standard home insurance policy can provide coverage for wind and projectiles.

Your choices for dealing with a flood are limited — you can be proactive and purchase flood insurance to help you recoup your loss in the event of a flood, or you can hope for assistance from the government if a flood occurs. Unfortunately, government assistance is only an option if the president declares the flood as a national disaster. Given the limited opportunity for government assistance, you may decide flood insurance is worth the investment because you have the peace of mind of knowing your home will be covered, no matter what, in the event of a flood.

When you purchase flood insurance, you can insure your home for up to $250,000 and your personal property for up to $100,000. Flood insurance is not just an option for homeowners — if you rent your home, condominium, or apartment, you can purchase coverage for your personal property for up to $100,000.

Flood insurance covers structural damage to your home; the repair or replacement of mechanicals, such as furnaces, water heaters, and air conditioners; the cleanup of debris; and the repair or replacement of flooring caused by a flood.

You can determine your flood risk and find out more about flood insurance by visiting **www.floodsmart.gov**.

Earthquake

Earthquakes are also excluded by most insurance policies. Earthquake policies are available that will cover your home in the event of a loss; however, they often carry high deductibles, which limits their effectiveness in indemnifying you for damage or a loss caused by an earthquake.

Because earthquakes are common in California, it is the state in which earthquake policies are most frequently purchased. Because of the high demand for earthquake coverage in California, the California Earthquake Authority (CEA) was developed in 2003 to provide information and advocacy for California residents seeking this coverage. If you are a California resident and are in need of earthquake insurance, you can learn more about the CEA online at **www.earthquakeauthority.com**.

Some insurance companies will also allow you to purchase an earthquake endorsement on your standard home insurance policy. In areas where earthquakes rarely occur, the endorsement will be less expensive than in areas with a higher likelihood of earthquakes.

Examine the odds of an earthquake occurring in your area when deciding if you need this endorsement or not. If you live in California or any other high-risk area, it may be worth the additional premium required to purchase this insurance. If you are not living near a fault line, or an earthquake has never occurred in your area, it is probably not worth the extra cost to purchase earthquake insurance.

The financial implications of civil calamity are potential loss of job; inability to pay bills; potential for bankruptcy, foreclosure, and repossession; and draining of family savings.

Take precautions

Because every area of the country is different, find out what is most likely to happen in your area and insure your belongings accordingly. Homeowner's insurance in some coastal areas is expensive and may even be out of reach for homeowners with a modest income. It is not wise to remain in a home for which you do not have adequate insurance, hoping that nothing bad happens. It is an extremely risky choice that could cause you to lose your home and belongings. Simply put, if you cannot afford homeowner's insurance in a given area, you cannot afford to live there. Many people who live along the Gulf Coast discovered there was an increase in their insurance premium following devastating hurricanes and were forced to move.

Although it is essential to protect your family through homeowner's insurance, it is also important to use other preventative measures for your home. For example, in 2004, the Atlantic Coast experienced one of the most costly, deadly hurricane seasons on record. But many residents purchased hurricane shutters for their homes at the beginning of the season and outlined evacuation and financial plans in case a natural disaster struck. For tornado protection, many families take precautions by picking a safe place in their home to hide during a tornado, and even have these safe places reinforced and made stronger.

In the event of a serious disaster, you may not be able to work for several days, or even weeks. Some form of public assistance may be available through FEMA and the Red Cross for food, shelter, and medical attention, but these will be used by the entire community and will likely end soon after the disaster. If you have a rainy day fund, however, you will have a source for your living expenses while you recover. This is especially important if you are unable to work, or if the natural disaster left costly damages to your home and other assets.

In some cases, you may be forced to move to another area, much like New Orleans residents were forced to do after Hurricane Katrina. This can be difficult and wrenching, especially because you are forced to rebuild your life with next to nothing. If this should happen, use whatever support is available to you, including government financial and counseling assistance.

How to prevent or overcome the financial implications of natural disasters:

- Secure a homeowner's or renter's insurance policy.
- Learn the details of your insurance and plan for the worst.
- Seek and apply for government assistance programs.
- Rely on savings to get you through.
- Set up an emergency plan for the entire family.
- Do not turn to credit cards for supplemental income.

Do not forget: Organizations like the Federal Emergency Management Agency (FEMA), **www.fema.gov**, and the American Red Cross, **www.red-cross.org,** specialize in helping families who have been affected by these disasters. They also offer important tips to protect your family and home, and can help you create a recovery plan for this type of financial disaster.

Chapter 2

The Basics of Bankruptcy

If you are considering bankruptcy as a way to get out of your devastating financial situation, this chapter is for you. Simply put, bankruptcy allows a debtor to eliminate either all of his or her debts — or simply a portion of them. It is a legitimate way to prevent the impending threat of foreclosures and repossessions, allowing you to move forward with your life. But are you sure bankruptcy is your best solution? Are you ready to put up with social stigma, legal fees, and the black mark on your credit that is associated with filing? There may be better options for you, so before you decide, consider all aspects of bankruptcy.

What is Bankruptcy?

Bankruptcy is a legal proceeding for a person or business that is unable to repay outstanding debts. Once the bankruptcy proceedings are complete, the debtor is relieved of the debt that was incurred prior to filing. For example, if an individual had $75,000 in loans and credit card debt that he owed, this sum would be dismissed, and he would be cleared of debt by filing for bankruptcy. The point of most forms of bankruptcy is to wipe out your existing debts, allowing you to make a fresh start. If you are granted bankruptcy, you do not have to pay the unsecured debts that you ran up before you filed your bankruptcy. However, you are responsible for all debts that are compiled after bankruptcy is filed.

It sounds simple, but it is not really that basic. Bankruptcy laws have evolved from legal proceedings that allowed creditors to seize and sell property (and then throw the debtor into prison), to laws that allow debtors a fresh start. U.S. bankruptcy laws are amended, or re-written, from time to time. In October 2005, a major revision went into effect that added hurdles to the process by which a debtor can be relieved of debt. Overall, the 2005 law made it harder for people to file for bankruptcy and required all debtors to get credit counseling before filling for bankruptcy. As with all revisions in the law, there are court challenges and interpretations that mold the actual processes and determine the true meaning of the law. Each state has its own bankruptcy regulations, which means the bankruptcy process is complicated and subject to change. Yet, the fundamentals are the same: debt relief and a new beginning.

Who Can File for Bankruptcy?

You may wonder exactly the amount of debt you will need to have before you are able to qualify for bankruptcy. The truth is, anyone can file for bankruptcy, and there is no minimum amount of debt required. The laws implemented in 2005, however, have changed some people's ability to file for bankruptcy. There used to be no specific policy that stipulated whether a judge could dismiss a bankruptcy case. But after the 2005 revisions, there are clear rules that tell who is eligible for Chapter 7 bankruptcy, as well as who needs to file Chapter 13. There are also other types of bankruptcy that can be filed, Chapter 11 and Chapter 12, as a way of preventing complete financial misfortune for you and your family. The U.S. Code sets up four different types of bankruptcy so that each type, or chapter, applies to different people or situations. Before deciding to file for bankruptcy, make sure you know which chapter you are eligible for.

The effects of bankruptcy on your family are:

- Wipes away previous debts, allowing your family to start fresh.
- Can help your family get out of a dire financial situation.
- Social stigma may be associated with filing for bankruptcy.

How Bankruptcy Works

If you are considering bankruptcy, consult an attorney who specializes in that area and learn your options. You may have legal rights that you are not aware of, or you may be enduring illegal or unsound threats from creditors. For example, if a creditor calls you and threatens to obtain a "warrant" regarding your debt, you do not want to assume that a "warrant" is another word for "arrest," when it is actually a technical filing in civil court. Legal consultants know how the law works and the games that creditors will play, and they will help you to understand what you are actually filing for and what proceedings there are.

Per Title 11 of the U.S. Code (also known as the bankruptcy code), when filing for bankruptcy, you will be required to list all of your creditors, along with the amounts owed. If you leave anyone out, you risk not having that debt cleared away during the bankruptcy process. You may have the option of affirming some debts, which means you agree to pay the loan as planned. If you seek protection under Chapter 7, you will not be able turn around and file again just because you discovered that you really cannot pay your mortgage. But if you are filing under Chapter 13, the payment plan, you will have more flexibility in re-negotiating terms of your payments — although your debts are not forgiven, but just paid down over time.

It is important to note that sometimes you may be able to file for multiple types of bankruptcy — for example, filing for protection under Chapter 7 to eliminate unsecured debts, then filing for protection under Chapter 13 to devise a plan to pay off taxes.

What to Do Before You Can File for Bankruptcy

1. Consult a lawyer.

2. Address all information about your finances and assets; be accurate when providing your lawyer with this information.

3. Complete, sign, and carefully review the court documents.

4. File a petition with the bankruptcy court.

Once you have completed these four steps, you are under the protection of the bankruptcy court, which means your creditors no longer have the right to come after you. This is called an automatic stay on collections actions, and it includes home foreclosures, vehicle repossessions, and other such collections or debt enforcement. But, do not mistake this for being able to live rent-free with a car you are no longer have to make payments on. All this means is that the creditor cannot come after you for the money that is owed up to that point. If you stop making mortgage, rent, or car payments after you file for bankruptcy, but continue to live in the house or drive the vehicle, the creditor can petition the court to either lift the stay or to rene-gotiate the loan. In addition, do not forget that if you decide to keep the house or the car, you must affirm the loan, which requires approval of the creditor and your commitment to remain current on future payments.

In addition to continue paying for the property you wish to keep, you also need to keep making insurance payments on policies that cover your property. If you do not maintain such coverage, a creditor may petition the court to lift the stay to reclaim the now-uninsured property.

Within a few weeks of your filing, there will be a meeting of creditors. During this meeting, the people or entities to which you owe money will be allowed to provide their comments and input about your filing. Creditors rarely show up for these meetings because in most cases, you are affirming certain loans or renegotiating terms of existing mortgages or car loans, which your attorney will have already handled with the lenders. Still, they may show up, anyway. Discuss all of this with your lawyer, and be prepared for the meeting. Chapter 7 proceedings normally last a few months before qualified debts are gone.

What is the Definition of a Bankruptcy Discharge?

A bankruptcy discharge is when you, the debtor, are released from being responsible for certain types of debts. It essentially means that the person in debt is not legally required to pay any debts that have been waived by the court. Thus, the creditors are legally prevented from trying to take action and collect a debt that has been cleared. In this case, no legal action will be taken, and communication with the person who was formally in debt may not take place. This includes communication such as phone calls, in-person contact, letters, or e-mails.

Although the individual in debt is no longer liable for debts that have been discharged, a lien that has been avoided in the bankruptcy case will still remain after the closing of the case. This is also defined as when a property has a charge placed upon it in order to secure the payment of a debt.

Top Five Bankruptcy Questions

Anyone considering filing for bankruptcy is sure to have a multitude of questions about the process, and you are most likely no different. Review these frequently asked questions about bankruptcy before deciding to file:

1. **Will my credit be affected if I file for bankruptcy?** Yes. According to the United States bankruptcy laws, credit bureaus can report your bankruptcy for up to ten years from the date you filed.

2. **Will I ever be able to buy another home?** Regardless of whether you lose your home due to bankruptcy or not, you have a good chance of being able to secure a mortgage again in the future. As long as you have an income high enough to qualify, you can usually apply for a mortgage about 4 years after filing bankruptcy.

3. **Is filing for bankruptcy a long process?** No, your petition can be filed in just a few days. After that, you will find that the creditors stop harassing you and the process begins.

4. **Can I cancel bankruptcy after I already filed?** If you file Chapter 7, you can never dismiss it, unless the courts decided that it is in the creditors' best interest.

5. **Is filing for bankruptcy expensive?** Not at all. You have to pay the courts a filing fee — $274 for Chapter 7 and $189 for Chapter 13. You may also have lawyer fees.

The Myths Associated with Bankruptcy

The term "bankruptcy" can mean a lot of different things to a lot of different people. There is no shame in filing for relief under the federal bankruptcy laws, but according to **www.bankrate.com**, there are many misconceptions associated with filing:

1. **All of your debts will be wiped away when filing for Chapter 7 bankruptcy:** Even the most successful bankruptcy case does not wipe away every debt. In fact, certain types of debts — like alimony, student loans, child support, and fraud-related debts — cannot be erased.

2. **You will lose everything:** Many people believe that if they file for bankruptcy, the government will sell all their assets, and they will have to start over. Though each state has different bankruptcy laws, every state has exemptions that protect certain kinds of assets. This includes your house, car (up to a certain value), retirement savings, clothing, and household items.

3. **You will never get credit again:** But credit card companies will never completely stop sending you those solicitations. Believe it or not, credit card offers will come in again; however, they will be from subprime lenders who may try to charge you high interest rates. It is also important to remember that if you hold a zero-balance credit card on the day you file for bankruptcy, it is not necessary to list it as a creditor. Thus, you may actually be able to keep that card, even after the bankruptcy.

4. **Both you and your spouse have to file for bankruptcy:** This depends on your situation. If you hold a large amount of debt that is only in your name, and not in your spouse's name, then only you need to file for bankruptcy. However, if you have debts that you are both liable for and want to have them cleared, you should file together.

5. **Only irresponsible people file for bankruptcy:** Because nine out of ten bankruptcies are the result of three of the personal financial hardships — medical bills, job loss, or divorce — only a small portion of bankruptcies can be traced directly to financial irresponsibility. Usually, people who file for bankruptcy are those who have struggled to pay their bills and keep falling further behind.

6. **You can only file for bankruptcy once:** The old bankruptcy laws allowed you to file every six years. New laws, however, state that you can go through a Chapter 7 bankruptcy filing only one time in an eight-year period.

Types of Bankruptcy: Chapter 7

This type of bankruptcy is usually considered the fastest way to get out of a financial crisis and start over. This type of bankruptcy accounts for up to 65 percent of all consumer banking filings, making it the most common way people get rid of their debt through bankruptcy filings. From a debtor's point of view, Chapter 7 is the way to go. It eliminates most of your debt, and you do not have to make payments on loans and other obligations, such as credit card debt. Often referred to as liquidation bankruptcy, Chapter 7 allows the bankruptcy court to sell all of the property you own that is considered non-exempt. The proceeds are then given to your creditors. Simply put: It cancels all of your debts in just about four to six months. Usually, the reason why this process can move quickly is because the debtor does not have many assets to lose. The law that went into effect in 2005, however, makes it harder to obtain relief under Chapter 7, forcing many people to file under Chapter 13.

When filing for Chapter 7 bankruptcy, you are generally allowed to keep your home, vehicle, and other things that are essential for your day-to-day life. But remember that if you have any money that is still owed on these items, you may be required to affirm the existing loans, meaning you will not be allowed to wipe out debt on them. In other words, you will still have to make the house and car payments. Additionally, when you file for Chapter 7 bankruptcy, you lose your right to file another bankruptcy petition later to wipe out debts you have affirmed in your initial filing; you will be stuck with them. Also, be sure to keep in the back of your mind that fact that not everyone is approved for Chapter 7 bankruptcy. If this happens, your only option is to file for Chapter 13.

The Chapter 7 process will require you to complete a short credit counseling course that will cost about $50, depending on your state. The U.S. Department of Justice (**www.usdoj.gov**) maintains a list of agencies that perform counseling duties and have been permitted to provide financial counseling for individuals seeking protection under bankruptcy laws. If you file under Chapter 7, you will be required to provide the court with a certificate proving that you have completed the required counseling within 180 days of filing.

If you have an attorney, he or she will gather the information you have provided, such as income, debts, assets, and other property, and prepare the proper forms for the court — known as schedules — as a method of organizing your personal information. It is important that the information you provide to your attorney, and therefore to the court, be completely accurate and complete. Misrepresentation of your financial reality before a bankruptcy court is a crime that can produce penalties, including reinstatement of debt. If you lie on your bankruptcy petition, you are also guilty of perjury. If you are acting on your own behalf without benefit of an attorney, you must still meet every one of the court's legal requirements while staying truthful in your filing.

Types of Bankruptcy: Chapter 13

Also defined as a wage earner's plan, Chapter 13 bankruptcy requires you to pay some or all of your debts to creditors over a set timeline. If you are an individual with a regular income, this process lets you restructure your debts and use future income to pay off your creditors. Depending on your circumstances, it usually offers lower or no-interest repayment plans over a period of three to five years.

Chapter 13 is a formal, court-ordered payment plan. You must have some verifiable income with which the court can work to put the plan together. You do not have to be a salaried worker to qualify; you can be retired with a pension or even self-employed. The primary goal of Chapter 13 is to pay off your debts under a court-approved payment plan. Under Chapter 13, you will be permitted to keep your assets while the plan is in effect, unlike Chapter 7 where, in theory, the court may order some of your property to be seized and sold to settle the outstanding amount of all, or part, of your debts.

Qualifying numbers, which is what type of bankruptcy you are eligible for, will be adjusted periodically, so be sure to determine the current qualifying requirements when you prepare to file. If you are confused about what portions of your debt are secured and unsecured, determine whether the creditor can take back the property if you do not make payments. For instance, if you fail to make car payments, the vehicle can be repossessed. Therefore, a car loan is secured debt. The items you buy with your credit card at a big-box store, however, is not secured, meaning the credit card company is not going to take back the sweater if you fail to pay the card's balance.

You will be unable to file under Chapter 13 if:

- Your debt level is above the limits in place at the time you file your petition. If that is the case, you may qualify for protection under Chapter 11, which is the bankruptcy filing commonly used by corporations undergoing financial reorganization.

- You have had another bankruptcy case within the past 180 days that was dismissed due to a violated order of the court — for example, you did not respond to a motion or make the required payments. There are other legal restrictions for stock-brokers and commodities brokers.

As with Chapter 7, you must prove to the court that you have completed a required credit-counseling course during the bankruptcy filing process. Additionally, as with Chapter 7, you must file a completed petition with the bankruptcy court. In the petition is a list of creditors, your statement of completed credit counseling, pay stubs, and additional required forms. You must also determine what your plan is to repay your debts and file it, based on estimated future income. You must file this plan within 15 days of your bankruptcy filing — if not, the court may dismiss your petition altogether, so it is wise to prepare all of your documentation at the same time and be ready to fully explain to the court how you will meet your financial obligations. Under your proposal, you will promise to make payments every month, most likely for three years, but the period could be expanded to five years depending on your level of debt and other factors.

Steve was laid off from his job and was not able to afford his mortgage payments.Steve files for Chapter 7 and is required to file a repayment plan. After this plan is filed, and the court confirms the plan, it is up to Steve to make sure his plan succeeds. Here is a breakdown of Steve's repayment plan:

- Set up a monthly budget so that money can be used to pay the trustee.
- Make regular payments to the trustee in the amount of $500 per month.
- Trustee will be paid using payroll deductions to ensure that the deadline is met each month.
- Trustee uses the money that Steve sends to pay Steve's creditors.

Bankruptcy to-do list:

It is important to compile a list of everything you will need to do when filing for bankruptcy.

1. You will list the source, amount, and frequency of your income and other financial assets.
2. You must also list your expenses: things such as rent or mortgage, car payments, utilities, and insurance, to name a few.
3. Also, make a detailed list of all of your living expenses — food, shelter, taxes, transportation, clothing, medical care, and more.
4. Provide a list of all your property.
5. List all your creditors and the amount of your claims.

Keep in mind that when filing your Chapter 13 proposal, your plan must be detailed and accurate. You will be making your Chapter 13 payments based on the disposable income you expect. That will be the difference between what you bring in and what you pay out for normal living expenses. Be careful when you put this plan together: The creditors who will be invited to meet with you and the trustee who will be appointed by the court to review your petition will almost certainly challenge your numbers, especially if you grant yourself a large monthly "entertainment" budget. This is an area where your attorney's input will be important, because the new bankruptcy laws restrict what you may declare "fair and reasonable living expenses." Be aware that your Chapter 13 plan will consume all of your disposable income over the life of the plan, which usually runs from three to five years.

If you plan to renegotiate a mortgage or car loan, do it before you file your Chapter 13 plan. Once the court accepts your plan, you may not renegotiate with lenders; you are locked in. Your attorney will advise you about ways to communicate with lenders during this process. You may find that once they become aware of your pending bankruptcy filing, they will be willing to renegotiate your loan, particularly if you are on the cusp of Chapter 7 but are exploring your options under Chapter 13.

Within 30 days of filing for Chapter 13, you must begin making payments under your plan. You must remain current in your payments during the entire process and beyond, until the bankruptcy petition has been satisfied.

As you move through the Chapter 13 process, the court will appoint a trustee who is a legally named individual to work with you. Anyone can become a trustee, but you must apply through the Justice Department to the U.S. Trustee Program. The trustee's role varies by district, but he or she will likely look over your plan, try to determine whether the numbers are realistic, and arrange for monthly payment. The payment may be through an automatic deduction from your paycheck. That may not be a bad thing, given that you will not have an opportunity to spend the money on something else and slide into default on your bankruptcy agreement. The trustee will schedule a meeting with you, your attorney, and your creditors. You are required to attend the meeting, which will most likely last under an hour. The trustee's job is to implement a workable payment schedule. He or she has a vested interest in a successful outcome because the trustee will be paid a percentage of the monthly payment as compensation for the work performed.

You will also be required to produce two forms of identification: a picture ID and your social security card, or a copy of it. You must prove that you have filed tax returns over the previous four years. If you have not, the bankruptcy proceedings will come to a halt until you are current on your tax returns. Be aware that tax obligations almost certainly survive bankruptcy, whether Chapter 13 or Chapter 7, so you should not delay the filing of your tax returns in hopes that bankruptcy will somehow get you off the hook. Remember: The tax collector never goes away.

Some of your creditors may object to your payment schedule and question your planned living expenses. It may be that your plan will only pay a portion of what you owe them, so they will demand more money and suggest that your personal expenses be cut to increase payments to creditors. Credit card companies may also show up, hoping to challenge your payment plan. Be prepared to document your financial proposal and negotiate with your creditors. Each change in your plan will require submission of a modified Chapter 13 plan. The trustee will work with you and your attorney and will communicate with your creditors. The trustee is not the one who will rule on your plan, however. That decision belongs to the judge in the bankruptcy court. It is important to note that 94 of the federal judicial districts take care of bankruptcy matters, and these are where bankruptcy cases are filed in bankruptcy court. They are not able to be filed in individual state courts.

You will be required to attend at least one court hearing under Chapter 13. During the Chapter 13 hearing, the judge will review your plan and either approve it or send you back to make modifications if it does not meet the legal requirements, as listed in the following chart. Chances are slim that the trustee will have missed anything this major, but it can happen.

It is important to understand that entering a Chapter 13 bankruptcy process will require patience and commitment. There will be legal and filing fees. As per provisions of the Fair Debt Collection Practices Act, once you file for bankruptcy, the creditors are not legally allowed to call and harass you for your debts. This law was set up to protect your rights and help you move on. However, while your creditors are legally prevented from making angry telephone calls to you, you may have to face them across a conference table. Remember, you are in the process of solving a serious financial crisis, and in the end, you will survive, and even prosper.

Another important consideration is the automatic stay. When an automatic stay comes into effect, the debtor cannot pursue foreclosures, repossessions, judgments, and other debts. The collection is literally stopped — but keep in mind that the stay may only be effective for a certain period of time.

Remember that there are many myths and misconceptions associated with bankruptcy. If you are considering going this route, your best bet is to study all the types of bankruptcy available to you and consult an attorney that specializes in this area to go over your options.

What Type of Bankruptcy is Right for You?

Now that you know what each type of bankruptcy filing entails, it is time to compare the two major types. Take a look at the differences between Chapter 7 and Chapter 13 so you can decide which one is best for you:

You own valuable property that is considered nonexempt:

- **Chapter 7:** You must give up the property and pay the trustee its fair market value.
- **Chapter 13:** You are able to keep your property.

Some of your personal loans include co-debtors:

- **Chapter 7:** Your co-debtor will also be contacted by the creditor and required to make a payment.
- **Chapter 13:** Your co-debtor will not be required to make a payment.

You owe child support, alimony, student loans, restitution, or criminal fines:

- **Chapter 7:** You will still need to pay these debts.
- **Chapter 13:** You must pay these debts in full after filing.

The Means Test

The requirements pertaining to Chapter 7 relief include a means test, which is a measure of your ability to pay your bills. The means test is a form on which you compute your average income during the previous six months. The average will then be matched against the median income for your state. Median means half of the workers in your state earn more and half earn less. For example, the median income for a single male in the United States in 2007 was $50,233, while nationwide the median household income was $48,201. Your state's numbers may be higher or lower, depending on income levels where you live. Such income levels tend to vary by region. People who reside in the state of California often have higher incomes than individuals who live in Mississippi, and the bankruptcy laws take those income differences into account when the means test is applied. Keep in mind that the court will also decide on your income by averaging the six months prior to filing the petition, whether you are employed or not. If you find that your income is less than your state's median, you will not have a problem filing under Chapter 7. However, if your income is higher than your state's median, you must use a complicated formula — also known as the means test — to see just where you will fall in the bankruptcy process. This is where a good attorney is helpful.

To get a sense of how the means test works, use a means test calculator, like the one at **www.legalconsumer.com/bankruptcy/nolo**. You can add in your zip code, and the calculator will help you determine if filing for Chapter 7 is an option for you. Based on the number of people in your household, your average monthly income, your veteran status, and your non-consumer debts, you can instantly see if filing Chapter 7 is a good option for you. To determine your eligibility, the main thing you need to be concerned with is whether your household income is less than the median household income in your state. If it is, you are able to file for Chapter 7. You can find this information on the Web site of the U.S. Census Bureau, at **www.census.gov/hhes/www/income/income.html**.

Because Chapter 7 offers complete relief, the new law restricts this relief to people who are in dire straights and cannot pay even a small portion of their debts. This means that if your income is higher than your state's median number, the court may decide that you belong under Chapter 13, where you will be legally responsible to pay off all or some of your bills. Again, be completely honest in providing income information. Your attorney should be prepared to advise you on this issue and tell you if there are any unusual aspects to your filing.

It is also important to note that under the bankruptcy laws, you need to determine how much income you make each month and compare it with your state's median income for a comparable household. If your income is lower than (or the same as) the median, then you are eligible to file for Chapter 7. If your income is more than the medium, you will be required to pass the means test described earlier. Before you can go through the process of filing your bankruptcy petition or work out a court-approved payment plan, you must know whether you qualify under the law to address your debts under the bankruptcy statutes. If you make $250,000 per year and want to wipe out $20,000 in debts and move on, you may find that a judge will have no sympathy for you and throw out your petition. If, on the other hand, you make $20,000 per year and have $250,000 in debts, bankruptcy court might be the best place to go.

The main element in a Chapter 7 filing is how much your income is. This is not as straightforward as you might think. As mentioned earlier, the laws, effective in 2005, require income to be measured as an average of your pay for the six months leading up to the time you filed. So, the law requires you to list your income for the previous six months, add it up, divide it by six, then multiply it by 12 to arrive at what is assumed your annual income. You then compare that number to your state's median income. If you are at or below the median, you will not be required to meet the so-called means test, which is a stricter standard to qualify for Chapter 7 protection. Here is an example:

Income — Household Total			
	Husband	**Wife**	**Total**
January	$4,000	$3,000	$7,000
February	$4,000	$3,000	$7,000
March	$4,000	$3,000	$7,000
April	$1,500	$3,000	$4,500
May	$1,500	$2,000	$3,500
June	$0	$2,000	$2,000
Totals	$15,000	$16,000	$31,000
6-month average	$2,500	$2,666	$5,166
Annual	$30,000	$31,996	$61,996

This example can be flexible, but to look at the best example, assume the household consists of a man, wife, and two children. Obviously, they are experiencing a severe financial crisis caused by a dramatic drop in income, from $7,000 per month in January to $2,000 per month in June. That is why they are behind on their bills and are seeking bankruptcy protection. But, under the law, their income is assumed to be an average of the six months prior to filing, so instead of reflecting that this family is currently living on $2,000 per month, the six-month average shows an income of $5,666, which is a difference of $3,666 between reality and assumption. Nevertheless, this is the figure the bankruptcy court will use to determine eligibility under Chapter 7.

We must now compare this figure to the median income for this family's state as determined by the U.S. Census Bureau. The bankruptcy court's clerk has the information, or you may find it at the Web site for the U.S. Department of Justice (**www.usdoj.gov**). For this example, we will use the national median income figure for a four-person family, $50,233 as of 2007. Using this number, the family's income average, as unrealistic as it is, qualifies for protection under Chapter 7 without the requirement of a means test. Conversely, if this couple had no children and was filing as a two-person household, the national median income figure would drop to $48,316, which is well below the median, forcing them into the means test. Some income is not counted in the means test:

1. Social security benefits
2. Proceeds to terrorism victims (such from as the September 11 attacks)
3. Proceeds to people who were victims of crimes or war

In early 2009, a law went into affect that no longer requires disabled veterans from taking the means test. To qualify, the debts must have been incurred during homeland defense or active duty. If this does not pertain to you, the categories below must be listed as income:

1. Wages, salaries, bonuses, commissions, and fees.

2. Retirement income (but not Social Security).

3. Tax refunds.

4. Rental income (net).

5. Child support or other such payments.

6. Payments under insurance accident and health plans.

7. Gifts.

8. Scholarships and other educational benefits.

9. All business income.

10. All funds that anyone, including family members, contributes to your monthly expenses. This includes money you receive from your spouse if you are not filing jointly, even if that money is used solely for household or other common expenses.

11. Unemployment compensation (although there are ongoing legal questions about this one).

If the total of your monthly income is higher than a salary, adding such aspects as rental income or child support, you must carefully calculate every source of cash you have available for the purposes of bankruptcy qualification and potential payment plans. By now, you may be asking yourself: How much more complicated can it get? If you do not have a lawyer at this point, you are at least beginning to understand why most people are represented by attorneys during bankruptcy proceedings.

As you proceed through the means test to seek qualification under Chapter 7, or even Chapter 13, you must maneuver through a minefield of government-allowed expenses and formulas to determine your eligibility for one chapter or another.

If your income each month is the same as or below your state's median, then you are qualified for Chapter 7. If your income is even one dollar above the median, you are required to use the means test in order to evaluate your income. You begin with your estimated annual income and then subtract your allowed expense value. Your spending allowances are determined by the Internal Revenue Service (IRS). As it turns out, when the new bankruptcy laws were being drafted, Congress decided to incorporate the standards used by the IRS in tax cases. The IRS (**www.irs.gov**) uses its own standards to determine acceptable monthly expenses for someone who is facing payments for back taxes. Generally, normal monthly expenses include rent, housing payments, utilities, automobile payments, insurance, taxes, food, and other basic necessities deemed necessary in order to live. The numbers are adjusted every year. The bankruptcy law subjects you to those standards, which are based on monthly income and family size, among others. There are additional expenses that are allowed, such as educational expenses for minor children and payments to IRS, but there is a long list of qualifications and limits.

Your averaged income will be compared against your expenses that are allowable, and the difference will be considered your disposable income. If the number is less than $100 per month, you have passed the means test. If it is more than $100 but less than $166.67, a formula will be applied to that will help determine the impact of certain payments to the total amount of debt. If the number is more than $166.67, you will not be eligible for Chapter 7 and will move to Chapter 13.

Types of Bankruptcy: Chapter 11

Also known as reorganization bankruptcy, Chapter 11 applies to corporations that need to file for financial restructuring. You often hear about Chapter 11 on the news when large corporations are in financial trouble. In this case, the corporation's assets are sold to pay creditors, and sometimes the company is allowed to remain open in order to earn revenue and keep their employees.

On occasion, individuals with very high debt loads may also qualify for this category of bankruptcy. However, if a petition for a prior bankruptcy has already been dismissed because the debtor is unable to agree with court orders or make an appearance in court, then that person is not eligible to file under Chapter 11. Also, if creditors tried to take back property that they held liens on, and the individual was voluntarily dismissed from court, this is also not a situation that is eligible to file for Chapter 11. Finally, anyone who received an approved agency's credit counseling no more than 180 days before the bankruptcy was filed for is not able to file Chapter 11.

Types of Bankruptcy: Chapter 12

Chapter 12 is also known as the "family fisherman" or "family farmer" bankruptcy. It is a special kind of bankruptcy that covers farmers or fishermen who are financially distressed but also have a regular annual income. In order to qualify, individuals must have debt that makes up at least 80 percent occupational costs, and they must owe less than $3,544,525 for farming and $1,642,500 for fishing. Added to the bankruptcy code in 1986, it is very similar to Chapter 13 in that you follow a plan to pay off creditors, although it provides a higher debt limitation. Chapter 12 enables family farmers or fisherman who are in detrimental financial situations to make an installment repayment plan to creditors over the time period of three to five years.

Under the Bankruptcy Code, these workers fall into two categories. The first is a farmer/fisherman or a farmer/fisherman and their spouse. The second is a partnership/corporation. For farmers/fishermen in the first category, they are required to meet the following criteria on the date that they filed the petition in order to qualify for Chapter 12:

- The farmer/fisherman, or their spouse, must work in a farming or commercial fishing operation.

- The total debts of the operation (both secured and unsecured) must not be higher than $3,544,525 (if a farming operation) or $1,642,500 (if a commercial fishing operation).

- For family farmers, no less than 50 percent of the total fixed debts (exclusive of debt for the debtor's home) must be related to the farming or commercial fishing operation. For family fisherman, this number is at least 80 percent.

- The gross income from the commercial fishing or farming operation must be more than 50 percent (either of the individual or the husband and wife) for the preceding tax year. Specifically for family farmers, each of the 2nd and 3rd prior tax years must have been derived from the farming or commercial fishing operation.

Chapter 7

Basics: Allows the bankruptcy court to sell all of the property that is not exempt. Have the money from the sale distributed to your creditors.

Price estimation:

- $300 to file.
- $1,000 - $2,000 in legal fees.

Process:

- The debtor must file bankruptcy documents in bankruptcy court.
- Creditors are advised that petition has been filed.
- The debtor and creditors meet at court.
- All non-exempt assets are sold.
- The debtor is discharged and most debts are eliminated, usually 60 to 90 days after the initial meeting.

Requirements:

- A $300 filing fee must be paid (Form 3A) — applicant can pay in installments (Form 3B).
- A voluntary petition must be filled out (Form 1).
- A list of all creditors must be provided.
- A statement of social security number must be filled out (Form 21).
- Must complete credit counseling and provide certificate and debt repayment plan.
- A notice by bankruptcy petition preparer to debtor must be filled out (Form 19B).
- A disclosure of compensation paid needs to be completed (Form B280).

Chapter 13

Basics: The type of bankruptcy that requires you to pay a set amount of your debts to creditors over a pre-determined timeline, usually three to five years.

Price estimation:

- $235 case filing fee.

- $39 miscellaneous administrative fee.

- Miscellaneous legal fees, which depend on the individual lawyer.

Process:

- The debtor must file bankruptcy documents in bankruptcy court.

- Fill out all paperwork: schedules of liabilities and assets, timeline of current expenditures and income, schedules of executory contracts and unexpired leases (for example, rental leases, cell phone contracts, auto leases, and rent-to-own agreements), and a financial affairs statement.

- Automatic stay comes into effect, which means the debtor can not pursue foreclosures, repossessions, judgments, and other debts.

- 20 and 50 days after the person in debt files the claim, the trustee will hold a meeting that the debtor must attend to discuss the situation with creditors.

- All unsecured creditors must file claims within 90 days after the first date set for the meeting of creditors.

- Within 45 days of meeting with creditors, the bankruptcy judge will hold a confirmation hearing to decide whether the plan is feasible and meets the standards set in the bankruptcy code.

- The individual in debt must begin to make plan payments to the trustee within 30 days after filing the bankruptcy case.

Requirements:

In order to qualify for Chapter 13, you must fall into the following criteria. Please note that some of these sums may fluctuate over time to reflect any changes in the consumer price index:

- Have less than $336,900 in unsecured debt (this includes credit cards).
- Have secured debt less than $1,010,650 (this includes property mortgages and vehicle loans).
- Provide a certificate of credit counseling and a copy of a plan for debt repayment (determined in counseling).
- Provide the U.S. trustee with copies of the most recent transcript copies or tax returns, as well as tax returns filed during the case.

Chapter 11

Basics: The type of bankruptcy that applies to corporations that need to file for financial reorganizations.

Price:

- $1,039 fee to file.
- A minimum quarterly fee is required to be paid to the U.S. trustee (cost ranges from $250 to $10,000).

Process:

- A petition is filed with the bankruptcy court either voluntarily, where you choose to file bankruptcy (includes standard information like your name, social security number, residence, and your plan of repayment or intention to file one), or involuntarily, where you are required to file bankruptcy (in certain circumstances).
- A written disclosure statement, containing information about assets, liabilities, and business affairs, is filed with the court.
- A plan of reorganization is also filed with the bankruptcy court.
- A certificate that proves credit counseling attendance must be provided.

- Debtor becomes the "debtor in possession," which means that the debtor filed for bankruptcy but still possesses property with a lien.
- Debtor must report monthly income, operating expenses, etc. to the U.S. trustee.
- Automatic Stay comes into effect, meaning the debtor cannot pursue foreclosures, repossessions, judgments and other debts.
- A reorganization plan is put into place and creditors have the chance to vote on it.

Requirements:

- The filing fee must accompany all schedules and/or petitions, or individual debtors may submit an application to pay the filing fee in a series of installments.

- To pay the filing fees, cash, a cashier's check, a money order, or a check from an attorney's firm is required. Checks must be made payable to "Clerk, U.S. Bankruptcy Court."

Chapter 12

Basics: A special kind of bankruptcy that covers individuals in these job categories who are financially distressed but also have a regular annual income.

Price:

- $200 case filing fee .
- $39 miscellaneous administrative fee.

Process:

- To initiate a case, the debtor must submit a voluntary petition with the court.

- The following must be filed with the court: a schedule of their liabilities and assets, a schedule of current income and expenditures, a schedule of executory contracts and unexpired leases, and a statement of financial affairs.

- A meeting of the creditors is held between 20 and 35 days after the petition is filed for the creditors to ask the debtor and the trustee questions about the debtor's finances and payment plan.

- Within 45 days after the individual files the plan, a confirmation hearing will be held to discuss the plan that will be scheduled.

- 90 days after filing the petition, the debtor must file a plan of repayment that includes payments of fixed amounts to the trustee on a regular basis over a period of three to five years.

- After completing every payment, the Chapter 12 debtor will be granted a discharge of all debts.

Requirements:

- The person in debt is required to file a plan for repaying debts and reorganizing the farming operation.

- The plan may modify the terms of debt repayment of either secured or unsecured creditors and may be waived over a reasonable period of time.

Summary

Your basic choice is whether to file or try to work something out with your creditors before the matter of your debt goes to the legal system. This is the best option because it will keep the word "bankruptcy" out of your credit report. Contact your creditors, explain your situation, and ask if they are willing to work with you. The debt crisis that began to deepen in early 2008 resulted in creditors with more incentives to negotiate, so you may find that the people to whom you owe money will be willing to talk.

Still, it may not be possible to avoid the bankruptcy option for any number of reasons, and such circumstances are not necessarily a negative reflection on you or your ability to manage your money. If you have been hit with huge medical bills that you cannot pay, or if you have lost your job, you may need protection under the bankruptcy laws.

If you choose this option, which will it be: Chapter 7 or Chapter 13? Chapter 7 will wipe away most of your debts, but it will also place your assets at risk. Even though you may keep your home, depending on your state, you will not likely keep your place at the lake, or your boat. Chapter 7 will take place over a few months. Chapter 13, on the other hand, means you will be making payments to your creditors for three or five years, depending on your income and debt levels, but you will be able to keep your assets.

Either option will require a close examination of your debts, assets, projected income, and factors particular to your state. Either option will get your creditors off your back during the bankruptcy process, meaning they will not be calling you demanding payment. They may, though, demand payment through the court process and challenge certain parts of your bankruptcy filing, especially a Chapter 13 repayment plan that they feel unfairly excludes them or limits their payments.

Detailed Descriptions of the U.S. Bankruptcy Laws

As you may already know, in 2005 U.S. Congress made big enhancements to the laws of bankruptcy. If you had any knowledge of bankruptcy laws prior to 2005, you should put that knowledge aside, as most of the pre-existing bankruptcy laws were affected. There are some important enhancements, known as the Bankruptcy Abuse Prevention and Consumer Protection Act of 2005 (BAPCPA). Here are the three major changes:

- **Ticket out**: Before your bankruptcy can be filed, you must go to a financial education class known as a Debtor Reduction Class. Both the class and the teacher must be approved by the U.S. Trustees Office.

- **Ticket in**: This is a credit counseling class, conducted by a non-profit agency and approved by the office of the U.S. Trustees, that you must attend for six months if you are considering filing for bankruptcy. Once taken, you are eligible to file for bankruptcy.

- **Means test**: This test uses a formula that determines whether you can afford to pay up to 25 percent of your unsecured debt — for example, credit card bills. It also compares how much you earn with the average in your state. If your income is above your state's average, and you are able to pay up to 25 percent of your unsecured debt, you will not be allowed to file Chapter 7 bankruptcy.

These laws will affect the way you may file, as shown in the following list:

- New regulations have been imposed on lawyers, which means you may have to take more time to find an attorney who is willing to represent you in a bankruptcy case.

- You must finish a form that shows your average monthly income six months before the time when you filed. This is called your current monthly income statement.

- If you fail the means test under Chapter 7, your filing will be deemed as an abuse of the system, and your case will be dismissed.

- If you have filed for Chapter 13 and your current monthly income is more than your state's medium, you must commit to pay all your future income over a five-year plan.

- You must provide your previous four years federal and state tax returns when filing Chapter 13.

- You need to attend a budget management class before your Chapter 7 and Chapter 13 can be finalized.

- All child support or alimony obligations must remain current while your Chapter 13 bankruptcy petition is pending.

CASE STUDY: THE REALITY OF BANKRUPTCY

"Tommy"
Washington, D.C.
Note: The participant in this case study is a real person who has filed bankruptcy. The name of this participant has been changed to ensure his privacy.

"I lived in fear and desperation."

That is how Tommy describes his life before bankruptcy. Tommy made a lot of money a few years ago but, as he put it, "I wasted it." He did not pay his taxes, ran up a large, unsecured credit card bill, drove an expensive car, and lived beyond his means.

His unpaid taxes accrued penalties and interest that topped $100,000. The IRS placed a 75 percent lien on his salary. He had no money. He lived in fear of arrest, assuming that the government would charge him with failure to pay his taxes.

Finally, he talked to an attorney experienced in resolving serious financial matters. The attorney told him, "Your life isn't over." He filed first for protection under Chapter 7 to wipe away his unsecured debts, then he filed under Chapter 13 to arrange a payment plan for his taxes.

During his bankruptcy process, Tommy underwent a financial forensic examination that detailed all of his spending, down to the penny. He learned that it was the small things, like dog grooming and restaurant meals, that added up to big problems. It was a sobering experience.

"I was brutally honest because I had to be," he said.

Tommy now has a good job with the government, drives a reliable but inexpensive car, and has paid off most of his taxes. He makes his payments on time and has managed to separate his needs from his wants. He pays cash for most things but has a credit card with a modest limit in case of emergencies. He has no balance on it.

His advice to anyone in this position: Find a good attorney. "There's no shame in bankruptcy," he said.

What Can You Keep?

When people begin the process of bankruptcy, one of the first questions they ask is what they can keep. The first major consideration is your home. Bankruptcy laws are not drawn to throw you and your family out on the street. If you are a homeowner, there is a chance you can remain in your home — but you will not get out of paying your mortgage. If you are renting a home, your landlord may allow you to stay in your current dwelling.

Homestead exemptions

The benefits of a homestead is that it protects some or all of your home's equity — specifically from property taxes and creditors. Each state has its own homestead exemption; that is, what value the state will allow you to retain after bankruptcy. Some states let you keep your home no matter how much it is worth. Others place extremely tough restrictions on the homestead exemption: the difference between what you owe on your home and its fair market value.

Homestead exemptions apply only to your primary residence, not to vacation or second homes, investment property, or other real estate in which you have an interest.

If you live in a mobile home or on a boat, there is a good chance the homestead exemption will apply, but only if it is your primary residence. Your state's bankruptcy laws may affect your options. For example, if you live in Texas and owe debts to the federal government, the law is that the homestead is not protected from those debts. This is why it is important to consult with an attorney, or go to your state's Web site to get the right information for your state.

There are other technical requirements that vary by state and certain federal rules that may make Chapter 7 an unwise choice for anyone wishing to retain their home during the bankruptcy process.

To retain your home, you must be current on your home mortgage, as well as other encumbrances to the property, such as equity credit lines or second mortgages. You also will be required to renegotiate a new mortgage or affirm your mortgage with your lender — one that will survive the bankruptcy process and ensure that you to are able to meet the payments.

The wildcard exemption allows you to protect certain assets during the process of bankruptcy. This exemption varies by state, but it may allow you to apply these protections to your real estate. Most states have small amounts that fall into this category. Upon publication of this book, Maryland has no homestead exemption, but its wildcard is $5,500. Pennsylvania's wildcard is $300, California's is $1,000, and New Hampshire's is $1,000, but you get an extra $7,000 if you do not take advantage of other exemptions provided by the state of New Hampshire.

Be aware that the bankruptcy laws contain certain residency limits and restrictions that apply to when you bought your home and how long you have lived in the state. Again, laws vary by state, thus it is important to research your state's laws.

Should You File Jointly or Singly?

Many married couples believe that they are in debt together. However, all married couples must make a decision whether they will file for bankruptcy as a couple, or if only one of them will file. It is important to ask what either of these options will mean. If only one party has lost a job or has incurred huge medical bills, it may be wise to limit bankruptcy to that individual, therefore limiting the financial damage to the family. If both husband and wife are enduring the financial crisis, such as job loss, and there is no gain by filing singly, a joint filing may be in order. This is a personal decision based on individual family needs and circumstances, but there are some things you may want to consider:

- **The family home**: A number of states protect property that is jointly owned by husband and wife, and such property is not part of bankruptcy proceeding if only one person is filing; this is known as "tenancy by the entirety." It means that the home owned by both people can only become part of the bankruptcy estate if both people file. If only one files, the property is protected, no matter its value. Some states do not offer such protections.

- **Income standards**: These are different for individuals and couples. Individuals will have a lower means test, and they will be allowed a lower monthly expense level. You and your spouse will be seen as a single unit in a joint filing, and your combined incomes and debts will be factored into the process. If only one of you files, those numbers will change and, depending on your state, so will the assets you can lose or protect.

How Bankruptcy Affects Your Debts & Property

In a perfect world, you would file for bankruptcy, and all your debt would be wiped away while you are still allowed to keep your property. Unfortunately, it does not work out that way. Every situation is different, but take a look at how debt and property are affected when bankruptcy is filed.

Personal debts

The purpose of bankruptcy is to help you take control of your financial obligations. Generally speaking, bankruptcy will eliminate debts that arise before filing instead of after. So, if you decide that bankruptcy is your best option, it is important to be sure you file at the right time. Here is a list of debts and whether they are dischargeable, also known as excusable. However, it is important to always remember that this may vary depending on which type of bankruptcy you file for.

Employment taxes	Not dischargeable
Loans	Not dischargeable for Chapter 7 Dischargeable for Chapter 13
Student loans	Not dischargeable
Noncriminal restitution	Dischargeable
Marital property divisions	Not dischargeable
Real and personal property taxes	Not dischargeable

Personal property

One of the most painful parts of going through the bankruptcy process is having your personal property seized. From valuable items to sentimental things, there is no easy way to lose your personal possessions. Generally, most states let you keep most of your personal property, especially those things that have little or no value. These include items that you use to earn a living; your clothing; and your household goods. In order to have a grasp on what can and cannot be taken, it is important to determine which assets are property of your estate and which items are considered exemptions. Take a closer look at each:

- **Property of the estate**: This includes almost every asset you owned when you filed for bankruptcy. It also includes proceeds from the property of the estate, inheritances, life insurance proceeds, and marital property division.

- **Exemptions**: The bankruptcy code offers a list of exemptions, but it is critical to keep in mind that each state has its own. In fact, a large number of states actually have removed themselves from the bankruptcy code exemptions, which means that the residents of those states can only rely on state exemptions. Some common exemptions include automobiles (currently the federal exemption allows each debtor claim $2,950 for a motor vehicle), household goods (the federal bankruptcy code exempts items up to $475 each and no more than $9,850 total), and inheritance.

Alternatives to Bankruptcy

While bankruptcy can be an essential way to get you out of a crippling financial situation and start over, it should always be considered as a last resort. As you probably already know, there are some major drawbacks to filing. Not only does filing for bankruptcy damage your credit rating, but it can also be used against you by prospective employers, force you to lose your personal belongings, and even damage the companies and individuals who have extended credit to you. Before you jump into bankruptcy with the belief that it is your only option, stop; it may not be the best, or only, solution for you. Here are some alternatives to consider:

Create a budget: While this seems like a simple solution, and possibly one that you are past, you may be surprised. Many people are not aware of where they are spending their money each month. Take a long, hard look at your monthly income and expenses and see if there is any room to pay off your existing debts over the next three to five years — which is a common rule of thumb.

Ask for help from a family member: Look at the support system around you and consider whether anyone may be able to help you out. From generous family members to employers to friends, these people may be in a willing position to pay your debts temporarily without suffering financial hardship themselves. However, it is important to caution that you are always putting your relationship with family members at risk if you do not pay off their loans.

Refinance your loans: If you currently have loans (mortgage, auto, student) that you are in good standing with — meaning that you are up-to-date with your payments — you may be able to refinance with better terms. This can help you find the money to pay off your existing debts.

Sell off some of your assets: Ask yourself if you have anything you would be able to sell to pay off creditors. Even if it does not cover all your debts, it may be enough to get balances down and keep certain creditors happy for a while. Remember that if you file for bankruptcy, there will be assets that you would lose during the process. Instead of losing them due to bankruptcy, use them to deter filing.

Negotiate with your creditors: Surprisingly enough, many creditors will consider negotiating to allow you some time to get back on your feet. Call your creditors and see if they will work with you before you resort to filing bankruptcy.

Create a repayment plan: While it may seem daunting to negotiate with creditors on your own, there are resources out there that can help you. Nonprofit organizations exist specifically to help people manage their debt. The U.S. Department of Justice offers a list of approved credit counseling agencies (**www.usdoj.gov/ust/eo/bapcpa/ccde/cc_approved.htm**). These organizations are on your side and will give you a method to help work out repayment plans that both the debtor and creditor can live with.

Other organizations that may help are:

- *National Foundation for Credit Counseling*
  Supports the national agenda for financially responsible behavior and helps members deliver high-quality financial education and counseling services.
  (**www.nfcc.org**)

- *Money Management International*
  An organization that has been helping people take charge of their finances since 1958.
  (**www.moneymanagement.org**)

- *American Consumer Credit Counseling*
  A non-profit that helps people take control of their money and plan for tomorrow.
  (**www.consumercredit.com**)

Tap into your retirement plans: If you feel confident that you will be able to repay the funds in the time required by the plan provider, it may be a good option to consider. But because there are tax consequences involved in taking a distribution from a retirement savings plan, this should always be considered as a last option.

Negotiating with the IRS

The task of having to contact and negotiate with the IRS may seem intimidating. However, it is an essential part of the process if you want to get yourself back on track financially.

If you owe the IRS money, the collection notices start about five weeks after the tax was due. The first notification you will receive is their "Intent to Levy," which means to seize your property. If your payment is not received by the deadline, you will be contacted by a local revenue office or an automatic collection system that will try to negotiate with you. In many cases, the local revenue office will agree to an installment payment plan with you. This is usually an option for outstanding taxes of less than $25,000, and it requires that you:

- Make all payments on time — both current and future.
- Agree that any future refunds be applied to your unpaid taxes.
- Provide updated financial information when requested.

If the offer is not approved, you must stop trying to negotiate on your own and seek professional help from a lawyer or accountant. These professionals have the expertise in dealing with the IRS and will help you endure the process, which is generally to complete a Collection Information Statement. This statement will provide the IRS with a clear picture of your assets, income, and living expenses.

If you owe taxes to the IRS, the government has ten years to collect the money. Once that period of time is over, unless the IRS files to renew the tax, they can no longer collect these tax amounts. Therefore, you need to be clear about when your statute of limitations begins and when it expires. It is important to look into your state's laws because in some states, the period to collect the tax can be renewed. For example, in California, it can be renewed twice for a total of 30 years.

Do You Need a Lawyer?

If you are going through the process of filing for bankruptcy, you do not necessarily need a lawyer. However, in practice, it is a smart idea. Bankruptcy is a complicated process that requires time and attention to detail. You can obtain all bankruptcy forms either online or from certain office supply stores. Be aware that each state has its own requirements that are melded into the federal statutes, and it is important that you meet the requirements of your state. Each bankruptcy court has what are known as "local rules" and you must become familiar with them. You may be required to see the clerk of the court's office and request permission to read them. It may not be possible or practical to obtain your own copy of these lengthy documents. Again, in theory, you can proceed through the bankruptcy process by yourself, but it may not be wise.

How to find a good bankruptcy lawyer

- Do not wait until the last minute; take your time researching options.
- Check the bar association for referrals.
- Make sure the lawyer is certified by the American Bankruptcy Institute.
- Ask lots of questions.

- Make sure your fees are outlined.
- Stay involved in the process at every stage.

If you choose to use the services of an attorney, look for one who specializes in bankruptcy issues. Not all lawyers are the same, and the person who once represented you for a traffic issue may not be competent to handle your bankruptcy. Be aware that hiring an attorney who specializes in this area will almost certainly save you money in the end by maneuvering your case through the court and knowing the system and how it works. There will be documents to complete, creditor meetings, hearings, and requirements particular to that court, among other things.

Most attorneys offer a free consultation to discuss your needs, so meet with several of them and be honest as you present your situation. Bring a list of all of your debts — not just monthly payments, but debt totals. Bring a list of your assets, such as your home, vehicle(s), computers, stocks, 401(k) benefits, and anything else that the court or your creditors will consider an asset. If you have a lease for an apartment, house, or a vehicle, or any other documents that can be considered a financial commitment, bring a copy of them. Your prospective attorney will need every detail of your financial life.

Most people will have a few credit cards, a vehicle loan, a home lease or mortgage, a consumer loan or two, possibly student loans, and other common debt. Some people will have unusual debt loads or personal financial standings that the lawyer must be made aware of, such as unpaid tax bills or liens and judgments. A lawyer whom you are considering to represent you must be aware of everything in your financial history.

If you look through the phone book's yellow directory, you will see pages of ads for attorneys. Stay away from the ones who advertise that they handle everything from drunken driving cases to divorce, wills, and "all your legal needs." Look for someone who specializes in bankruptcies. The Internet is a good place to start researching. Call your local bar association to ask for a referral to an attorney who specializes in bankruptcy. Also, ask friends or relatives if they know of any good lawyers.

When you find an attorney, inquire about their fees; some attorneys may charge a small fee for the first consultation. You can decide whether it would be worth it to pay the fee or to choose lawyers whose first consultation is free. What you are looking for is the best possible legal representation, not the best price. You should feel comfortable with the attorney you are considering, so ask yourself these questions after your initial meeting:

- Does he or she seem sympathetic?

- Is he or she abrupt and judgmental?

- Do you feel as though you are getting personal attention, or are just another name on a form?

- Ask each attorney how long they have been representing bankruptcy clients and whether most of their clients are debtors or creditors.

Finally, what is this going to cost you? Lawyers are free to charge whatever they want. Fortunately, there are a lot of them, and they compete against each other. Try to get an indication of the lawyer's fees for common bankruptcy services when you are setting the appointment. You will perhaps be told something about every case being different, and there is no way to determine in advance what the total will be. If you get that answer, press for an estimate. Many bankruptcy lawyers will tell you in advance what you are going to pay. This figure may be stated after your initial meeting. You will no doubt be required to pay up-front, in advance and in full. The lawyers know that your financial assets are precarious, and they want to ensure that they are paid for their services.

Do not look for the cheapest lawyer in town. Whomever you choose is going to save you a lot of money in the long run, and quality representation is what you need. Do not choose the most expensive lawyer, either, no matter how nice he or she looks in that expensive suit. Someone who has experience, good recommendations, and a reasonable price is a good choice.

CASE STUDY: FROM A LAWYER'S PERSPECTIVE

Edward Gonzalez
Attorney
2405 Eye St. N.W.
Suite 1A
Washington, D.C. 20037
(202) 822-4970

Edward Gonzalez is a former IRS lawyer who now works in private practice serving clients in Washington, D.C., Maryland, and Virginia. He specializes in tax and bankruptcy law and his services address financial distress involving individuals and small businesses.

Gonzalez said the sub-prime mortgage crisis that exploded during the first half of 2008 is the cause of many of the financial problems that his clients are experiencing. Many of them were not aware of the downside of their loans and took on too much debt, which created a financial crisis when the real estate market began its downward trend.

He said his clients are from all ethnic groups and all income levels, adding that the one thing they all have in common is "a lack of financial education." They have fallen into the trap of living paycheck-to-paycheck and always counting on their next check to pay the bills. If the car breaks down or they lose their job, they are then unable to meet their obligations.

What is a typical outcome for Gonzalez's clients? Bankruptcy, because they have already borrowed from lenders.

"Ask for truth in lending statements from lenders. Know about any adjustments in rates or payments. Ask yourself, 'What am I borrowing for?'" Gonzalez said about borrowing from lenders.

Gonzalez said lenders who are communicating with late-paying borrowers often use bullying tactics such as aggressive telephone calls, threats of "warrants" that produce a fear of arrest, garnishment of wages, and so on. Attorneys who specialize in these matters can obtain stays to stop such actions, at least until matters have been sorted through and agreements have been reached.

He said credit counseling agencies can work, but he cautions against using such an agency if it demands substantial up-front fees or makes promises that appear to be too good to be true. As a tax expert, he warns against using any of the firms whose television ads promise to settle your tax bill for pennies on the dollar. "They are come-ons, and they don't work," he said.

Important Things to Keep in Mind After You File for Bankruptcy

In order to successfully re-establish your credit after a bankruptcy and get back on track, there are a number of important details you should keep in mind. Read this list closely and refer to it often. It can have a great impact on how successfully you come out of the process.

1. **Pay your bills in a timely manner**: This is the No. 1 most important thing that lenders look for when reviewing your credit report. It is your way of showing them that you have changed your spending habits after bankruptcy. It is also critical to understand that some bills are more important than others. For example, you do not ever want to pay a mortgage bill or car loan late. However, paying your gym fee late may not be as big of a deal. Remember, if the company reports your pay-

ments to the credit bureaus, then you want to pay it on time. Review your credit report to see which of your lenders do this.

2. **Consider only "mainstream" credit**: When shopping around for creditors, it is important to stick with the reputable ones. These are known as "mainstream" creditors and usually are the ones that report to the credit bureaus. Stay away from such lenders that offer only high-interest financing and other questionable practices, such as "rent-to-own" and "pay here and pay us" auto dealers.

3. **Know your discharge date**: When you file for bankruptcy, there are two dates — the filing date and the discharge date. It is the discharge date that is the most important, as everything begins from this point. For example, if an auto retailer's policy is to provide loans to a people who have filed bankruptcy after one year, it is one year after your discharge. Know that date like the back of your hand!

4. **Avoid co-signing**: You are at a point where you need to re-establish your own credit — not help someone else with theirs. Therefore, if you are asked to co-sign on someone's loan, just say no. Right now, you need to focus on getting financed yourself.

5. **Know when to stop with new credit**: If your goal is to buy a new car and get a mortgage on a new home, you will need more than just a bank card. Take small steps to establish credit with a bank loan and savings accounts, then move on to the car loan and mortgage. By concentrating on the necessities, you can feel like you are moving at a pace that is right for you.

Summary

Remember that bankruptcy is a last resort — not an "easy out" that many Americans think it is. Although bankruptcy will wipe out many of your debts, do not forget that it will not wipe away your tax bill. In fact, it is unlikely that the back taxes you owe will be forgiven in a bankruptcy proceeding; the IRS will be first in line. Remember that the IRS sets the standards for your monthly expenses during your Chapter 13 payment period. You must also meet alimony and child support obligations: They will not go away, and nor will debt incurred through fraud.

Certain court judgments will be wiped out, such as those incurred through lawsuits, as long as no fraud or criminal activity was involved on your part. If you file for Chapter 7, you must wait eight years to file another bankruptcy petition. If you file for Chapter 13, you have the flexibility to amend your payment schedule with approval of the court. However, you will not be given relief under Chapter 13 if you have been given previous debt relief under Chapter 7 within four years of your new filing or two years of a previous Chapter 13 filing. Bottom line: Think carefully before making the decision to go down the bankruptcy path.

Chapter 3

The Fundamentals of Foreclosure

If you are reading this chapter, you may be on the brink of foreclosing on your home — or you are currently going through the process. Whatever your situation, foreclosure can put both an emotional and financial strain on any family. This chapter will help you deal with a foreclosure and provide actionable steps to overcome it.

What is Foreclosure?

This is defined as the legal process when a homeowner who has not made the required payments of both the interest and principal on their mortgage loses the title to their home. The lender holds the note on the property, which means that the lender outright owns the property. Because of this note, the lender has the right to take it back and sell it if you fall behind on the payment terms outlined in your mortgage agreement.

There is nothing scarier to a homeowner than the thought of foreclosure. Unfortunately, it happens every day, and not just in low-income areas of the country. It is everywhere — from rural America to Park Avenue. There are lots of reasons why Americans end up having to foreclose on a home.

Maybe it is due to a job loss, a medial emergency, or a predatory lending. Whatever the reason, there are ways to protect your home from being foreclosed on.

The word "foreclosure" was all over the news during the first half of 2008, as the real estate mortgage meltdown swept through many areas of the country. Lenders made unwise or even foolish loans to people who did not have the resources to make monthly payments. Adjustable rate mortgages (ARMs) contained clauses that allowed lenders to boost interest rates to a point where monthly payments were out of reach of the homeowners who had agreed to the loans.

The effects of foreclosure on your family are:

- Loss of family home.
- Adjustment to moving into a rental.
- Embarrassment associated with this social stigma.

The financial implications of foreclosure will appear on your credit report; make your credit score lower; and wipe out your home equity.

The Dos and Don'ts of Foreclosure

No homeowner wants to be faced with the emotional and financial burden of losing their home. Consider these dos and don'ts when faced with foreclosure:

DO — **Work out a deal with the lender**: Instead of losing money at a foreclosure sale, your lender may be open to working out a payment plan. This is even more of an option now that the government has come up with set criteria for interest rates, loan terms, and principals down in order to make buying — and keeping — a home more affordable.

DON'T — **Sign over your property title**: If a company promises you that once your mortgage becomes current, they will resign your home back to you, do not believe it. Because the home will no longer be in your name, whatever happens to the property is out of your control.

DO — **Consider filing Chapter 7 bankruptcy**: Filing for this type of bankruptcy will not guarantee that you keep your home, but it can help delay the foreclosure sale by a few months, which will keep a roof over your head. Remember, by filing bankruptcy, any debt to the lender will be wiped out. It is important to note that filing for bankruptcy does not automatically mean you will foreclose on your house. However, if you fail to make payments to your lender, foreclosure is imminent.

DON'T — **Get help from a non-HUD-approved counselor**: A HUD-approved counselor has been legally approved by the U.S. Department of Housing and Urban Development (HUD) and can offer advice on buying a home, renting, foreclosures, credit, defaults, and reverse mortgages. Non-legitimate housing counselors charge big fees and may take advantage of your situation. Avoid them at all cost by making sure you go with a HUD-approved counselor.

DO — **Consider filing Chapter 13 bankruptcy**: If you are confident that you can make the overdue mortgage payments, as well as the future mortgage payments, then Chapter 13 bankruptcy is your best bet. This lets you keep your assets and repay your debts over three to five years.

Judicial foreclosure

If you have financed your home loan through a mortgage, you will probably have a judicial foreclosure. This type of foreclosure is a lawsuit against
you due to failure to pay your mortgage. A judicial foreclosure is generally
thought to be more expensive and time-consuming for the lender who is
trying to take back, or repossess, the property. This is because the lender
must file the papers in court and must notify the borrower during the
entire the process. This process can take up to two years, although it will
most likely be closer to one year. During this time, you will have the chance
to come to another solution with your lender.

Be aware that real estate law varies by state. Also, foreclosure may be different for multi-residential properties, such as apartment complexes that fall
into default or commercial buildings whose owners are not current on their
loans. If your home loan is secured by a mortgage and you live in one of the
following states, then a judicial foreclosure will most likely apply:

States where judicial foreclosures apply	
Alabama	Alaska
Arizona	Arkansas
California	Connecticut
Delaware	Florida
Illinois	Indiana
Iowa	Kansas
Kentucky	Louisiana
Maine	Maryland
Massachusetts	Michigan
Minnesota	Mississippi
Missouri	Montana
Nebraska	Nevada
New Jersey	New Mexico
New York	North Carolina

North Dakota	Ohio
Oklahoma	Oregon
Pennsylvania	Rhode Island
South Carolina	South Dakota
Texas	Utah
Vermont	Virginia
Washington	West Virginia
Wisconsin	Wyoming

Assume that the property in question is a residence occupied by the people who have taken out the mortgage on that property. In this case, despite what may seem like a horrible circumstance, the system is weighted in your favor. To start, the lender has to file a foreclosure lawsuit in the local court. This is not something they want to go through for a number of reasons, with cost being the primary one. It costs money to bring a lawsuit, and it takes a long time to obtain a resolution. Also, no money is coming in on this property during this time, and once a judgment is rendered, the lender must then go through the process of selling the property. In the current market, there is a good chance that the property's value will decline during this period, making the lender's loss even larger.

While judicial foreclosures cannot usually be permanently thrown off course, they can be delayed by a significant amount of time. If you feel that you have good reason to fight the foreclosure — perhaps because you have evidence that you were not behind on your payments — it will drag out the time it takes to resolve the case one way or another. See the following timeline for a standard judicial foreclosure:

Typical judicial foreclosure process

To give you a good sense of a judicial foreclosure process, take a look at this example. Steve is 32 years old and lives in Kentucky. He recently got laid off from his job and now is unable to afford his mortgage payments.

- **Month 1:** Steve loses his job.

- **Month 2:** Steve misses his first mortgage payment.

- **Month 5:** Steve has now missed three mortgage payments, and his lender sent him a written notice that he must contact them to work out a solution.

- **Month 7:** Steve does not contact the lender, then receives a ten-day notice of intent to begin foreclosure proceedings from his lender. Steve sees no other option and agrees to begin the foreclosure process.

- **Month 8:** Steve is notified that the lender has filed a foreclosure complaint and is served with a summons to appear in court.

- **Month 9:** Steve files a response and asks for a trial. However, he is unable to pay his legal bills, so he retracts the response, and the court issues a default judgment to authorize the sale of the home.

- **Month 10:** Steve receives an official notice that tells him his lender will begin to sell the property.

- **Month 11:** The house is put up for sale at an auction and is sold.

- **Month 12:** Steve is forced to vacate the property immediately.

In one year's time, Steve has lost his home. If he had contacted his lender to work out a solution early in the process, he may have been able to come up with a plan to keep his home.

Nonjudicial foreclosure

If your loan is secured by a deed of trust, the foreclosure will probably be nonjudicial.

A nonjudicial foreclosure is a process in which your lender does not have to go to court to take your home. In this case, the lender needs to publicly advertise their intent to foreclose prior to an auction. Not all states allow such foreclosures, and those that do will have strict rules for the lender. If your loan is secured by a deed of trust, which is a document that some states use instead of a mortgage, then you signed a promissory note (an agreement to pay back a certain amount by a certain date, and a deed of trust when you closed on the property. These documents will specify the rights of the lender to take action against the property if you, the borrower, fail to meet the terms of the loan. Alternatively, your mortgage may contain a clause that allows the lender to sell the property if you are not able to keep on top of your payments. You should carefully review your agreement for the word "forfeiture." The forfeiture section will spell out the rights of the lender and your rights under your sales and purchase contract. Either option will permit the lender to seek relief without going to court. With foreclosures becoming more common, many lenders are taking steps to protect themselves by placing "anti-forfeiture" provisions in their loan documents. This means that the mortgagor (person taking out the mortgage) states that he or she, or any person living in or involved with the mortgaged property, has done anything that would result in foreclosure. The agreement generally states that the mortgagor will not carry out unlawful activity during loan the period, and that they will defend the mortgagee (the lender) from loss or damage. The nonjudicial foreclosure process usually takes a few months — not the year or two that is common for judicial foreclosure.

The process begins with a notice of default. The lender will have a trustee, or third party, begin the process by notifying you that the bank, or lender, intends to sell your house because you have defaulted on the loan; this is the start of the foreclosure process. Be aware that the lender must submit a copy of the default notice with the recorder's office for your county. If, for any reason, the trustee fails to file such a notice, you have the right to stop the foreclosure process and force the trustee or the lender to begin the process all over again with the notice of default being filed at the recorder's office. This is a small, technical detail, but one that can buy you time because you have to get a third party involved. Of course, this will only work if the trustee or lender makes the mistake of not filing the notice. The notice will outline exactly what you owe in back payments and will in all probability order you to continue paying taxes and insurance on the property during the foreclosure process.

The bank also may post the notice of default on or near your property, and will also post a notice in a local newspaper. The notice will include your name, the name of your lender, a legal description of the property, the amount owed, the interest rate, the date of the sale, and other relevant information. The situation is now very serious. The bank wants its money and is prepared to force you into selling your home to get it. If you have not contacted your lender by now, do it immediately. You still have some options, but the clock is ticking.

It is important to consider that not every state offers their residents the right to a nonjudicial foreclosure. The following chart outlines the states in which this process is customary:

States where nonjudicial foreclosures apply	
Alabama	Alaska
Arizona	Arkansas
California	Colorado
D.C.	Georgia
Hawaii	Idaho
Michigan	Minnesota
Mississippi	Missouri
Montana	Nevada
New Hampshire	North Carolina
Oklahoma	Oregon
Rhode Island	South Dakota
Tennessee	Texas
Utah	Vermont
Virginia	Washington
West Virginia	Wisconsin
Wyoming	

Typical nonjudicial foreclosure process

Sarah lives in California and is injured off the job. Due to her injury, she is unable to work and finds that she is unable to make her mortgage payments.

- **Month 1:** Sarah misses her first mortgage payments.

- **Month 3:** Sarah has now missed three mortgage payments; her lender sends her a mandatory Notice of Default, which gives her 90 days to make up the missed payments.

- **Month 5:** Sarah does not make up the missed payments and receives a notice of intent to sell the property at an auction. Ten days later, the home is put up for sale at an auction and is sold.

As you can see, a nonjudicial foreclosure requires no time in court and can be a much faster process than a judicial foreclosure.

Descriptions of the U.S. Foreclosure Laws

Each state has its own foreclosure laws, but what it comes down to is whether the state uses mortgages or deeds of trust to purchase the property. The following chart, based on information found at **www.foreclosurelaw.org**, indicates foreclosure laws of each state. If you are going through the foreclosure process, make sure that you contact your state for more specific information.

State	Primary Security	Average Timeline	Judicial Foreclosure?	Nonjudicial Foreclosure?	Right of Redemption?	Deficiency Judgments Allowed?
AL	Deed of Trust / Mortgage	30-60 Days	Yes	Yes	12 Months	Yes
AK	Deed of Trust / Mortgage	90 Days	Yes	Yes	Varies	Varies
AZ	Deed of Trust / Mortgage	90 Days	Yes	Yes	None	Varies
AR	Deed of Trust / Mortgage	120 Days	Yes	Yes	Varies	Varies
CA	Deed of Trust / Mortgage	120 Days	Yes	Yes	Varies	Varies
CO	Deed of Trust / Mortgage	4 Months	Yes	Yes	Yes	Yes
CT	Mortgage	60 Days	Yes	No	No	Yes
DC	Deed of Trust	60 Days	No	Yes	No	Yes
DE	Mortgage	90 Days	Yes	No	No	No
FL	Mortgage	180 Days	Yes	No	Yes	Yes

GA	Deed of Trust / Mortgage	90 Days	Yes	Yes	Yes	Yes
HI	Deed of Trust / Mortgage	60 Days	Yes	Yes	No	Yes
ID	Deed of Trust	150 Days	No	Yes	Yes	Yes
IL	Mortgage	210 Days	Yes	No	No	Yes
IA	Mortgage	150 Days	Yes	No	No	No
IN	Mortgage	150 Days	Yes	No	Yes	Yes
KS	Mortgage	120 Days	Yes	No	Yes	Yes
KY	Mortgage	Varies	Yes	No	Yes	Yes
LA	Mortgage	60 Days	Yes	No	No	Yes
ME	Mortgage	90 Days	Yes	No	Yes	Yes
MD	Deed of Trust / Mortgage	90 Days	Yes	Yes	No	Yes
MA	Deed of Trust / Mortgage	90 Days	Yes	Yes	No	No
MI	Deed of Trust / Mortgage	60 Days	Yes	Yes	Yes	Varies
MN	Deed of Trust / Mortgage	60 Days	Yes	Yes	Yes	Yes
MS	Deed of Trust / Mortgage	60 Days	Yes	Yes	No	No
MO	Deed of Trust / Mortgage	60 Days	Yes	Yes	Yes	No
MT	Deed of Trust / Mortgage	150 Days	Yes	Yes	No	Varies
NE	Mortgage	180 Days	Yes	No	Yes	No

NV	Deed of Trust / Mortgage	120 Days	Yes	Yes	Yes	Yes
NH	Deed of Trust / Mortgage	60 Days	Yes	Yes	No	Yes
NJ	Mortgage	90 Days	Yes	No	Yes	Yes
NM	Mortgage	120 Days	Yes	No	Yes	Yes
NY	Deed of Trust / Mortgage	120 Days	Yes	Yes	No	Yes
NC	Deed of Trust / Mortgage	60 Days	Yes	Yes	Yes	Varies
ND	Mortgage	90 Days	Yes	No	Yes	Yes
OH	Mortgage	150 Days	Yes	No	Yes	Yes
OK	Deed of Trust / Mortgage	90 Days	Yes	Yes	No	Varies
OR	Deed of Trust / Mortgage	180 Days	Yes	Yes	Yes	Yes
PA	Mortgage	90 Days	Yes	No	No	Yes
RI	Deed of Trust / Mortgage	60 Days	Yes	Yes	Varies	Yes
SC	Mortgage	Varies	Yes	No	No	Yes
SD	Deed of Trust / Mortgage	90 Days	Yes	Yes	Varies	Varies
TN	Deed of Trust / Mortgage	60 Days	Yes	Yes	Yes	Yes
TX	Deed of Trust / Mortgage	60 Days	Yes	Yes	No	Yes
UT	Deed of Trust / Mortgage	Varies	Yes	Yes	Yes	Yes
VT	Deed of Trust / Mortgage	210 Days	Yes	Yes	Yes	Yes

VA	Deed of Trust / Mortgage	60 Days	Yes	Yes	Varies	Yes
WA	Deed of Trust / Mortgage	120 Days	Yes	Yes	Yes	Yes
WV	Deed of Trust / Mortgage	60 Days	Yes	Yes	No	No
WI	Deed of Trust / Mortgage	90 Days	Yes	Yes	Yes	Yes
WY	Deed of Trust / Mortgage	90 Days	Yes	Yes	Yes	Yes

CASE STUDY: THE FACES OF FORECLOSURE

Terence Brian Garvey
Attorney
839C Quince Orchard Blvd.
Gaithersburg, MD 20878
(301) 948-1227

Terence Garvey has been practicing bankruptcy law for 25 years. In July 2007, he saw a surge in one category of financial crisis.

"Foreclosure skyrocketed," he said. A weak real estate market produced a wave of clients who could no longer make their mortgage payments and were receiving foreclosure notices. It was a problem that swept across the state of Maryland, causing the legislature to change the laws to slow down the foreclosure process.

Garvey said the new laws offer some breathing room for troubled homeowners to ask for protection under Chapter 13. The amount owed as late payments can be separated into a Chapter 13 filing, and a payment schedule can be worked out to pay it off over a five-year period. The homeowner makes separate payments for that debt but must also remain current on the mortgage payments that resume when the homeowner works out his or her debt plan.

Garvey believes that many of his clients should never have obtained the large mortgages that were approved without any proof of income or ability to pay. Some of the loans were for as much as $800,000.

Other clients are real estate speculators who bet that the market would continue to go up. It did not. They lost the bet and are facing bankruptcy or foreclosure. Another group walking through Garvey's door is the mortgage bankers who approved some of the loans that economists say were too lenient and helped create the housing meltdown.

Mortgage banking was hit hard by the real estate slowdown, and many men and women who work in that sector suffered reduced incomes, meaning they could not pay their own mortgages. Because of this, these people turned to the protection offered by bankruptcy laws. Garvey said by the time his clients walk through his door, their problems are already severe, and they look to him for help. "It's a matter of trying to cut your losses," he said.

Interest

Home loans and interest rates are important, as an interest rate can often be the reason why an individual needs to foreclose on a home. There are two basic forms of interest on home loans. The first is the fixed rate. This means the interest on the loan remains unchanged for the duration of the loan. For example, if you have a 6 percent rate at the beginning, it will remain at 6 percent for the 30 years it will take to pay it off. This can be a good option for people who plan on staying in their home for many years and want to lock in one steady rate.

The second type of interest is adjustable. This interest rate will be reset at designated intervals during the life of the loan. If you have a 30-year loan, your interest rate may fluctuate after one year, three years, or whatever the terms instruct. The adjustment may be pinned to some other financial instrument, the prime rate, or a rate the lender designates. Adjustable rate mortgages, or ARMs, offer homebuyers an introductory rate that offers a low initial payment on the assumption that a higher payment later will be within the means of the homebuyer.

Because there are few people who have the cash on-hand to purchase something as expensive as a home, most Americans borrow money in the form of mortgages. In fact, mortgages are the engines that drive the real estate market in the United States and worldwide. In good times, with good lending practices, the percentage of homes that slide into foreclosure is low and normally confined to those who have suffered an unfortunate financial crisis over which they have no control. That began to change in 2007, and it bloomed into a full-blown national crisis in 2008. In 2009, it was worse than ever.

What happened?

Two major events occurred. First, mortgage interest rates sank to historic lows. This made it easier for people to buy homes, so more people went house shopping. Second, the increase of demand for real estate caused the prices to go up in a classic, market-driven boom. Higher prices created an atmosphere of speculation, so investors began snapping up properties, which led to even higher prices and more demand.

From a purely financial point of view, without regard for historic realities, lenders saw opportunities to take advantage of a rising, out-of-control market. This misguided, delusional business policy produced a situation in which virtually anyone could get a home loan, regardless of ability to pay. This was based on the assumption that the price of real estate would continue to rise dramatically, the home could be refinanced in a year or so for substantially more money, and all would be made right.

Lenders created loans in the so-called subprime market (when borrowers with less-than-stellar credit were able to get unconventional loans). This made it possible for a couple earning a combined $20,000 a year to purchase a home costing ten times that amount, with awfully little — if any — money down. In some cases, the couple could obtain a loan for $220,000 — even more than the price of the house. All of this happened under the assumption that home prices would continue to rise dramatically.

How did they qualify for so much money? The lenders created "interest only" (when the interest is only paid on a loan periodically and the principal is paid at the end of the loan's terms), or "introductory interest rate" loans (when a low interest rate is initially offered for a pre-set introductory period) that began with small monthly payments. Some have argued that these payments were unrealistically low, and that these loans amounted to misrepresentation at best and fraud at worst. Nevertheless, many loans were made like this; as a result, more people bought houses, which drove up prices even more, until the bubble burst. The simplest explanation is that prices finally reached a tipping point, and they could not be sustained. Added to that is the maturing of adjustable rate mortgages, which occurs when a low interest rate is given at the beginning of the loan, usually five or seven years, and after a specified period of time, the rate goes up. In some cases, this is caused by monthly payments to double or even triple overnight. Homeowners could no longer afford to live in their houses after the initial, unrealistically low introductory rate matured into a huge monthly obligation.

The problem spread across the country, particularly in areas where subprime loans were most common; this is the type of loan discussed above. Why would lenders be so aggressive in offering these loans? Mortgage companies make money every time they close a loan. The more loans they close, the more money they make; it was a classic bubble market. Everyone saw dollar signs and assumed the graph line would continue to rise. Even high-end, blue-chip financial companies were caught up in the housing market, and they took significant financial losses when the value of all that paper crashed.

Prices dropped just as many subprime ARMs were raising monthly payments. Suddenly, many people could not afford their homes, which they could not refinance because they were upside down, meaning their houses were no longer worth what they owed on them. The couple above still made $20,000, and they still owed $220,000 on their home, which was now worth $180,000. Their monthly payment now represented two-thirds of their income, and so the trend continued. You can adjust the figures any number of ways, but they still do not work. All in all, it is a dangerous trap that many Americans were caught in — regardless of their income.

Talk to your lender

Believe it or not, your lender does not want you to foreclose on your home and will be willing to work with you. Once you know why you are unable to pay your mortgage and whether your situation is permanent or temporary, it is absolutely essential that you communicate with your lender. If you see a resolution down the road, suggest an accommodation, such as delayed or reduced payments, or even a re-negotiation of the loan. You may not get anywhere, but it is worth a try. Many lenders are flexible in such cases because they do not want to take your home and try to sell it. Even in a strong real estate market, lenders do not want to be in the position of seller — they lend, not sell. You may discover that the financial entity that originated your mortgage no longer owns or even manages it. Your loan may have been bought and sold many times over, and bundled into a number of other loans and used as a financial instrument on Wall Street.

Now that you and others are behind on payments, the big financial firm that controls the loan is bankrupt or almost bankrupt.

Someone, somewhere, is in a position to make a decision about your loan. Call the customer service number on your monthly statement to ask where you can go to discuss your loan. It is possible that the only answer you will receive is, "Pay the bill," but keep trying. If your interest rate is through the roof, or you are facing a balloon payment as part of your loan structure, ask if the lender will lower your interest rate or restructure the loan. You may have more leverage than you realize.

Maintain a record of every contact you have with your lender, even if the contact is with someone who said, "She is not in right now." Write down names, telephone numbers, dates, and times. It is important that you show good faith in dealing with lenders, even if they have begun the foreclosure process. Moreover, it is better to communicate with your lender than to maintain a policy of silence. Ignoring the mortgage holder may cause them to feel as though they have no alternative but to take back your home. If you receive a letter from your lender, no matter how unpleasant it may be, respond immediately by stating your circumstances and desire to resolve the problem. Keep the original copy, and send your response along with a copy of the lender's letter. Respond directly to the person who sent you the letter and keep a copy of your response. You are creating a paper trail that may help you if the process goes before a court. You are proving your desire to work with your lender.

The person you deal with in the early stages of this process is not likely to be anyone who can make a decision about your loan. This person's job is to send out this type of letter, not to negotiate with debtors who are behind on their payments. Once you have responded and stated your circumstances and intentions, your case may move up the corporate ladder to that person's boss, moving on from there. By maintaining a paper trail of timely responses and explanations, you will put yourself in a better position once your loan comes to the attention of someone who can actually make a decision about your case.

Summary

Remember, when it comes to the threat of foreclosure, communication is key. Regularly contact your lender, and do not ignore late payment letters, notices, or threats. If you cannot make your payments, tell your lender what your situation is and when it will improve. Ask to renegotiate your loan. Offer a payment plan. Keep copies of all correspondence with your lender, and maintain a log of all telephone calls, along with names, dates, and topics discussed. Make sure the person you are talking to has the authority to make a decision. If not, find out who does. By keeping the lines of communication open, you will be in a better position to keep your home.

Chapter 4

Your Housing Options

If you are facing foreclosure because of factors beyond your control, you may have no choice but to accept the loss of your house and move on. Job loss, medical catastrophes, and even divorce can put people into this situation. If you have no satisfactory income to make your house payments, you are in a bad spot. If you are facing huge medical bills that are draining your income, you may be in an untenable situation (although seeking bankruptcy protection may be a way out for you). In cases of divorce, you may accept foreclosure, or another difficult process, simply because your former spouse forces the issue. Divorce is a key cause of foreclosure because it means lower household income for both parties and, occasionally, the party who is responsible for making the house payment cannot or will not.

If you are facing foreclosure because you lost $50,000 in Atlantic City or ran up too many credit card bills, you must begin the process of cleaning up your finances, and that may or may not permit you to make things right with your lender(s). Look at your income opposed to your bills and decide how important it is for you to keep your house.

Once you understand why you are facing foreclosure and have determined whether you have the financial resources to work with your lender, you must decide if you want to keep your home. It may be in your best interest to allow the foreclosure to proceed, particularly if it is a nonjudicial foreclosure. In that case, the lender cannot go after you for the difference between what your house sells for and what you owe on your loan. Remember, under a judicial foreclosure, the lender may seek this type of damage against you, but not under a nonjudicial procedure, which is a simple sale. Your state will have its own particular laws.

Look Again at Your Resources

Assume you are working and you want to save your home because it is worth more than you owe. You have a serious debt problem, though, and you cannot meet all of your monthly commitments, one of which is your mortgage payment. You are behind on all of your bills and have been doling out your cash to whoever screams the loudest, but you are still being called by people who demand money, and now your home is threatened with foreclosure. The car company is threatening to take back your vehicle. The credit card companies are threatening lawsuits. You may be considering bankruptcy; perhaps a little reflection can avoid that. You may have to prioritize your bills. What is most important to you: your home or your car? Perhaps your credit card company will be willing to extend your payment period. Allowing your car to be repossessed to save your home might not be a bad option. If you removed your car and credit card payments from your monthly bills, maybe then you would be able to pay your mortgage. That scenario would in turn put you in a better position to negotiate with your banker. Although none of these options is ideal, you may be forced to make hard choices as you move ahead.

Get help from the government

The good news is that even in what probably seems like a horrible financial mess, you are not alone. The Federal Housing Administration (FHA) was given more flexibility in 2007 to insure mortgage loans so that people affected by foreclosure could take their high-interest home loans and refinance them into lower interest rates. Because a large portion of the U.S. economy is driven by home ownership, having too many people default on their mortgages can affect the economy as a whole. Be sure to take advantage of the government-offered foreclosure assistance programs.

Local government assistance

The best place to start when you need help with your foreclosure is on the local county level. Start by contacting the county register of deeds and inquire as to whether they know of any programs to assist homeowners in your area. They may be able to point you in the direction of free or affordable legal services as well.

State government assistance

If you have looked into local options and have not found any that will work for you, then your next move is to contact your state housing authority. They may be able to help you find a more affordable loan or can give you information on local resources you may have not yet heard about.

Federal government assistance

If you find that going straight to the top is your best bet, then call or visit the Web site of the U.S. Department of Housing and Urban Development (HUD). They offer free or low-cost housing consulting. You can speak to a housing counselor to get assistance in understanding the foreclosure laws and your options, better managing your finances, and negotiating with your lender. Your state may also offer programs to help residents affected by foreclosures. The following is a list of some state-specific programs. Be sure to check with your state to see if they others that could help you.

Colorado	The Home Stretch Program: **www.chfainfo.com**
Connecticut	CT Families Program: **www.chfa.org**
Delware	Delaware Emergency Mortgage Assistance Program (DEMAP): **www.destatehousing.com/services/hb_demap.shtml**
Idaho	Idaho Housing and Finance Association Advantage Loan Program: **www.ihfa.org/idamortgage/loan_program.asp**
Illinois	Homeowner Assistance Initiative: **www.ihda.org/ViewPage.aspx?PageID=257**
Maryland	Lifeline Refinance Mortgage: **www.dhcd.state.md.us/lifeline**
Massachusetts	Home Saver Foreclosure Prevention Program: **www.masshousing.com**
Michigan	MSHDA Assist Refinance Program: **www.michigan.gov/mshda**
Montana	Foreclosure Prevention Loan: **www.banking.mt.gov/foreclosureprevention.mcpx**
New Jersey	Homeownership Preservation Refinance Program: **www.state.nj.us/dobi/njhope**
New York	Keep the Dream Mortgage Program: **www.nyhomes.org/index.aspx?page=489**
Pennsylvania	Refinance to an Affordable Loan (REAL) Program and Homeowner Equity Recovery Opportunity (HERO) Program: **www.phfa.org/consumers/homeowners/real.aspx**
Rhode Island	Home Saver Loan Program: **www.rhodeislandhousing.org**

Selling Your Home

Talk to a good real estate agent, one who has experience in your market and can offer sound advice. Explain your situation and ask the agent what he or she thinks is the likelihood that you will sell your house in a reasonable period for a price you can live with — but be prepared for bad news. If houses in your neighborhood were selling for $150,000 a year ago, they may be selling for $130,000 or even lower today. If there are many houses on the market in your neighborhood — and some of them are foreclosures — the chances for a quick sale will be bleak. If, on the other hand, you are in a desirable neighborhood where few houses are on the market, you may be in a good position for a sale.

The price you list your home for will be extremely important. You should determine the minimum number you must make in order to walk away from the property. Based on your local real estate market, your realtor will help you assess the best price according to the market's supply and demand. If you list the price of your home too high, no one will buy it. If it is too low, you may not make enough to make it worthwhile.

Visit similar houses that are on the market to compare yours to the others. Ask your real estate agent about staging your home. This is a process of sprucing up the place to make it look better than the other homes on the market. It may involve paint and serious removal of clutter.

Investors may be an option, even though they are unlikely to offer top dollar. What they do offer is a quick sale and, depending on price and equity, you may be served well by it. Your real estate agent should know the market and who the serious investors are, so seek their counsel on these matters. Serious investors will be familiar with the foreclosure market. They are the ones who buy this type of property. If your home is priced right, they may decide it is easier to deal with you than to work through the hassles of a foreclosed home.

If you decide to sell, contact your lender to explain your decision and what you are asking for the house, and also ask for time to sell it on your own. The lender may decide it will be cheaper to let you sell the place than to drag the foreclosure out to its conclusion and pay all of the fees involved. Your lender will compare your asking price to the other homes for sale in your neighborhood and will most likely reject your request if you are listing your home for a significantly higher price than your neighbors are. Your bank wants to get your home off its books as fast as possible.

Short sale

A short sale is the bank's agreeing to accept less than you owe and wipe out your mortgage. Obviously, this is appealing if your outstanding mortgage balance is higher than the total loan's value, or if you have little or no equity. Say you owe $120,000 on your home. The current market value is $115,000; you are behind $5,000. From the bank's point of view, losses are inevitable. There is the cost of foreclosure, which includes lawyers, the trustee, filing fees, and real estate agents to sell and fix it, just to name a few expenses. During this period, nothing is coming in on the loan, so the bank is eating the cost of managing the loan without enjoying any benefit. This is not what banks are in business to do.

If you have an offer from an investor for, say, $100,000, it is worth consideration. You cannot offer the bank the full amount because you will have to pay the real estate agent who listed your home and any other costs associated with the sale, but you do have something to present to the bank. In this case, say the figure is $90,000. Why would the bank accept $90,000 to pay off a $120,000 loan? As stated above, they almost certainly will not —

but they might. If someone at the bank looks at the numbers and decides that $90,000 is about all they will end up with at the conclusion of the foreclosure process, they may see this as the best option, and certainly one that gets them out of this property.

The auction

If you have attempted to determine a plan for payment with your lender and they have ignored your requests for more time, a payment schedule, or a renegotiation of the loan, your home may go up for sale at a foreclosure auction. Now it is time to accept that foreclosure is a reality. Each state has a required period between the notice of default and the sale, and if your lender violates that requirement, you will have a case to halt the sale.

The trustee or an auctioneer will announce the sale and describe the property. He or she will state terms of the sale and whether cash is required for payment. Your home will most likely be sold "as is," meaning the buyer gets the property without any warranties and promises to fix things that are broken.

The bidding opens with your lender making a bid of whatever you owe, or a number that represents a bottom for the sale; then, others make their bids. You went into the sale owing the bank $120,000. The lender has assessed fees and interest in addition to that, along with the costs associated with the foreclosure. So, with the costs of foreclosure included, the new figure that you owe the bank to satisfy the debt is at $130,000. If someone bids a higher figure, you will get the difference between what you owed and the sale price. If the winning bid was below the number the bank has set, you owe nothing following the foreclosure, and the debt is cleared.

Finding New Housing Options

Once you have accepted the fact that foreclosure is a reality, your first order of business is to find yourself acceptable housing that is within your budget and fulfills your family's needs.

If your state offers a redemption period, you may have the ability to live in your house free for that period. These periods vary greatly. For example, the state of Alabama offers a redemption period that is up to 12 months, while the state of Indiana offers three months. Many states, such as Missouri, Virginia, and Oregon, offer no redemption period at all, so be sure to check with your individual state. This is a golden opportunity to save some money for a deposit on another house. Therefore, when it is time to move, you will be in a better financial situation.

However, if the state you live in does not offer a redemption period, you must move out of your house immediately after the house is sold at auction. Therefore, you need to determine next steps — such as to whether you can temporarily stay with family or friends, rent a home, or relocate. And although having your house sold and being forced out on the street may seem like the end of the world, look at it this way: It is actually a chance to put the foreclosure behind you and make a fresh start.

Living with family or friends

Before you do anything, you may want to consider the support of family and friends to get back on your feet, at least temporarily. Perhaps there is someone who has a little extra space and will allow you and your family to move in. This will take a huge financial burden off you while also providing you with the emotional support you need to get back on track. Though this is not an ideal situation, and probably not something you should consider for the long term, it may be a great way to start fresh again.

Finding a rental

Purchasing another home so soon after a foreclosure may not be the best option. Not only has your credit gone down, but you may not have the nest egg you need to put money down on a home. Therefore, finding a suitable rental will be necessary. Look in the newspaper, online, and in your town for appropriate rental properties. Landlords usually want a few months' rent up-front in addition to a security deposit, so keep that in mind when you are looking. Renting a home is a great way to ensure you do not go down the same path you just came out of.

When looking for a place to rent, ask yourself these questions:

- What are your needs?
- Where do you want to live?
- How much can you afford?

You must be realistic about what you can afford to pay monthly, and avoid the temptation to go-for-broke, so to speak, and try to rent the most luxurious place on your list. Unlike the irresponsible lenders who offered huge loans with exotic interest structures to homeowners who were forced into foreclosure, landlords are more cautious in approving applications. Large property management companies will use an income formula to determine how much rent you can afford — probably 25 to 30 percent of your income. If you make $3,000 per month, you would be advised to look at property that would consume no more than one-third of that, or something around $1,000 or less. This is not to say that with enough digging, you cannot find a landlord who is willing to accept you for more than that, but most responsible landlords will not.

Relocating

There is nothing like starting fresh. In some cases, having gone through such an emotional ordeal leaves families with the desire to leave the situation behind and move on. Maybe you have always dreamed of living in the Southwest and see this as your opportunity, or maybe the area you have been living in has been hit hard by the recent dismal economy. Whatever your situation, here are some steps to consider when thinking about relocating:

- **How is the economy in that area?** If you are starting fresh, you want to be sure you can find a new job quickly so that you are not without income for any period of time.

- **Do you have family or friends nearby?** Because you have just come out of an emotional foreclosure process, it will be important to have a solid support system around you. If you are considering making a move to a new area, having friends and family already there can make the transition much easier.

- **How is the housing market?** Because you may need to find a rental at first, make sure you are moving to an area that offers adequate rental opportunities. Also, if you find that you like the area and want to stay, make sure the real estate market is not inflated so that when you are ready to buy a home, you are buying at a good price.

Living assistance

Each state administers its own living assistance program, and each state uses its own name for the program, although temporary Assistance for Needy Families is a common name. Other examples include North Carolina Work First, California CalWORKS, and Iowa Family Investment

(FIP). You can find a list of the programs offered for your state on the U.S. Department of Health and Human Services Administration for Children & Families page at **www.acf.hhs.gov/programs/ofa/states/tnfnames. htm**. Although most of these programs are managed by state and local social services departments (with each setting its own rules), the following are general guidelines that apply to most locations. To receive living assistance payments, you must:

- Be responsible for a child under the age of 19 or be pregnant.

- Have no or low income.

- Be unemployed, underemployed, or likely of losing a job soon.

- Have the legal right to live in the United States, and live in the state in which you are applying.

Most states require that participants enroll in some type of training or work program to continue to qualify for living assistance payments. These programs are designed to help people move on to earning money as quickly as possible so that they can leave the program.

Know Your Rights as a Renter

Because you may be jumping back into the rental market for the first time in years, it is important to know your rights as a renter. Millions of people rent or lease their residences, offices, and other facilities where they live, work, or play. But just as one must be vigilant during the purchase of property, one must also be vigilant during the rental process to protect your rights and know your options and responsibilities. This section will walk you through the process of renting property, either because you chose to or because you were forced to through foreclosure or other financial calamity.

Why you can be rejected

In many parts of the country, the rental market may be just as competitive as the real estate market — if not more so. When it comes to renting a house or apartment, you are at the sole discretion of the landlord. They can reject almost anyone they believe will not be a good renter for their property for just about any reason.

For example, many states have laws that limit the number of people who can live in a residence based upon the number of bedrooms in the unit. A common such restriction is two people per bedroom, plus one. Under this restriction, a two-bedroom apartment would accommodate five people — two in each bedroom, plus one. Your area may have this limit, one that is different, or no limit at all. A real estate professional who specializes in rental properties will know the landlord/tenant laws in your area.

In addition to occupancy, here are the primary reasons you can be rejected for a lease:

- Poor credit history
- Negative items on your credit report
- Recent bankruptcy
- History of late rental payments
- Eviction(s)
- Criminal convictions
- Lawsuits against you
- Drug addiction
- Pets
- Too many people on the lease
- Unmarried couples or alternative lifestyles

The Fair Housing Act

This law helps renters get equal treatment when being considered as renters or purchasers of real estate. It covers almost all scenarios and types of housing, and it is set up to protect you — especially if you have filed for bankruptcy or foreclosure. Visit the HUD, also known as the U.S. Department of Housing and Urban Development (**www.hud.gov**), to find out what the affordable rental options are in your state, and to get a list of ways that you can get assistance in renting.

Tips to Impress the Landlord

You may have to go the extra distance to convince a property owner or manager to accept your application, particularly if you have some negative issues in your credit history. Just because you were late on a few payments or recently filed for bankruptcy does not mean you are doomed to live in substandard housing. Everyone has a case to make.

As you can imagine, the landlord or property manager's job is to find the best renters. It is your job to convince this person that, despite the issues outlined above, you would be a good renter. Here are some tips to help you:

- **Address negative items up-front**: If there are negative items on your credit report, you must address them individually. Late payments to credit card companies and missed car payments can be attributed to factors that are no longer relevant. For example, say you were unemployed then, but have a steady job now. Bankruptcy may have wiped away your debts, so you have more financial resources and can confidently sign a lease.

- **Fix any credit errors**: If there any errors on your credit report, you must correct them by contacting the reporting agency and, if necessary, the creditor who filed the erroneous report. You have the right to correct such errors or file letters of explanation in cases where you and a creditor have a disagreement over a bill or payment.

- **Get letters of recommendation**: Ask friends, former landlords, your employer, and anyone else who will vouch for you for letters of recommendation. You may find that even if you have been late with a rent payment or two, your former landlord will be willing to say something nice about you, assuming you are still on speaking terms.

- **Make finding a rental your top priority**: Consider the process akin to looking for a job. Show up on time. Wear decent clothes. Be polite. Be accommodating. Smile. Landlords often deal with unreasonable renters who demand the moon in exchange for their monthly check; so showing a measure of respect and refraining from issuing a long list of demands may bring you to the front of the line.

- **Use bargaining power**: To make yourself look more desirable, offer to pay several months rent up-front as a good faith gesture. If that does not work with your budget, offer to paint the home or clean up the yard. By doing this kind of thing, you level the field of potential renters by offsetting your weaknesses with something that will benefit the landlord.

Signing the Lease

It is often said that the devil is in the details, and that is true of your lease. There is more to the deal than the monthly rent. Your lease is a legal contract that binds you and the landlord to the terms. For instance, a two-year lease does not give you the right to move out after 12 months. A non-smoking clause does not give you the right to take up cigars in your apartment. On the other hand, your landlord must also comply with the terms of the lease and cannot evict you unless you violate the terms of the agreement. That is the reason why it is essential to know exactly what you are agreeing to.

Many renters are not aware that there is a difference between a lease and a rental agreement:

- **Rental agreement**: This term refers to a short-term arrangement of a month or two and is usually used for month-to-month living situations or vacation rentals. It offers you a level of flexibility to move if you decide to, but the downside is that your landlord can raise your rent with only a 30-day notice or change the terms of the agreement — therefore, the flexibility works both ways.

- **Lease**: This refers to a longer-term agreement and locks you in legally for a longer period of time — usually one or two years. This provides a measure of security for both you and the landlord. You may be able to move out early by paying a penalty fee, and the landlord can always evict you for failure to pay the rent or live up to the terms that were outlined in the agreement.

Your lease may also include other terms and restrictions, such as no smoking, no pets, no long-term guests (whom the landlord will consider residents), no loud noises, and no band practice, among other things. It will also spell out the terms of eviction should you violate the conditions laid out by the property owner. It is important that you understand these terms to avoid a surprise notice ordering you out. Here is one area where verbal agreements may be worthless because it will be your word against hers or his. Be sure all of your rights and the conditions of the lease are clear and understandable, which may be a challenge in the sometimes-legalistic language of real estate documents.

Utilities

Do not forget that when negotiating the lease, utilities are another matter to be settled before you sign the lease. Large complexes will have policies that are spelled out in printed material and rental agreements. Some pay for all or part of the utilities. It is common for renters to pay electricity, but not gas. Some landlords pay nothing at all, and others pay everything except telephone and cable. Individual property owners may be willing to negotiate utilities. If you are renting a single-family house, be prepared to foot the entire utility bill. Larger apartment developments are more likely to absorb some portion of the utility cost because they have more tenants and may be able to afford to pay things like heat or cooling.

The deposit

The sole purpose of a rental deposit is to protect the landlord in case you damage the property or move out in the middle of the night before your lease is up; some communities regulate such deposits. There may be a limit on how much you can be required to pay, and there may even be a requirement that the landlord pay interest on your deposit. Normally, your deposit will equal one month's rent. If your rent is $800 per month, you will be required to leave a deposit in that amount with your landlord until you move out. The lease may spell out reasons why the landlord can withhold all or part of your deposit. For example, you may find that the lease commits you to pay for the professional cleanup of the place after you move out. The cost of the cleanup will be taken from your deposit, as will the cost to repair or replace anything that is broken or damaged. This may include pet stains, dirty ovens, and mold in the bathroom.

Your lease may contain rent increase clauses. Your landlord may offer an initial six months at a lower rate, then an increased monthly rent for the final six months, for example. Be aware that you may be required to increase your deposit as your monthly rent goes up to comply with the lease provision of one-month's rent. If your initial rent is $700, you may be required to put down a like deposit, but if your rent goes to $800 six months or a year later, your landlord may ask for another $100. This is only an example, and your lease may state other terms, but be prepared to increase your security deposit along with your rent.

Also, some landlords require even more at the lease signing. Yours may ask for the security deposit, as well as the first month's and last month's rent. Again, this is to protect the landlord. Many renters will give the required 30-day notice to move out after their lease is up, then not pay the last month's rent, assuming that their deposit will cover it. The landlord is left holding the bag, so to speak, if the unit is damaged or dirty, and the deposit was used to pay the last monthly rent bill.

Before you sign your lease, be aware of the entire amount you will be required to pay, and educate yourself about the terms of the lease. This will help avoid problems later.

Steer Clear of Scammers

Unfortunately, when you go through a foreclosure, it may become public knowledge — either by word of mouth or in the newspaper, depending on your community. Even worse, as soon as news of your foreclosure gets out, the scam artists come calling. Con artists are looking for people who exhibit fear, desperation, trust, and pride; they try to make them their targets. If a situation looks or feels too good to be true, there is a very good chance it is.

It is understandable that after having gone through such an emotionally overwhelming process, you are looking for a way out of this crisis — a way to save your home. And when a con artist shows up on your doorstep promising to make it all go away, it can be very tempting. Telephone calls pour in with the same offer. Do not be fooled. These people are not trying to help you; they are hoping to take advantage of you during a vulnerable period in your life.

There are a number of variations on the scam, but it comes down to a promise to help you save your house in return for something, possibly your home itself, but the offer may not look that way in the beginning. Here are some scams you may come across:

- **Negotiating with your bank**: A salesperson claiming to have experience negotiating with lenders and guaranteeing a satisfactory resolution to your problem — for a fee, of course.

- **Saving your house**: In this instance, you may be paying a fee of hundreds of dollars to someone who will do no more than what you have already done, which is to send a letter to your lender. Sometimes, the scammer will simply take your money and vanish.

- **Clearing up your credit**: This type of scam promises that if you pay a fee and sign the house over, the foreclosure will no longer be against you — hence saving your credit.

- **Buying the house for you**: This scam may offer to buy your home from you, lease it to you, and give you the option to purchase it back. Usually these scams require you to secure a larger loan than you originally had — resulting in a higher payment and potentially a higher mortgage interest rate.

Bottom line: Do not sign away your home, no matter how charming the offer. Ask yourself why a perfect stranger would show up at your door to do you a favor. It is naïve to believe the answer is because people are just nice. These offers are from people who prey on the desperate, and they know that homeowners in crisis will listen to even the most outrageous schemes in hopes that the foreclosure nightmare will go away.

At best, these people are at the fringe of the financial services sector. At worst, they are crooks. Dealing with them can be like doing business with payday lenders. They get far more than they give and you are likely to end up worse off than you are now. The best way to solve your problem is by working directly with your lender or the trustee acting on the lender's behalf. Half-baked, quick-solution schemes are not the answer to your problems.

Staying current with government regulations

Passed in July 2008 in response to a struggling economy and a housing market that was spiraling out of control, the U.S. government passed the Housing and Economic Recovery Act of 2008. The act was a step toward ensuring that the lifestyles Americans had grown accustomed to were once again affordable, as it established plans for relief for hundreds of thousands of U.S. citizens who found themselves facing foreclosure.

If you are facing foreclosure, or are on the brink, the Housing and Economic Recovery Act is your friend. It can help you refinance into a fixed, 30-year mortgage that is up to 90 percent of your home's value. If you are in an interest-only mortgage, or a high-interest-rate loan, this act is a great way to lock into a mortgage that puts your financial needs first. Best of all, it prevents any financing surprises from creeping up down the line. For more information about the Housing and Economic Recovery Act, visit **www.hud.gov/news/recoveryactfaq.cfm**.

Other housing acts that you should be aware of are:

- **The S.A.F.E. Mortgage Licensing Act**: This would create a federal registry and establish minimum national standards for all residential mortgage brokers and lenders;

- **The Foreclosure Prevention Act**: This would provide assistance for communities devastated by foreclosures, foreclosure counseling for families in need, programs to help returning soldiers avoid foreclosure, FHA modernization, and mortgage disclosure enhancements;

- **The Housing Assistance Tax Act of 2008**: This would provide tax benefits for homeowners, homebuyers, and homebuilders. It is aimed at helping the housing market recover and giving you the ability to get into a mortgage that provides lower fixed-interest rates — and does not surprise you with escalating costs down the line.

Redemption: Buying Back Your Home

Some states have a redemption period following a foreclosure sale. This is a period of time in which you may buy back your home. You will purchase the property from the person or entity that bought it at auction, not from your original lender. This is generally a hassle for investors who purchase homes at foreclosure auctions because during the redemption period, they are legally vulnerable. Most foreclosed homes are not redeemed because most people who have been evicted from their homes move on to other residences, but now and then, someone who truly does want their home back will be able to reclaim it.

If you decide to reclaim your home during the redemption period, you can sell the property or keep it as your residence. Though some states do not offer a redemption period, you may have the option to take back the property after auction by paying your past due balances before the sale.

CASE STUDY: AMERICAN DREAM DILEMMA

"Krystal"
Chicago, Illinois

Krystal is a woman who been caught up in the red tape often associated with bankruptcy. She owned two properties, one in Phoenix, Arizona, and one in Chicago, Illinois. In order to support her business, she re-financed the Phoenix property. The business failed, and she was separated from her corporate IT position. Prior to separating from the IT position, she was planning to file a Chapter 13. After the separation, a Chapter 7 became her only option.

During this period, Krystal finished a patent for a product that she had worked on for most of her adult life (**www.theheelshield.com**). Because she had been unemployed since 2007, she realized she had to make her patented product become her mechanism for earning money. While Krystal receives a pension check that is less than $1,000 per month, she has given up on finding a position in the downward economy. She lives in her Chicago property with her daughter and her daughter's husband, as foreclosure took the Phoenix property. No one in the household is working, and both her daughter and son-in-law have been laid off from their jobs. They are expecting a baby and have no real means of supporting the child. Krystal's dilemma is that she does not get enough money from her pension check to file for Chapter 13 bankruptcy. Therefore, her only option is to file Chapter 7. Unfortunately, this means the court will take her patent away, which is her only way to make a living in the future.

Krystal applied for a loan modification through her mortgage lender in December. She was told it would take 90 days for someone to contact her. After she finally received a call, she was unable to reach the original caller. At the time this book was rewritten, Krystal was still unable to get back in contact with the bank, as her case had someone fallen through the cracks. In Krystal's case, there is still no outcome other than the fact that she is relying on her business venture. While it is still yet to be determined if the court will take Krystal's patent away, she is holding out hope that she will get the loan through her mortgage lender. If not, she will need to rely on her pension and hope the economy picks up. As Krystal said, "(I am) a victim of the economy."

Summary

You may decide to allow foreclosure because you cannot produce the financial resources to keep your house, or because you determine that you owe far more than the house is worth and have no hope of becoming current on your loan. Look into whether selling your home during the foreclosure process is feasible. You may have a right to buy back your home, even after someone has bought it at a foreclosure auction. Imagine how great it would feel to have that mortgage lender hand you the keys to your very own home again.

Chapter 5

The Real Facts on Repossession

Repossession is a pretty simple concept. Basically, if you have taken out a loan on a possession, whether it is a car or other personal properties, and fail to follow the terms of the loan agreement, then you run the risk of having it taken away. If you are currently facing the threat of repossession, either on your car or on other properties, then this section can help you become knowledgeable on the process and give you tips and action steps to prevent it or get your goods back.

The effects of repossession on your family are:

- Loss of possessions.
- Financial and emotional stress associated with needing to regain possessions.
- Embarrassment associated with this social stigma.

The financial implications of repossession are that your credit score may be affected; you can be sued for the money you may still owe; and you may be in need of replacing the item with a new one.

What is Repossession?

Repossession is comparable to foreclosure — they both involve the seizing of a property used as collateral in a debt. In the case of your home, the house and land are the collateral. In an auto loan, the vehicle is collateral. If you are not able to meet the loan's terms, the lender has the right to take the property. It is as simple as that.

When you finance an item, your agreement will spell out the circumstances under which the possession may be taken back. It will be in the fine print. State law may permit the lender to ask you to waive certain rights, such as permitting the repossessor to come onto your property or enter your garage when state law prohibits such access, unless such restrictions are waived.

Sometimes repossession happens simply with one missed payment. Although every loan agreement is different, the best strategy to safeguard yourself is to read the terms of the agreement so you are clear on exactly what will happen if a payment is missed or late. Some auto loans actually state that they will repossess a vehicle after just one missed payment. Once the item is taken, it is difficult and expensive to get back. Therefore, it is important to always be up-front with your creditor if you know you will be late with a payment. It is much easier to come up with a plan for repayment with your financer rather than try to get your vehicle or other possession back.

How the U.S. Repossession Laws Can Affect You

If you are being faced with repossession, it is important for you to understand the laws. Though every state has its own specific set of repossession legalities, there are two types you must be aware of: voluntary and involuntary repossession.

- **Voluntary repossession:** When you fall behind on your loan payments, a creditor will contact you to discuss repossession. If you agree to the repossession and allow the creditor to take over ownership of the property, then voluntary repossession has occurred. In this case the lender does not take your vehicle or home, but instead you have granted it to them instead of paying back the money loaned to you by the creditor.

- **Involuntary repossession:** If you are in a situation where the creditor forcefully takes away the property against your will, this is called involuntary repossession. This is a less preferable option because it does not give you the choice of working amicably with the lender. It also means that you may have to provide the money for the expenses incurred by the loan provider during the repossession.

Your creditor, or the entity that holds your loan, has the right to do what they want with the item; it is considered theirs, not yours at this point. They may keep it as compensation for what you owe, or they may sell it.

In some states, they will be required to conduct a sale that meets minimum market requirements, such as an auction. Selling the car for $100 and then claiming you owe $7,900 on an $8,000 debt will not meet the standard. Selling the car at a public auction for $5,000 and going after you for the remaining $3,000 meets the standard in states where such standards exist.

Repossession Companies

Repossession companies are the businesses hired to take back your vehicle or other possessions. You may have heard horror stories associated with some repossession companies — often dubbed "repos." State laws vary, and many provide protection from repossession companies that use overly aggressive action the seize property. Many states will not permit repossession companies to take drastic measures, such as knocking on your door at 2 a.m. or breaking into your garage to taking your car. However, these are real companies, and their jobs are to take back your possessions. Bottom line: Because they are generally paid based on the repossession of each item, their top priority is to get the item back.

Repossession of Automobiles

There are many types of items that can be repossessed — furniture, boats, homes, appliances — but one of the main items of repossession is automobiles. If you have been late on monthly payments, you run the risk of having your car or truck taken away. Laws vary by state; in some cases, repossessions are lawful if you are one second late on your payment. It is unlikely that a lender will be that eager to take back a vehicle, but it can happen. It is important to note that creditors can take back your car without any warning and without having to go to court.

Always read the fine print

The agreement you signed will spell out your monthly payment and the date on which it is due. Some states require a grace period of a few days, during which no penalty may be imposed. One example is the car payment due on the first day of each month. If your state provides a five-day grace period, then you, in reality, have until the fifth of the month to get your payment to the lender or the entity that holds the note on your car. Be aware that the grace period is a consumer benefit, not a modification to your contract, and your lender may be indisposed to grant another hour should you be chronically late with your payment.

The agreement, or loan contract, may either be transferred to a third party or sold, much in the way home loans are bought and sold. The terms of the loan will remain constant even if the note's holder is not the originator of the loan. If you purchased your vehicle from a local dealer who wrote up your loan, you may discover that the dealer has sold the loan to a company several states away and is not in a position to assist you, should you be unable to make a payment.

Vehicle loans take many forms and contain all kinds of interest rates, penalties, benefits (mostly for the lender), and rights for both parties. If your credit history is less than stellar, you will in all probability face high interest rates. Some states cap the allowable interest rate, but they can still be over 20 percent, particularly for those with the worst credit histories and prior repossessions.

What about the property in the vehicle?

Your creditor (or lessor) cannot legally keep personal property that was located inside the car or truck when it is repossessed. This would include your watch, computer, or any other item that is not installed in the vehicle. If you had an expensive radio installed in place of the original, it will likely be considered part of the vehicle, not a personal item. If you have a plug-in satellite radio device that can be easily removed, it will be considered a personal item. Again, state laws vary, but as a common rule, personal property in a vehicle is protected from the entity that repossesses a vehicle, and care must be taken to protect it. Such care would preclude a repo man from leaving the door open in an open lot to provide access to anyone who happens to walk by.

The repossession is limited to the property that was used as collateral, and nothing more. In the event that a lender offers to settle everything if you throw in your laptop or some other item, get it in writing and specify that the debt will be considered paid in full. Make sure you get everything written down in contract form, and obtain a statement releasing you from any liens on the vehicle.

If your vehicle is repossessed and you later discover that certain personal items are unaccounted for, such as computers, MP3 players, and navigation devices, then you may be entitled to compensation. This will vary by state, so look into your state laws to see if you are able to get your personal items back. It is wise to consult an attorney to review your options.

Other Repossessions

Although vehicles make up the bulk of repossessions, any secured loan can result in the lender taking back an item if the borrower fails to make payments. Some items that can be repossessed include:

- **Appliances**: refrigerators, ovens, microwaves
- **Furniture**: beds, couches, dining room sets
- **Household equipment**: lawn mowers, snow blowers, tractors
- **Recreation items**: boats, jet skis, motorcycles
- **Electronic items**: televisions, stereo systems, computers

Basically, for anything that you took out on loan, that product is the security on the loan and is subject to repossession. Once you have put your signature on a legal contract, you are bound by its terms. Unscrupulous lenders or retailers may impose pre-payment penalties, charge-backs, interest premiums, and all sorts of gimmicks that will double or triple the actual cost of the item.

Consider Jim for an example. He passes by an electronics store and notices a new computer on sale. Though Jim has a computer at home, his is a slightly older model, and he would like to have an upgraded machine. The store is offering a 0-percent-down financing program. Jim becomes tempted into purchasing the new model — even though he does not essentially need it and is currently wrestling with some credit card debt. Nevertheless, he is seduced by the offer of what appears to be a reasonable monthly payment, and he ignores the high interest rate and fees. Jim signs up for a three-year, rent-to-own agreement and goes home with his new computer. A few months later, the payments begin to get more costly and he is unable to make them. Jim skips two payments.

Soon Jim gets a letter from the retailer asking if maybe he "overlooked" the scheduled payment. The next one is less pleasant. The third one is nasty, and the fourth demands that the computer be returned. It points out penalties that are outlined in the agreement that Jim signed and numerous other fees associated with breach of agreement. The retailer or holder of the note or lease has also notified the crediting rating services, so Jim's credit report is suddenly in jeopardy. It is fairly simple to see how the decision to bring home the newest computer can spiral out of control.

How To Get Your Possessions Back

If you are wondering whether it is even possible to get your possession back, the good news is that it is possible. However, you will most likely have to pay the entire note, plus whatever expenses the lender has incurred to repossess the vehicle, including the cost of towing it away from your home, and any court costs or legal fees. If you owe $8,000 on the car, for example, your lender will want all of it, plus the additional amount. If you had that much cash available to you, it is unlikely the vehicle would be in repossession, but you do have a right to pay it off, with additional fees, to get it back.

In some states, though, that right may be nothing more than the right to attend the auction at which the vehicle is being sold and bid on it. This will put you in an awkward position because you will be still be legally liable for the difference between the sale price at auction and what you owe on the original loan. Say you attend the auction and win the bidding with an offer of $5,000. You will be required to pay in cash. That money goes to the lender, minus the auction fees. You will still be held responsible for the $3,000 difference of what the auction brought and what you owed when the vehicle was repossessed, and the lender can go to court to get a judgment against you for that money. In other words, there is no financial incentive for you to show up at the auction to bid on your own car.

Some states require that the lender give you appropriate notice of the time and place of the sale of your item. There may even be such a require-ment in the event of a private sale to an individual. Normally, states with such requirements will give you the right to re-instate your loan if you can pay off the back payments and all fees incurred by the lender during the repossession process. This is before the sale of the vehicle. These fees may include towing, storage, and detailing, among other things, which can total hundreds of dollars.

You may still owe money

Here is where the price you paid and the interest rate you were charged come into focus. Use a vehicle as an example. You may still owe more than what your vehicle is worth. There are a wide range of reasons for this, and it is not uncommon for cars and trucks to drop in value or, in the case of used vehicles purchased by desperate buyers, to be worth less than the price paid.

When the lender sells your vehicle, the proceeds go toward paying what you owe on it. The difference, called the deficiency, remains in the books, making you liable. The amount will include all the costs and fees associated with the repossession, including legal fees and court filing obligations. You may be hit with a claim for hundreds or even thousands of dollars and, in many states, the lender has the right to sue and obtain a judgment against you. This may give him or her the right to claim some other property of yours, or even file a lien against your home. You will be notified of the date of the court hearing and will have an opportunity to defend yourself. If your lender has violated the law during the repossession process, this is the time to explain what happened to the judge. If there are extenuating circumstances, the judge may, under state law, give you a break. Again, discussing this with an attorney is a wise course of action under these conditions.

How repossession can affect your credit

If a judgment is rendered against you, it will be entered into your credit report, along with the repossession. Your state may have laws that specify your rights and the rights of someone who has won a judgment against you, and how such a judgment may be satisfied. In some cases, the judgment may be negotiated, and the lender may accept a lower amount. There is no harm in asking. Be sure to get any agreement in writing. Your ultimate goal is to get this matter resolved and be free of any liens and judgments.

Some states allow holders of judgments to go to your employer to garnish a portion of your salary to satisfy the judgment. This is more likely to happen if you ignore attempts to collect or fail to make payments that you agreed upon. It can also be quite embarrassing. If possible, negotiate a settlement or payment schedule before the process comes that far.

In the highly unlikely event that the vehicle is sold for more than you owe, you are entitled to the difference, minus the costs associated with the repossession, in most states.

Ways to Prevent or Overcome Repossession

- **Communicate with creditors**: It is never a good idea to ignore letters and telephone calls.

- **Talk to your creditor**: Ask if you can make partial payments until you are back on track financially.

- **Do not let lenders know that you no longer want the item and will give it back**: They do not want the item; they want your payment.

If you have found yourself at risk for repossession, or have already had your items taken back, there are resources that can help. Consider the following:

- **Private lawyers:** Look for those who specialize in repossession laws. See the Fair Debt for Consumers group at **http://fairdebtforconsumers.com**.

- **Non-profit organizations:** Look into the American Recovery Association at **www.repo.org** and the National Foundation for Credit Counseling at **http://nfcc.org**.

- **General Web sites:** Try **www.expertlaw.com**.

Summary

As this chapter has taught you, repossession is essentially the same as foreclosure. It is the process of one party reclaiming property from another, usually because payments are late or have been missed entirely. Most commonly, it is a vehicle that is repossessed, but anything that has been used as collateral in a loan is subject to repossession, including furniture, appliances, and computers. Items purchased using a non-secured credit card are not liable to be repossessed because such cards, as the description implies, are non-secured, meaning the money is not being lent against a tangible asset.

Because repossession is the result of failure to comply with the terms of a purchase agreement — commonly a failure to make payments on time or at all — it occurs only on secured loans. That means the loan is guaranteed by a product such as a car or an appliance that, in the event of default, is seized and subject to sale by the lender to help satisfy the loan.

Read and understand the terms of every contract you sign. Do not be lured into making a bad deal because the initial monthly payment is low or is "interest-free." Such deals are offered to consumers because retailers and lenders believe they will make money, not because they want to be nice guys. Lenders count on consumers who will not pay off "six-month-same-as-cash" or similar contracts before the interest or payment grace period expires. If that happens, consumers are subject to high interest rates that begin on the first day of the loan. Such deals may also come with a high base price for the product because the so-called bargain is the financing, not the price of the item being purchased, hence the easy trap of repossession. Suddenly, not being able to pay off a loan due to an agreement that snowballs into more than you expected can lead to debt — and then the reclaiming of your possessions.

As with foreclosure, always communicate with your lender(s) if you are having trouble making the monthly payments. Do not ignore telephone calls and letters. Explain your situation, and offer a plan to become current on your loan. It truly is your best bet for keeping your possessions.

Chapter 6

Overcoming Eviction

E viction is a legal court action used by a landlord to remove a tenant from a home, apartment, or room. Essentially, eviction is a form of repossession or foreclosure. The landlord takes back the property by forcing the tenant to move out. You can be evicted for many reasons. Failure to pay the rent is the most common, but landlords have the right to evict tenants who are noisy, offend other tenants, create unsanitary conditions that affect other tenants, and so on.

If you have found yourself in a situation where you cannot pay the rent because of job loss, illness, or any other reason, use the information you learn in the chapter to figure out ways to prevent or overcome eviction.

The effects of eviction on your family are:

- Loss of home.
- Potential to be uprooted from community.
- Embarrassment associated with this social stigma.

The financial implications of eviction are effects on your credit score; loss of your security deposit; more money needed to be put down on the next apartment; potential for having to put higher deposits on future rental property; or increased rental payments.

Detailed Descriptions of the U.S. Eviction Laws

Although each state has different eviction laws — and it is important that you check with your individual state — if you have violated your lease or rental agreement, then there are essentially three main categories of termination notices that you may be in jeopardy of receiving. They are:

1. **Pay-rent-or-quit notices**: This type of notice is usually given to renters who, simply put, have not paid their rent. If you receive this type of notice, you will have three to five days to pay the landlord your rent or to move out of the property.

2. **Cure-or-quit notices**: This type of notice is typically given if the renter violates a specific term or condition of the rental agreement or lease. Some examples would be violating the no-pets clause or making excessive noise. If you have received this notice, you generally have a certain amount of time to correct the violation.

3. **Unconditional quit notices**: This type of notice orders you to vacate the property immediately. You have no chance to pay your rent or correct the violation. In most states, unconditional quit notices are only permissible if the renter has done one of the following:

a. Been a regular violator of a major clause within a lease or rental agreement.

b. Continued to be late in paying the rent on more than one occasion.

c. Caused serious physical damage to the premises.

d. Has been found to have engaged in serious illegal activity — for example, dealing drugs on the premises.

There are times when a renter will be forced to move out, and the reasons vary, from justifiable to illegal to the owner's personal financial misfortune.

Justifiable evictions

Also known as legal evictions, justifiable evictions occur because the renter(s) have violated the terms of the lease, most commonly by not paying the rent. Everyone who signs the lease is responsible for abiding by its terms. If you have roommates and one or more of them moves out, gets a dog, makes too much noise, or offends other tenants, all of you may be held responsible and be evicted. It is advisable to make sure before you move in that you get along well with your roommates and can live with them. Your landlord must approve of any multi-person living arrangement and be aware of who is living in the rental property, or you may be deemed to be in violation of your lease, subjecting you to eviction.

If you are self-employed, you may face restrictions on doing business in your rental unit. Retail sales that involve deliveries and pickups, customers coming and going, and other activities that may irritate or inconvenience your neighbors may subject you to eviction, as will other business activity that make loud noises or otherwise call attention to you. If you work computer or perform other self-employment activities that are quiet unlikely to bother others, you may be legally within your rights to

out of your home. Your landlord should be aware of your business activities to avoid any misunderstandings.

Some communities have special landlord/tenant courts that make decisions about issues involving rental properties. If this is the case where you live, you will appear before such a court if your landlord attempts to evict you. If you file a court action against your landlord, you may also find yourself in landlord/tenant court. Nonetheless, small-claims court is also an option available to you to force him or her into making certain repairs and returning all or a portion of your deposit. Your landlord may also take you to small claims court to force you into making certain payments. Again, do all you can to avoid going to court.

Is Eviction Legal?

If you have violated the terms of your lease, chances are the eviction is legal. You and your landlord may have extremely different versions of what actually took place and whether there was an actual or imagined incident. Obviously, if you have not paid your rent for three months, your landlord has valid grounds for evicting you. If, conversely, you have had a frequent overnight guest whom your landlord considers a resident, but you consider only an occasional guest, there may be grounds for discussion. It is important for all parties to recognize that the lease is a legal document, and it binds you to the terms you signed.

Many states allow tenants several days to pay back rent. During this time, you may stop the eviction process by giving your landlord a check for what you owe. Be sure the check is good and will clear the bank. Presenting your landlord with a bad check can create problems including bad-check criminal charges.

Some states offer no grace period whatsoever, and you may be facing eviction if you are just a single day late in your rent. A landlord who will evict someone under such flimsy circumstances is not likely to be that understanding about anything else, so maybe finding somewhere else to live is not a bad idea. Do not count on a good recommendation, though.

Lease restrictions

If your lease contains restrictions on the number of people living in the place and you have exceeded that number, your landlord has a legal right to evict you. Having some friends over for Super Bowl weekend most likely will not fall under this category, but if your friends stay through March Madness, your landlord may have a valid complaint. If you have read your lease, you will know the limit on the number of people who may live with you, and under what circumstances they may stay over or even reside in an apartment or house.

Additionally, your landlord has a right to evict you if you break other rules of the lease — such as loud music, frequent loud arguments, or foul odors. You may feel the same way about your neighbors who act in this manner. Who wants to live around people who attract rats, or whose loud music makes having a peaceful home impossible?

The same standard may apply to smoking. If your lease contains a no-smoking clause and you or a roommate takes up smoking, you may be subject to eviction. Pets are objectionable for several reasons. Dogs bark and irritate others. Cats can scratch furniture and ruin carpets. If your landlord outlines in the terms of the lease that these conditions are not permitted, you can be evicted if you break the rules.

Nearly every lease or rental agreement will permit the landlord to evict you for criminal behavior. This applies to the use of illegal drugs, violations of weapons laws, and your running a gambling pool out of your home. Do not expect the landlord/tenant court to show much sympathy if your landlord evicts you for criminal acts committed in your unit.

Some leases contain moral clauses that may or may not be legal, depending on state or local laws and the wording of the clause. Essentially, such clauses give the landlord the right to evict you for acts committed on or off the premises. For instance, if you are charged with possession of an illegal substance, you may find yourself facing eviction, regardless of where you were caught. Such clauses may not violate your rights under state or federal laws and restrict your personal liberties under the law. In other words, you may not be evicted for conduct that is legal and unrestricted under landlord/tenant laws.

Illegal Evictions

Just as the terms of the lease apply to you, they apply to your landlord. You must both comply with federal, state, and local landlord/tenant laws — and be governed by them.

Your landlord may not evict you before your lease ends simply because someone else is offering to pay a higher rent for the place or replace the bathroom tile for free. He or she may not increase your rent or change the terms of the lease before the lease is up, unless you both agree. That standard applies to all aspects of your rental agreement or lease.

Your landlord may not evict you because you demand necessary repairs or for any other reason that can be categorized as retaliation for demanding what is justly due. Some states permit the withholding of rent to force the landlord to make necessary repairs, but some communities require that rent withheld in this manner be put into an account of escrow (a separate trust account that is held in the borrower's name) to be paid to the landlord once repairs are made. Such laws are designed to ensure that tenants do not use their complaints as excuses to live rent-free.

It is not uncommon for landlords and tenants to argue. What appears to be a clear-cut need for a new bathtub to you appears to be a case of normal wear and tear and nothing that requires action to the landlord. Other things may be more serious. For instance, a substandard heating system or faulty electrical outlet may require an intense conversation. Older residences that have been rental units for many years may not have been maintained well and might have serious repair issues. These are the types of issues that are best addressed before you sign the lease and move in, but if your landlord has failed to make improvements that are spelled out in your lease, you have every right to take action. In fact, some apartment complexes will give residents a walk-through checklist to fill out before moving in. Be aware that such action must comply with the law. Starting an argument or having a physical encounter is not allowed. Sending the landlord a letter outlining your complaint, however, is proper. The letter will simply inform her or him that you intend to pursue the matter in landlord/tenant court, and it is within bounds. It is not legal for your landlord to evict you for exercising your rights as a tenant.

In many communities, you have the right to withhold rent and move out if your unit becomes uninhabitable, as defined by state or municipal law. This is not limited to fire and flood, and it may include mold and lack of heat during winter months, among other things. You also may have a legal right to receive a full refund of your deposit, plus interest.

It is important to note that tempers may flare during the process of negotiating improvements to a rental unit. Things may be said and done that, in the clear light of reflection, were better left unsaid and undone. If your matter goes before a court for resolution, be confident that both sides of the story will be told. That means you will have an opportunity to explain how you were wronged, and your landlord will have a chance to tell the court all of the things you have done, even if they were in the heat of the moment. It is best to negotiate disputes rather than litigate them.

How to Work Out a Solution with the Landlord

The most common reason tenants are evicted is failure to pay the rent in a timely manner. In a small number of cases, landlords are simply unreasonable and unwilling to grant tenants any slack. In most cases, though, landlords begin the eviction process as a last resort. They are not in business to throw people out. Many tenants do not communicate with their landlords because they are embarrassed by their inability to pay the rent on time or want to avoid their landlord's reaction, which would be understandably negative.

As with all other credit issues, it will not help you to withdraw and hope it just goes away. Here are some ideas to work things out with the landlord:

- **Be up-front**: It is always best to address your financial difficulties in a forthright manner. That means telling your landlord if you are having financial problems and how you plan to become current on your rent. Failure to answer the telephone or door is a fast track to eviction because the landlord will assume you are a hopeless case and want you out.

- **Come up with a plan**: If you have lost your job and cannot pay your rent, explain your situation and what you are doing about it. If you are actively looking for another job and have bright prospects, tell your landlord. By being up-front with your landlord, you can set their mind at ease that you fully intend to honor the terms of your lease.

- **Negotiate**: If you believe your landlord has not lived up to the terms of the lease, the negotiation with him or her will be about what you believe to be the violation of the rental agreement. It could be a faulty furnace, bad plumbing, or some other complaint the landlord has failed to address. The landlord, on the other hand, may demand the rent check before any repairs are made or other issues are addressed. If that is the case, you have a classic standoff and would be advised to seek a solution that benefits both sides — such as partial rent payment with the intent to pay the rest after repairs are made.

Mediation

If relations between you and your landlord have become so strained that you cannot talk to each other, you may need to bring in a mediator — a third party who has no stake in the outcome. This could be someone whom both of you trust and respect, or it could be an outsider who you believe will listen to all of the facts and make recommendations without bias to one side or another. Remember that any fees associated with the mediation should be paid equally; if one of you pays all mediation fees, the outcome may be questioned if the one who pays also prevails on the issues. In fact, it will actually look like the person who paid for the mediation fees was really paying for the mediator to take their side.

Mediation can work if the issues are resolvable. If the property in question is uninhabitable, then there is not much to discuss other than the return of your deposit, and things are likely to play out in your favor. If your goal in mediation is to simply convince your landlord to allow you to keep a horse in your living room, you almost certainly will not get your way, however.

Mediation is one step away from the courtroom, a kind of second-to-last resort. Both sides must agree to it and be willing to accept the mediator's recommendations, although mediation does not automatically commit both sides to the third party's findings. Mediation may actually be a great way for the two parties to come up with a mutual solution of their own.

Arbitration

Arbitration is an alternative to mediation. It is a bit more formal, and its findings can be binding on both parties if the resolution is ordered by the court. Arbitration can be court-ordered or an alternative to a formal court preceding. Under this scheme, an arbitrator will be selected or appointed, hear both sides, and make a decision. Depending on the laws of your state and the terms of your agreement upon entering the arbitration, the outcome can have the force of law, and you and your landlord will have no choice but to accept it.

Court

Some states and communities have established landlord/tenant courts that only hear such cases; others hear these cases in general or district courts. Federal, state, and community landlord/tenant laws will apply. Most courts will strongly recommend mediation, arbitration, or some other out-of-court settlement. The process of eviction through the courts can be time-consuming and costly, especially for the landlord, who will most likely hire an attorney to move the case quickly through the court system.

The process begins when you, the tenant, receive an eviction notice. Land-lord/tenant laws routinely set a specific timetable, and the clock begins to run once you are legally notified that your landlord plans to evict you, regardless of when you actually receive and read the notice. You may have a few days in which to make past rent payments to satisfy the landlord, or you may not; it is completely dependent upon the terms of your lease and your landlord. You always have the option of attempting to contact your landlord to discuss issues or seek mediation, as outlined above.

If your landlord is determined to evict you, he or she may try to speed up the process to get you out, assuming that you will not pay any more rent. For example, he or she may serve you with a Notice to Vacate in order to get you out of the property. The court process takes time, and the landlord is losing money.

The court may or may not have the authority to order the landlord to make repairs, if that is the reason you have withheld rent. State and municipal laws will determine what powers the court has in these matters. You will be allowed to testify at the hearing as to why you withheld your rent checks and the court may determine that your requests are justified and order the landlord to fix the place up.

You should know that the court option is not limited to your landlord. If you have a serious or ongoing dispute over clearly stated terms of your lease, and the property owner or manager refuses to address these issues, you may take him or her to court. Small claims court may be a good option because these courts, by design, are easier to use and understand. You fill out a form at the office of the clerk, the other party is notified by the court, and a date is set. Both sides appear and state their case. You may present witnesses and evidence, such as photographs of holes in the ceiling or a statement from a furnace company. The judge will hear both sides and make a ruling. It is not uncommon for both sides to file competing claims on the same or similar issues. For instance, you may take him or her to court over furnace issues, and your landlord may counter-sue you for back rent (rent that was not paid to the landlord). Normally, both cases are settled at the same time, but if your state requires that different courts hear small claims and landlord/tenant issues, the process may be dragged into different courtrooms. Some small claims courts have mandatory, on-the-spot mediation to resolve issues even in the minutes before the judge hears the case. The point is to bring pressure to both sides, forcing them to talk it out and find common ground.

Eviction Through Foreclosure

The real estate crisis that began in 2007 and intensified in 2008 produced a wave of evictions that were not the fault of the renters who leased apartments and homes. The owners of these properties became unable to make their payments and lost the properties through foreclosure and, in some cases, the banks evicted the people who had leased the property.

Many of the people who bought these properties were speculators who assumed that the wild rise in real estate prices would continue, which led them to sign mortgages they could not pay, even with the rental income they received from the property. These mortgages may have had adjustable interest rates that boosted monthly payments to unreasonable levels, called "balloon payments." For whatever reason, the owner/speculator lost the property, and the bank now owns it and wants to get rid of it. Property occupied by renters who hold a lease is harder to sell than an empty house, due to the fact that the residents have a lease, so banks evict the tenants. It may be perfectly legal, but it is an onerous burden for the tenant who is forced to move out.

If you have found yourself in this situation, try to work with the bank or new owner to give yourself a bit more time to get a new place to move to.

This is one eviction circumstance that will not be considered negative on your credit score and credit report because it was not your fault. A prospective landlord will not hold it against you.

How to Find a New Place to Live

If all of the above fail and you are forced to move out, you must be proactive in finding a new place before the marshal shows up to put your possessions in the street. Most evictions take place at a specific date and time. Some local laws require the landlord to pay a certain number of movers to remove all property from the premises and place it on nearby public property — most likely the curb. You do not want to wait for this to happen. You will be given a few days' notice; use this time wisely. Hanging around your apartment and hoping the eviction will not take place will only make matters worse.

If you have been evicted, you probably will not receive your deposit back. If the eviction was the result of a court ruling, your deposit will most likely be awarded to your landlord to help compensate for missed rent payments.

You now are back where you started on the topic of rentals. You need a place to live, and the same issues, like previous evictions or foreclosures, that you faced as you chose the place that evicted you are in play, along with the added complication of the eviction you have just experienced. The first issue you must address is your ability to pay the rent in your new apartment or house. Do not be shocked to find that a prospective landlord might want a higher deposit and may even raise the monthly rent because of your eviction. This is not illegal in most places, unless rent controls (which limit the amount of rent and rent increases that a landlord can charge) restrict the amount a landlord may charge.

Ways to Prevent or Overcome Eviction

- Honor the terms outlined in your lease.
- Read your lease and know your rights.
- Contact your landlord if you have trouble paying rent.
- Do not rent a place that exceeds your monthly income by one-third.

Summary

If you were evicted because you violated the terms of your lease by being loud or having a pet, you must address that issue with a prospective landlord. He or she will want to know whether you will honor a new lease. If you like loud music, perhaps you should consider a place that is more isolated. If you must keep your dog, look for a place that accepts pets. Do what you must to avoid a repeat of the situation that got you evicted. Bottom line: If your landlord outlines in the terms of the lease that certain conditions, like having a pet or loud music, are not permitted, then you can be evicted if you break the rules.

 # Chapter 7

How to Rebuild Your Credit

C redit is simply a contractual agreement between you and a lender where you take something of value and agree to repay the lender in the future. When you apply for credit, the lender looks at your credit history to determine if you are a good loan candidate and to see how reliable you have been in the past. The lender weighs the level of risk associated with extending credit to you. If you have a poor history of repaying loans, your credit is considered less than ideal, which may mean you will not be approved for the loan.

Why Your Credit Score is Essential

Simply put: The higher your credit score, the better your opportunity for getting good rates on loans. When lenders look at your score, it is a reflection of how financially responsible you have been. Lenders then use your credit history to determine how responsible you are likely to be in the future. Therefore, when you have good credit, lenders are more likely to give you a better rate than someone who has a lower credit score. In turn, you save money.

It is important to remember that your credit report will set the tone for your financial life. It determines your loan eligibility, interest rate, and may even determine the cost of your auto insurance or ability to get a "pay later" deal. Any late payment to any lender may trigger higher interest rates on the credit cards you now hold. Thus, it is essential that you are aware of what things are in credit report and correct any errors that may be in them. You may discover that a creditor has mistakenly claimed late payments, or that someone has stolen your identity to obtain credit cards and has run up huge bills that you know nothing about. If you have blemishes on your credit report that can be explained, send letters outlining the circumstances. You have a right to explain such problems. You also have the right — and should always make it a priority — to correct mistakes.

If you have failed to pay a bill because the item was returned as unacceptable or the service was not provided, you have the right to explain it. Occasionally, what should be a simple consumer complaint about shoddy goods or services will turn up on someone's credit report because the merchant is angry or spiteful. For example, say you ordered a piece of jewelry online that was deemed "final sale," and it did not live up to your expectations upon receipt. If you returned it, a merchant could take measures to penalize your credit report — even though you feel that you are taking steps to protect yourself financially. Even if the merchant is unyielding, it is possible to correct this mistake. Be aware that this process can be time-consuming and frustrating, but in the end, you will be doing yourself a favor.

How your credit score is calculated

There are many factors in your credit score. Major financial difficulties such as bankruptcies and foreclosures will affect your score, but so will your debt-to-available-credit ratio. This is the percentage of available credit that you have actually borrowed. Say, for instance, that you have a credit card limit (the maximum amount you can charge) of $10,000. If you are maxed out, meaning that you have no more credit available, your score will be lower than if you owed only $2,500 on your $10,000 limit.

General credit score ratings

Though credit scores in excess of 700 points fall into the norm of credit risks and are typically necessary to acquire more financing options and better interest rates, lower scores do not necessarily prevent an individual from obtaining credit financing. Lenders and creditors provide financing options to suit a variety of credit profiles. Credit scores among the U.S. population in 2003 averaged as follows:

Up to 499	1%	650 - 699	16%
500 - 549	5%	700 - 749	20%
550 - 599	7%	750 - 799	29%
600 - 649	11%	Over 800	11%

Therefore, if you have a low-debt level — such as the $2,500 that we mentioned earlier — your credit score could potentially be in the 800 and above range. However, if you were maxed out on one — or, worse, multiple credit cards — your credit score could potentially be in the 500 and below range. As you can see, your everyday money management has a huge impact on your credit.

The history of your accounts will also be factored into your score. A brand-new account that is current with no late notices may have a lower score than a long-term account with late payments that were in the distant past. That is because the older account will be seen as a better indicator of your ability and willingness to pay off your debt. If you pay only the monthly minimums, your score may suffer. If you have often been late on your payments, your score will suffer. Also, having multiple cards that are maxed out will affect your credit score more than having one open with a small balance.

If you have recently obtained a credit card, this could be seen as a need for money and may bring down your score, especially if you already have a number of credit cards that are maxed out. People who have maxed-out credit cards can still get new ones at very high interest rates. Do not do this, as it will take already-bad credit and make it much worse.

It is also important to mention that some individuals who carry small balances on their cards and make timely payments can actually help their credit score. This is because it shows the credit bureaus that they are using credit wisely. On the other hand, people with no credit cards at all can hurt their credit score because they are not building credit at all.

The Federal Reserve, the nation's central bank, studied credit scores and reported that a score of 701 or above reflects only a 5 percent likelihood of payment delinquencies of the following two-year period from when the credit score was calculated. A score of 600 or below, however, reflects a 50 percent likelihood of delinquencies in the following two years. Your score is a reflection of the credit industry's opinion of your ability to pay your bills.

A low score will cost you money because the credit industry thinks you are a risky borrower and are more likely to walk away from your debts, so they hedge their bets by charging you more to borrow. The Federal Reserve reported that in 2004, a borrower with a credit score of 720 paid an almost 4 percent lower mortgage interest rate than a borrower with a credit score of 560. The difference in the monthly payments on this interest rate gap is huge, and every penny of this difference is a penalty for a bad credit history.

The good news is that you can begin the process of raising your credit score right now. If you are delinquent in your credit card payments, you can raise your score simply by becoming current. If you can pay off any of your credit cards, do it, and lower your debt ratio at the same time. If you discover errors on your report, be sure to call the credit reporting agencies to correct the mistakes. You should put your concerns and corrections in writing. Under the law, credit reporting agencies must report their findings and actions back to you, so be sure to stay on top of any correspondence with them.

Tips for Improving Your Credit Score

Any efforts made to pay down bills, take a second job, engage credit counseling, or file bankruptcy should be included in a credit repair plan, and the individual must then be responsible for acting on the planned activities. A credit repair plan should establish financial goals that indicate methods for spending and saving money in the near and far future. The credit repair plan should include a budget that is based realistically on the amount of income an individual has to work with. From that income, money should be allocated to the following:

- Necessary living expenses.

- Outstanding debts, such that they may be paid off as soon as possible.

- A savings plan to be used in emergency situations, such as illness or a loss of employment.

- A savings plan to be used in meeting established financial goals.

The most important step that you can take to help keep your credit score high, or to make your credit score better, is to make timely payments. When creditors assess your payment history, your credit score is the most important factor that is used to calculate it. If you have any payments that are more than 30 days past due, they will come up on your credit report and negatively affect your score. Generally these things will stay on your report for up to seven years — so even just one mistake now could be costly down the line. You may wonder how you get your credit score. It is broken down into the following categories:

1. **The credit you have in use:** 10 percent
2. **Your history of past payments:** 35 percent
3. **The length of your credit history:** 15 percent
4. **The total amount you have owed:** 30 percent
5. **The amount of new credit you have:** 10 percent

Stop borrowing money

The second most significant credit score factor is the overall amount you owe. Therefore, it should go without saying that it is critical to keep your borrowing at a minimum. If you currently have a high amount of out-standing debt, your priority must be to stop borrowing and work toward minimizing that balance. Though this is not always easy, it truly is the only way to improve your financial situation. Also, be sure to consider exactly how much of the credit that is available to you is being used. For example, having a high number of credit cards that are at the maximum, or are near-ing their total limits, will have a negative affect on your credit score. Hav-ing two credit cards each with a limit of $5,000 and a balance of $1,000 will look much better than just having one card with a $2,500 limit and a balance of $2,000.

Make sure you keep old accounts open

The duration of your credit history is another vital factor in your credit score. Therefore, it can actually help you to keep older accounts open, even though they have been paid off. While it is important that you keep your total number of accounts low, it may actually hurt your score more to close an old account rather than keep it open.

Use caution when opening new accounts

You probably already know that new credit is the least important factor in your score; however, it is still important for you to keep in mind. While shopping for a loan or credit card, do it relatively quickly. You do not want your credit report to show that you are always on the lookout for credit. Also, do not keep accounts open that you do not plan on using. While this may seem tempting to get an 10 percent off on a retail store card, keep in mind that the small amount of money you save may not matter when a high number of new accounts actually make your credit score lower.

Paying to see your credit score

Even though you have a legal right to see what is in your credit report once a year for free, that right does not extend to your credit score, which will determine whether you obtain credit from lenders and the interest rate they will establish for you. Under the law, the agencies that report credit are legally able to charge you a fee to see your score. Upon publication of this book, this fee was around $10 to access to your report. Credit reporting agencies have a virtual menu of services they would like to sell you, including alerts about inquiries and negative items, so it will be based on your discretion to decide just how intensely you want to monitor your credit, and if such monitoring is worth paying for.

Reviewing Your Credit Report

The Fair Credit Reporting Act (FCRA) mandates that individuals are able to receive a complimentary credit report once per year from the three major consumer reporting companies. These are:

- Equifax: **www.equifax.com**
- Experian: **www.experian.com**
- TransUnion: **www.transunion.com**

You may also order your free credit report each year by visiting **www.annualcreditreport.com**, calling the toll-free number at 1-877-322-8228, or filling the Annual Credit Report Request Form and sending it to: Annual Credit Report Request Service, P.O. Box 105281, Atlanta, GA 30348-5281.

Your credit report consists of basic information: your address, how well you pay your monthly bills, whether you have been placed under arrest or have had a lawsuit against you, or whether have had a prior bankruptcy. There are companies that sell this type of information to insurers, creditors, employers, and other businesses. These groups, in turn, use the data in your report to decide upon applications for employment, insurance, credit, and home rentals. Because you can legally request one complimentary credit report from each of the consumer reporting companies once per year, you may want to order them all at once. This is an easy and important way to check discrepancies.

Who May Access Your Credit Report?

Federal consumer laws limit access to individuals' credit reports, so, technically, yours is not available to nosy neighbors. But such reports are available to creditors, insurance companies, real estate management companies, or other potential landlords. Basically, anyone considering you for a loan, as well as potential, or current, employers, can check your credit report. There are limits for employers wanting to check your credit history, however — you must provide written permission for them to view your credit report.

It is assumed that anyone accessing your credit report is attempting to determine whether you are trustworthy enough to pay back a loan, pay your rent on time, or act as reliably as an employee.

You can see why it is essential that the information in the report be correct, even if some of it may not be positive. If you have a history of failing to meet financial obligations, you will have problems obtaining credit, insurance, or maybe even a job. If, however, your financial difficulties were the result of a medical catastrophe or something else that was not your fault, you will be in a much better position to explain these circumstances.

Thus, the severity of a negative item on your credit report will be an important indicator of your ability to pay back a loan or meet a financial commitment. Walking away from thousands of dollars in credit card debt will be seen as more serious than a dispute over medical bills.

CASE STUDY: CREDIT SCORE CRISIS

Nora Raum
Attorney
2007 N. 15th Street, Suite 201
Arlington, VA 22201
Phone (703) 243-2044
Fax (703) 243-5279
info@noraraum.com

Nora Raum has been a practicing attorney for 21 years, specializing in personal bankruptcies. She saw an increase in clients after the housing crisis that began in 2007 forced people to seek protection from creditors. Many of her clients are immigrants who fell victim to unscrupulous or poorly trained mortgage lenders, purchasing homes they could not afford and obtaining mortgages they were unable to pay. The result was bankruptcy and foreclosure.

Raum also has many clients who are professionals whose credit simply got out of control.

"Most people do not realize that the dollar you borrow today can become $10 tomorrow," she said, referring to high credit card interest rates.

She believes most people would benefit from courses that teach personal financial basics, such as how credit cards really work, how mortgages work, and how to budget your money. In fact, she believes such education should begin in middle school.

Her advice to anyone who wants to use borrowed money is to be cautious. "It doesn't take much to damage your credit rating. One late payment to the credit card company can produce a huge increase in your interest rate," she said.

Raum charges $100 for an initial consultation with prospective clients, advising them to bring documentation of all of their bills and debts. She then provides forms for them to take home and fill out, detailing their financial obligations and income.

Most of her clients file for Chapter 7 bankruptcy protection. Only a few file for Chapter 13 and, she said, most of the Chapter 13 filings fail because debtors have unrealistic expectations of their ability to pay off their debts over the three- to five-year period. As with most bankruptcy attorneys, she requires that her fee be paid in full before bankruptcy filing with a federal court. She said she does allow her clients to pay in increments as she is working with them to prepare the documents for filing.

Reviewing Your Report

Once you receive your report, you must sit down and carefully review it for errors. If you notice that there are items on your credit report that do not seem accurate, the information provider and consumer reporting companies are required to correct any incomplete or wrong information. It is a good idea to write to the information provider and consumer reporting company to let them know what information you believe to be inaccurate. Unless they consider your request to be fraudulent, they must look into the questionable items generally within 30 days. They are also required to send all of the relevant information about the inaccuracy to the organization or company where they originally got the information. Then the dispute will be investigated and reviewed, and the results will be reported back to the consumer reporting company. All of these companies will be contacted if the information provider finds the questionable items to be wrong. They will also provide you with the written breakdown and a free credit report if your query results in a change.

How long items stay on your report

If you read through credit report and see information that is negative and correct, these items will generally remain on your report for seven years. However, there are some exceptions to this rule:

- Filing for bankruptcy will remain on your credit report for 10 years.

- If there is information reported due to a job application where the salary is more than $20,000, it will have no time limitation.

- Any lawsuits or judgments against you can be reported for seven years — or until the statue of limitations tied to it expires (whichever comes first).

- If you have defaulted (not made payments) on your student loans, this may be reported for up to seven years after guarantor actions.

191

Outstanding tax liens will remain on your report for seven years from the date that they are compensated

How to add positive information

To help balance the negative items on your credit report and boost your credit score, it is always a good idea to add any positive information you have. For example, if you are paying off old credit cards, it may be a good idea to add one new account that you pay on time to help increase your score. What if you have really bad credit, and worry that a creditor will not provide you with any new loans? Consider an installment loan (a loan that is repaid in equal, periodic payments with a preset interest rate) from your bank or credit union — they will usually issue you one for the amount that you have in your savings account.

By borrowing the money from yourself and paying it back regularly, you are boosting your credit. You may also want to consider a secured credit card. This type of card is issued with a total credit limit based on how much you have in your savings account. Again, it is like borrowing money from yourself, but the results on your credit report will be worth it.

There is No Quick Fix

No matter where you are or how you got here, the rebuilding of your financial health will take time. That does not mean you must live under deplorable conditions until the time comes when your credit score climbs above 800. It does mean, however, that you must avoid the temptation to make matters worse, or succumb to offers of quick-fix schemes that are attractive on the surface but will only enrich the people who operate the scheme. The following are examples of some of the lures to avoid:

- "Bad credit? No problem! Your credit is guaranteed!"
- "We will erase your bad credit!"
- "We will remove bankruptcies, foreclosures, evictions, and repossessions from your credit report!"
- "We will give you a new credit identity!"

None of these claims are plausible. Your credit report is a legal history of your credit, spending, and ability to pay back loans. Creating a new identity to hide it is a fraud, and companies making such claims are scams. No one can make legitimate problems on your credit report go away; there is no magic bullet. Bankruptcies, foreclosures, and repossessions will stay on your report for years. Take the following as additional warning signs of scammers:

- A recommendation that you create a new identity to evade normal credit reporting

- A suggestion that you apply for a credit card using someone else's name

- A recommendation that you file challenges to all the items on your credit report

- Up-front fees for so-called "credit counseling"

The first two of the warning signs are illegal, the third is not productive and is a waste of time, and the fourth is a waste of money. If you attempt to create a false identity to get around negative elements of your credit history, you are exposing yourself to a host of legal difficulties that will make your credit issues seem quite small. Obtaining new federal tax identification accounts under false pretenses is fraud. Applying for a credit card under someone else's name may expose you to charges of identity theft, as well.

Credit counseling services

Credit counseling services are offered through many providers. A good place to look for a credit counselor is a federal bankruptcy court nearby, which maintains a list of reputable and approved credit counseling and education agencies. There may be a fee for their services, but the advice they offer will be legitimate, and the solutions and procedures they outline will be legal.

Under the Credit Repair Organizations Act, you are not required to pay for credit counseling services until the company has fulfilled the services for which it was contracted. Under the act, you have a period of three days during which you may withdraw any contract you have signed for such services.

Taking Other Important Financial Measures

Once you review and improve upon your credit report, you can also take measures to secure other important forms of financial collateral. The following are some of the main ones you will probably want to consider after coming out of financial misfortune:

Get approved for a new bank card

Although it may seem unlikely that a bank or creditor is going to issue you a new card, it is not entirely impossible. It is an important step to take to getting back on track financially. The bottom line is that a bank card can actually help you — if you are using it wisely, it will help your credit report. Depending on what your credit score is, it can have a big impact on the types of cards you may be able to get.

Mortgage a home after bankruptcy

You probably assume that getting a mortgage after bankruptcy is impossible. But believe it or not, many people have the ability to get mortgage services, even if it is just days after a bankruptcy discharge. There are some loan lenders and programs that require minimal time following a bankruptcy.

To speed up the process, be sure to continue paying bills on time — especially the items that were not discharged when you went through the bankruptcy process, like your home and your automobiles. It is also a smart idea to have a few credit items you pay on time. Also try to minimize the number of other debts that you have, such as bank loans and credit cards. A large amount of debt will make it more complicated to qualify for a mortgage.

When trying to determine if you are actually able to pay a mortgage, lenders will look at your debt-to-income ratio. They will also want all of the necessary documents quickly. These items include pay stubs and tax returns to show your income and that you have the ability to pay back the loan. They will also want to check information on your credit report to ensure that it is accurate. If you are unable to qualify for a loan at first, do not worry; this process can take time. You may want to wait about six months to one year following the discharge of bankruptcy for better results.

Find the best deals

If you find yourself in the position where you need to borrow money for a vehicle or another consumer item, shop around for optimal price and interest rates. Stay away from the high-profit add-ons that car dealers like to sell, such as extended third-party warranties, upgraded security systems, and other strategic schemes. Buy only what you need, and get the shortest loan available. A three-year car loan will cost you far less interest than a six-year loan, although the monthly payment will be higher.

Other factors remain the same. The value of the vehicle will depreciate at the same rate, and the cost of gasoline, maintenance, and repairs will be the same, but you will have saved a considerable sum on the interest. If you can pay cash for a car that gets good gasoline mileage and meets your needs, you will cut your transportation expenses by a significant amount. If you must finance, get the lowest interest rate on the shortest loan.

CASE STUDY: DROWNING IN DEBT

Sari Kurland
Attorney
211 Jersey Lane
Rockville, MD 20850
Phone 1-866-935-3435

Sari Kurland has been in legal practice since 1988 and is an expert on Chapter 13 bankruptcies, although she also represents individuals and small businesses in Chapter 7 cases before court. What do her clients have in common? "Too much debt. They can't pay their bills," she said.

Kurland has experienced an increase in the number of people who come to her for bankruptcy advice, she said. Her clients include government employees, small business owners, self-employed men and women, and independent truck drivers who were forced into bankruptcy by the high cost of diesel fuel in 2008.

She advises anyone who plans to borrow money for consumer goods or real estate to know the terms of the loan. Many people agree to high payments, even though they do not have the money to make the payments. She cites one client who obtained an $800 per month car loan on a monthly income of $1,300.

Another client obtained a home loan that was unrealistically high, and she advised this client to get rid of the home any way that she could, even if it meant turning it over to the lender.

Kurland said the Washington, D.C., area is very expensive, and many of her clients cannot afford the lifestyle they want, so they take on too much debt, live paycheck to paycheck, and suffer for it. She advises anyone who is in financial trouble to seek the advice of an expert.

Summary

Your credit report is a reflection of how financially responsible you have been. There is no legal way to remove information that is correct from your report. You have the right to examine your report and challenge items that are not true or are misleading, but if you have filed for bankruptcy or have been evicted, you have no legal way of removing it. Only time will cause it to melt away: ten years for bankruptcy, and seven years for most other negative items. During these periods, you will have to live with the reports.

You will discover, though, that as time passes and your credit performance improves, these items will have a smaller impact on your ability to obtain loans. Some shady "credit repair" companies will advise you to challenge every item on your credit report as a way to make it appear as though the entire report is riddled with inaccuracies; this does not work and will not improve your credit report. Legitimate, accurate information will remain, no matter how many letters you send. Remember, your credit report will set the tone for your financial life, so use credit wisely.

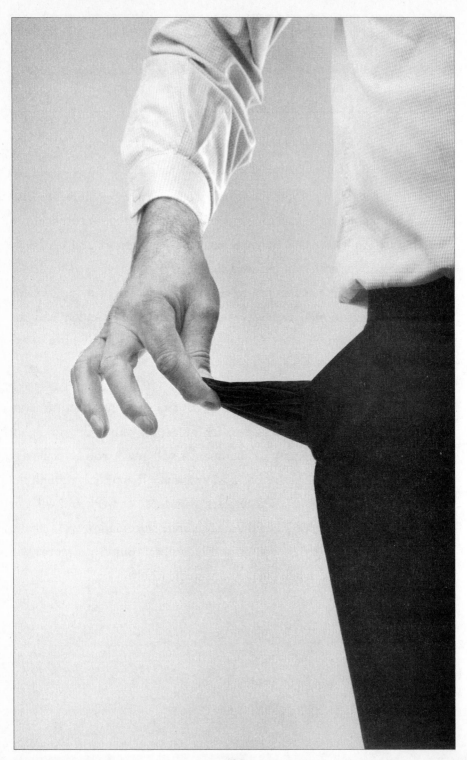

 # Chapter 8

How to Take Control of Your Debt

N ow it is time to take a long, hard look at your debt. This is the first step to accepting how far off track you have come — and it is essential to help you create a plan for taking control of your debt.

Start by getting to know your financial circumstances inside and out. Many people avoid facing reality and move from one month to the next, paying what they can and hoping for the best. Sooner or later, reality sets in, and they sit down in front of a stack of bills they cannot pay. If they lose their job or become ill or injured, the effect is more severe.

Use the following steps to determine where your financial recovery will begin:

1. Add up your monthly expenses and your debts.

2. List each debt; write down the balances and what you are paying on each debt each month. *See Appendix F for this worksheet.*

3. Determine if you are behind on your payments to any or all of them.

4. Include their interest rates.

5. Create a plan to begin paying off the debts with the highest interest rates first.

Finding Out if You Have Too Much Debt

Do you have debt that is making you feel weighed down? Is it preventing you from achieving your financial goals? A debit or a credit card can be an important tool that helps you to buy a car, finance a college education, purchase a home, and even give you the backing for other purchases. However, when you build up too much debt, rather than help you, it can hinder you.

If you think that all it takes to get out of your debt payments is to keep up with your debt payment, you are mistaken. Even though you are able to afford to make these payments as part of your budget, you are still putting stress on your savings and assets. That is because money that is used to pay off your credit card debt cannot be used anywhere else in your budget. That means if each month you are spending money on credit cards or other harmful debt, you are not putting it toward other areas of your finances that can be used to plan for the future and build wealth.

It may be hard for you to see when you have reached a serious crossroads with your debt circumstances. That is why should you be aware of some warning signs that can help you stay on top of your debt before it gets out of hand. Take a look at the following questions and ask yourself if any of them apply to you. If so, you need to take action to rectify the issue at hand.

Top 10 warning signs that you have too much debt

1. A lack of savings.

2. The ability to only make the minimum monthly credit card payment.

3. The continuation of making additional credit card purchases, even while you are trying to pay it off.

4. Just one of your credit cards is near, at, or over the credit limit.

5. You have been late in making payments on credit cards, bills, or other expenses.

6. You are not certain how much you actually have in total debt.

7. You have had to use cash advances from your credit cards to pay other bills.

8. You have bounced checks or overdrawn your bank accounts.

9. You have been denied credit in the recent past.

10. You are not honest with people in your life about your spending and debt.

Sometimes you will find that it is easier to reject the problem than to address it. Although paying down credit card debt can be an enormous challenge and can require hard work, you need to come to terms with the fact that you are in over your head, so you can begin to make positive changes. Putting it off will only make the problem worse.

Smart Ways to Eliminate Your Debt

With credit card annual rates of 20 percent or higher that are compounded monthly, debt can get out of control quickly. The good news is that you can pay it down — if you are determined. To help you get out of debt, follow the action items in this section.

Strive to pay off more than just the minimum

It is easy to get into the habit of paying only the least amount required on your credit card statement. But paying the minimum, generally about 2 or 3 percent of the balance you owe on the total card, is the worst thing you can do. The longer it takes you to pay off the charges, the more interest the bank makes — which costs you more over the long term.

Strive to put as much money as you can to your card each month. If your minimum payment is $110, see if you can find money to increase it to $150 or more. By taking a close look at your daily living expenses, there is a good chance you will be able to discover the extra money you need to increase your debt repayments. This may mean cutting back in some areas where you find that you are spending money on things that are not necessities. Not only will these increased payments save you a great amount of money in interest payments, but you will have the ability to get out of the debt much faster.

Be strategic with your debt payments

Sit down, get out a piece of paper, and take a long, hard look at your credit cards. Starting with the one with the lowest interest rate, determine if you have hit the highest limit on that card. If you have not, consider doing a balance transfer on a higher-interest bill to that card. This will let you remove some debt from a higher-interest rate credit card and pay it off with a card with a lower interest rate. If you are not sure if this is possible, ask your credit card company. Many permit this, and it is a smart way to pay off debt.

If your total balance is too large to be transferred over to one low-interest credit card, pay the minimum — the lowest amount due on every one of your cards — with the exception of one. Then, put most of your debt repayments on that one card, and pay it off as fast as you possibly can. Take a look at the example below:

Monthly budget for credit card payoffs	$800
Low-interest rate card #1	$150
Low-interest rate card #2	$150
High-interest rate card	$500

For example, if you have $20,000 in total debt, pay the minimum on the cards with the low interest rates — and make paying down the cards with the highest interest rate your top priority. If you have a monthly budget of $800 to put toward your debt, and you have two low-interest cards and one high-interest card, you could put $150 to the low-rate cards and $500 to the high-rate card.

After the balance on that card goes down to $0, move on to the next with the same plan for repayment. This method is called snowballing, and as your debts get smaller, the amount of money you have to pay them off will increase. Your payments will act like a snowball until all your debt is gone.

Another way to take higher-interest debt and put it on to a lower-interest credit card is by using some of the techniques banks offer. They offer ways to peak your interest and, if you are smart about your money management, it could be worth it. Transferring to a 3.9 percent interest rate from a 12 percent interest rate could mean extensive savings for you each month. By taking the money that you save in interest and applying it toward the principal each month, you can reduce your outstanding debt balance even more. Be sure to examine the offer closely before you sign up. Find out if the rate after the introductory period is higher than what you are paying now. If you learn that it is, you may have to go through the same exercise down the line.

Monitor your borrowing

Another important step to take is to regularly stay on top of your borrowing. This is a basic money-management strategy that often is overlooked. Whether it is due to the passage of time, or the fact that the financial crisis eases, some people find themselves slowly accumulating more debt. It can start small, with a purchase that cannot be paid off immediately, so a balance starts to build on a credit card. The process is easy, and before you know it, you are back where you began — with a huge credit card balance.

It is important to your financial future that you monitor your borrowing by closely examining each monthly statement and acknowledging that every fee and interest payment is money lost. It is the same as taking the cash out of your wallet and dropping it down the sewer: You get nothing for it.

Know what and why you are borrowing. Do not shop as a form of entertainment. Avoid the "I deserve it" rationale. You may well "deserve" it, but that is not the same as being able to afford it. When the bills come due, you will feel less enthusiastic about your spontaneous generosity to yourself. As you move into your new financial life, you must maintain your promise to spend wisely and responsibly.

Talk to your creditors

By now, you can assume that your creditors are aware that you are not paying — and perhaps cannot pay — your bills. If you have not spoken with them or contacted them by mail, they may wonder if you have taken off, leaving them high and dry. Without any reference point to your situation, they may already be ordering their attorneys to initiate legal action against you. You may already be in the name-calling phase of the proceedings. Put a stop to that.

Take out the list of creditors from the worksheet above and the latest copy of the most recent bills from each of them. The bills or statements will have customer-service telephone numbers or addresses. Start by sending letters to each of them. If the statement contains a telephone number but no address, call the number to request an address where you can contact the company by mail regarding your account. You may have to endure a maddening round of voicemail prompts, but keep pressing "zero." Eventually, you will be transferred to an actual person who should be able to provide you with a suitable address. The point of your call is to find an office to which you will send an explanation of your circumstances in your first attempts to resolving the problem. Chances are that the operator you will be talking to will not be able to resolve anything other than the limited options he or she has on the computer screen in front of him or her.

Once you have addresses for every creditor you owe, draft a letter that explains your situation and makes it clear that your intention is to resolve all outstanding issues. Avoid making specific promises that you may not be able to keep. For instance, do not promise to send the creditor $300 per month if you cannot fulfill that promise every month. It might make you and the creditor feel better, but you will only feel better until the first missed payment. It is better to be honest and keep your word, even if it means admitting you do not have the resources to put your creditors at ease.

If you have a home mortgage, you may have difficulty determining who actually owns your mortgage. These types of loans are routinely bought and sold, packaged and bundled, spun off, and woven into financial instruments that no longer resemble traditional home loans. You will, though, be getting a monthly bill from someone or some company that may only be managing or servicing your mortgage — but that statement will have an address on it, and that is a start. If you have no firm options, send your letter to the address on your mortgage statement, or call the customer service number listed on it.

If possible, avoid dealing with collection agencies. Your goal is to communicate with the creditor before your account is sold to a collection agency or similar entity that have bought your debt for pennies on the dollar, and are making profit by getting as much as they can from you to pay whatever portion of the debt is still considered "in play."

Sample letter to a creditor

To: Big Home Mortgage Company
#1 Homeowner Avenue
Hometown, USA 12345

Dear Sir or Madam,

Regarding account #111222333444555: I am currently experiencing financial difficulty and cannot bring my account to current status. It is my intention to bring this account to current status as soon as possible. I would like to speak to one of your representatives to discuss a mutually satisfactory solution to this temporary situation.

I can be reached during business hours at 555-333-8888 or evenings at 555-333-1212. My address is below. I look forward to talking with you to resolve this matter as quickly as possible.

Sincerely,
Behind Homeowner
Home Address

Note: In this letter, the term "current status" is used by lenders to describe a borrower who is caught up on payments.

The previous sample letter does not attempt to go into detail about why the payments are not current; its only function is notifying the lender that you are aware your payments are late, and you want to work with them to resolve the issues. It may be that after all is said and done, there is no acceptable solution other than foreclosure. Be aware, though, that banks do not want to own properties. They are in business to make money by lending money, not to own and sell houses. Therefore, most lending institutions are willing to talk with people who are having troubles. There are still those that are not, though, so be prepared for negative feedback. Regardless, by sending the letter, you will be on record as being aware of the situation and ready to work it out.

Do this with all of your creditors. Make them aware of your interest in a resolution and your acknowledgement of the status of your loan. You can expect telephone calls within days of mailing the letters. The calls will probably be from customer service representatives who will want you to make a bank transfer payment over the telephone. If you cannot make such a payment, tell them and ask them to mail you a specific payment schedule that reflects your inability to make payments immediately, but your intention to pay down the road. Do not expect universal warmth from the creditor's customer service representatives, but chances are that they will try to work something out with you.

You will discover that some of your creditors will want to work with you and be eager to receive payments, even if they are smaller than the agreed loan payments. Others may reject anything other than full payment right now. Any room you are given is space in which you can maneuver to recover or resolve your debt issues. The time spent communicating with your creditors accomplishes several things: It buys time for you to catch your breath; puts you on record as desiring to pay your bills; acknowledges your situation; and states your willingness to work things out. If the situation becomes truly drastic, all of these actions will work in your favor down the road.

Contact utility companies

You may find yourself in a situation where you cannot make your utility payments. These include such bills as electric, water, phone, and gas, and these companies will often allow you to go a few months before turning off your services and canceling your accounts. Some utility companies will also offer programs that allow customers with late accounts to make installment payments (equal periodic payments) over the course of many months. Consider this solution as well. The best step to take is contact them immediately and make them aware of your situation.

If you fall into the categories of low-income, or you are elderly, your utility company may offer special reduced rates for people in these categories. For example, some states will join forces with utility companies to help older people afford the cost of high winter heating bills. To find out if you qualify for such reduced rates, call your utility provider and ask. Your provider may also know of charities or religious groups that can help out. The bottom line is to contact your utility company immediately to find out what your options are.

Make car payments

When faced with the situation that you will have trouble making your auto payments, the first detail you want to consider is whether you have bought or leased your car.

If you purchased the car, here are some steps to take:

- **Sell**: Consider selling the car and paying off the lender who holds the title to your vehicle. Then you will have paid off the car and can use the remaining funds to purchase a more inexpensive vehicle.

- **Pay the difference**: If you find yourself "upside down," which means that you are in debt more from purchasing your car than you could sell the car for, try to pay the difference between the loan amount and the market value of your vehicle. That way, you can sell the car and will no longer have to make monthly auto payments.

- **Talk to the lender**: If selling the car is not an option, but you find yourself about to miss a payment, contact the lender as soon as you can. You do not want your car to get repossessed, and this can happen just a few hours after your payment was due with no required notice. If your vehicle is repossessed, you may be forced to pay the total balance that is due on the loan, in addition to towing and garage storage costs in order to get it back. If you are not able to do this, the creditor may sell the car. Your lender may grant you an extension or rewrite the loan to reduce your monthly payments.

If you leased the car, here are some steps to take:

- **Look at your lease agreement**: It will have information in it that describes what will happen if you are not able to default on your lease, or if you may need to terminate the lease agreement early. Keep in mind that there may be an early termination penalty — unless your dealer is open to selling you a car from their existing inventory.

- **Contact the dealer**: If you are not able to determine how much you owe, send a letter to the dealer to let them know you need to end your lease early, and inquire as to how much you still owe.

Pay student loans

While there are many different circumstances surrounding student loans, you must start by determining what type of student loan you have and when it originated. If you still owe money on your student loans and find yourself unable to pay them, you have a few options. You may be able to:

- Choose a new payment schedule that is a better fit with your income

- Defer your payments — which essentially means you are making an agreement with a lender to put off payments for a set period of time

- End your repayment obligation, under certain circumstances

Federal student loans come from three sources: the Department of Education, the campus you attend, and the bank. Depending on your loan type, your options differ on repayments, so be sure to contact your lender to learn what your specific loans types are. For example, a standard student loan tends to be the most economical type of payment plan and is generally level in terms of monthly payments. A graduated loan, however, allows you to repay your loan with reduced payments that may be interest-only. An extended loan offers the lowest monthly payments but is usually interest-only at first, or monthly payments of interest and principle. In this case, the overall cost of the loan is higher. Keep in mind that to protect your credit, your best bet is always to continue paying your loan in any format.

Stay on top of doctor bills

Medical bills can add up quickly and can often take people by surprise, especially because many people expect their health insurance companies to pay for these expenses. If you find yourself with extensive medical bills that you are unable to pay, contact the medical provider's office. They may be able to accept partial payments, drop late fees or interest, or even reduce the bill.

Take care of credit card payments

Believe it or not, credit card companies can be flexible with their customers — particularly if you have had good payment history in past years. If you find that you are unable to pay the minimum on your credit card, you must contact the lender immediately. They may be able to reduce your outstanding balance or let you skip a month or two without penalty. However, like in the cases previously mentioned, the key is contacting them before you default on your payment.

Deal with collection agencies

Collection agencies have always had a bad reputation. Fortunately, the Fair Debt Collection Practices Act determines when and how a debt collector is legally able to contact you. The laws prevent them from calling you before 8 a.m., after 9 p.m., or during the time that you are working. It is also unlawful for these collectors to use unfair practices, such as harassment, in order to collect a debt. If you send them a written letter asking them to stop contacting you, they must honor your request.

Making Sense of Taxes

No one likes to think about taxes. However, they are an essential part of your plan for total financial freedom. Many changes over the course of your life can have an impact on the amount of money you can have taken out of your taxes each pay period. Some events that may trigger changes in your tax status and may require you to change your withholding include:

Life Event	Tax Implications
The birth of a child	Claiming a child on your taxes means that a portion of your income is sheltered from taxes. In 2008, this was $3,500 per child.
Getting married or divorced	Many married couples receive a tax bonus, which lets them pay less on taxes than they would if they were each single.
Purchasing or selling a home	Buying a home means you can deduct the mortgage interest from your taxes. If you have sold a home and made a profit, you may be able to exclude up to $250,000 from your income.
An older child who cannot be claimed as a dependent any longer	If your child has turned 24, you can no longer claim him or her as a dependent. This means you are no longer eligible to have a portion of your taxes sheltered.
Any updates to your college savings or retirement contributions	Money in a college savings plan is free of taxes when withdrawn — provided it is used for education expenses. Money in a retirement plan grows free of taxes until the money is taken out.
A change in your employment	If you leave a company to start your own business, you will be considered an independent contractor and will be taxed accordingly using form 1099-MISC. Your vendors will pay you at 100 percent of your invoice, and you will then be responsible for paying taxes on your earnings quarterly.

Though some of these events may require that you pay more in taxes, others may provide you with the opportunity to receive additional tax breaks. Here are some guidelines for making sure that you are making the most of your taxes.

- **Withhold the right amount**: It is important to come to some sort of balance with your withholdings so that you receive little or no refund. That could entail having less money taken from your paycheck over the course of the year. If you are withholding more money than you need to, you are taking money from your pocket each paycheck and giving the IRS a free loan.

- **Remember state tax withholding**: Your W-4 will report your financial information to the IRS. Although your W-4 will affect your federal tax withholding, be sure to check with your current employer to see if any changes should to be made to your withholding for the state that you live in, too. Every state is different, so check with your state's guidelines closely. For example, some states have placed larger taxes on high-income earners. For more information on your state's tax law, visit **www.at-homeworks.com/state_tax.htm**.

A standard deduction versus itemizing your deductions

A standard deduction is an amount of income that is not subject to taxes. It is the amount that you can legally deduct from your taxable income and is based on how many dependents you have, the year you file your taxes, and your filing status. Going this route is easier and may be a better option if you have a single tax situation or do not own any real estate. However, when it comes to dropping your tax burden, taking the time to itemize deductions may be your best bet. By making the extra effort to itemize, you may be able to enjoy substantial savings.

When you itemize your deductions, you can take away the individual deduction's dollar amount. Some of these deductions consist of mortgage interest, medical expenses, and property taxes. If all of your allowed deductions are greater than the standard deduction when totaled up, your best bet would be to itemize.

The following is a list of expenses that can be itemized:

- Property tax

- State and local income tax

- Mortgage interest

- Charitable donations

- Medical expenses that are more than 7.5 percent of your adjusted gross income — which is the total of your qualified income minus any qualified deductions

- Miscellaneous expenses that are more than 2 percent of your income, such as work supplies, union dues, tax preparation fees, and legal fees

If you are wondering if you should itemize, know that it is purely up to you — it is ultimately based on your situation. Here are some tips to help you determine if itemizing would be worthwhile:

1. List your itemized expenses.

2. Add up your itemized deductions.

3. Compare the total amount to the standard deduction.

4. If the total amount of your itemized deductions is higher than the standard, then it may be wise to itemize.

5. If the total amount of your itemized deductions is lower than the standard, it is not a good idea to itemize.

It is important to remember that for most people, the greatest deductions come from property taxes and mortgage interest. Therefore, a smaller mortgage may help you reach over the standard deduction limit. Due to the fact that this can add up into more than the standard deduction by thousands of dollars, the tax savings are potentially significant.

If you cannot pay your taxes

If you have just finished preparing your tax return and find you cannot afford to pay your taxes, do not worry. Take these steps to alleviate the situation, and make sure you do not get hit with any fines:

- **Send in your return**: Even if you cannot pay the taxes that are currently due, be sure to send in your return by the filing deadline. If April 15 arrives and you have not paid at least 90 percent of your tax bill, you will receive penalties and interest for the amount that was not paid when you file. The penalty begins at 0.5 percent per month and can increase to a 1 percent rate per month of the amount you owe. Thus, you will want to be sure to file your taxes by the deadline.

- **Try to find the money**: Whether you owe $200 or $20,000, try to get the money. Some options include equity in your home, credit cards, or your savings account.

- **Buy yourself some time**: While it is always ideal to pay the taxes you own completely on time, there are occasions when all you need are a few weeks until the money is available. If you know you will have the money soon after the filing deadline, you may want to just wait until they send you the bill and pay it then. But be sure to request that extension officially. This is because the interest you pay will be relatively low compared to looking into another source for financing the money.

- **Think about an installment plan**: Uncle Sam would rather get the money over a period of time rather than not at all. Therefore, there is an installment plan for individuals who are not able to pay in full. You can even structure this plan as a direct deposit from your bank account to make the process even easier.

- **Your last resort**: The government does have an Offer in Compromise, which is an agreement between you, the taxpayer, and the IRS for extreme circumstances. If you request this option, you can offer to make either fixed payments or a lump-sum payment over a short period of time. This will require you to submit a complete personal financial statement and an application fee of $150.

Considering Debt Consolidation

You may want to consider debt consolidation, which is a method of combining all your outstanding debt and taking out one loan to pay it all off. This is a way of to reduce your debt by rolling all of it into a second mortgage or a home equity line of credit. But it is vital to keep in mind that these types of loans often require you to use your home as collateral. Also, if you are unable to make the payments — or if your payments are late — there is a chance that you could run the risk of losing your home.

It is also important to consider that the costs of these types of these loans can potentially escalate. In addition to the loan interest, you may have to pay something that is called "points." One point is usually equal to a single percent of the amount that you want to borrow. These types of loans may offer you some tax advantages that are not always an option with other kinds of credit and may be something to consider.

The art of negotiation

Debt negotiation is not the same as dealing with credit counseling agencies. It is important to note that these agencies can have a risk associated with them that may have negative, long-term implications on your credit report. In turn, this affects your chances of getting approved for credit.

Though many of these debt negotiation firms claim that they are nonprofit agencies working on your behalf, they are not. These firms may also claim they have the power to make arrangements to have your unsecured debt — generally your credit card debt — paid off at a rate of up to 50 percent of the balance you owe on the card.

These companies may describe themselves as nonprofit organizations, but the services they claim to provide may not be legitimate. There also is no real promise that your creditor will be willing to accept a portion of payment toward your debt. If not, you will need to explore other options. Also, if you stop making payments on unsecured debts, such as your credit cards, you will have interest and late fees added monthly to the debt you are already in. The end result is that your debt can suddenly triple. Because most debt negotiation firms charge fairly large fees — such as fees to establish the account, monthly service fees, and final fees that are usually a percentage of the funds you were supposed to have saved — you could end up owing more than you started with.

Setting a Budget

You may think that creating a budget is hard, but it is actually easier than you think. With a little planning, you will be able to achieve the goals you want. These three steps, combined with the following worksheet, can help you get started:

1. **Look at your income versus your spending:** The first step of your plan is to take a close look at where your money is going. Start by entering your monthly spending into categories — for example food, utilities, gas, clothing, etc. If you have a record of the exact amount of your spending each month, be sure to include it. If you do not have a record of your spending, provide an estimate. Keep in mind that while this first step provides an overall look at each spending category, you can always go into more detail on each category. For example, a miscellaneous category could include dining out, leisure activities, and other dispensable items. Once you have entered all your information in the current spending categories, fill in your current monthly income. Next, it is time to take a closer look at your finances.

2. **Analyze your financial situation:** Now that you have entered your current spending and income, and have made sure all the information is correct, take a closer look at where your money is actually going. This will help you look to the future and set realistic spending goals.

   Start by comparing your current spending with your income. If you are spending less than you earn, you are in good shape, and you may want to put the extra money away for your future

— like your employer's retirement plan, or an emergency fund. On the other hand, if you are spending more than you earn, reevaluate your spending habits and look for places where you can cut back. This will help you set spending goals for each category. Small cutbacks add up over time.

When cutting back, also be sure to consider your wants versus your needs. Before making a purchase, ask yourself if the item that has caught your interest is really a necessity. By addressing this question up-front, it may help you prioritize your spending, especially when you are faced with temptation. Also remember to pay yourself first. If you are given a pay increase or receive an income tax return, consider putting that money directly into your employer's retirement plan, or use it to pay off debt. That way, you will be less likely to miss the money, and it will automatically help you reach your overall goal of getting out of debt.

3. **Set future spending goals:** Once you know what you are spending your money on, set goals to prevent yourself from overspending. Look at your current spending, and make a plan as to how much you can save comfortably.

Again, you can either provide an overall goal for each spending category, or you may create a more detailed breakdown of your goals. Remember that some categories are more flexible than others.

Debt management worksheets

This is a sample monthly worksheet to help you stay on top of your expenses. When assessing your budget, take a close look at what the essentials are and what you can do with out. You may be surprised at where your money is going.

Sample Month Budget Worksheet	
Mortgage/Rent	$
Electric Bill	$
Telephone Bill	$
Cell Phone Bill	$
Cable/TV Bill	$
Heat/AC Bill	$
Student Loans	$
Car Loans	$
Car Insurance	$
Credit Card Payments	$
Groceries	$
Gas	$
Miscellaneous	$
	TOTAL

Income Versus Expenses	
Salary	$
Other Sources of Income	$
Total Expenses (from chart above)	$
	DIFFERENCE

Compare the two totals. If your monthly bills total $2,500 and your income is $2,600, you are in a stable financial position, even if you are not exactly floating in cash. If your monthly bills total $3,000 and your income is $2,600, you have some issues to address. If your bills total $6,000 and your income is $2,600, things are serious. Of course, these numbers are not real — yours may be much higher or lower. Either way, your course of action needs to be the same.

Let us assume the worst: You have bills you cannot pay. You sit at your kitchen table, staring at a pile of notices from creditors threatening to drag you into court, and the phone is ringing with calls from collection agencies that hire hostile-sounding people who demand that you send cash, right now, down the telephone wire. The mortgage company wants money, or the landlord is using the word "eviction," and the car company's repossession man is stalking you. Where do you begin?

Return to your list of expenses. It represents your monthly payments, but it does not represent your total debt. All the list tells you is how much you need each month. You have determined that you do not have sufficient income to meet these monthly obligations, so first address the larger issue of your total debt.

Debt Worksheet	
Real Estate Payoff	$
Car Loan Payoff	$
Student Loans Payoff	$
Miscellaneous Loans Payoff	$
	TOTAL

This worksheet assesses how much you owe right now. Be honest. Do not exempt any creditor, even a family member who may have given you $1,000 as a loan and expects to be paid back. By taking a close look at all your creditors, you will know where you stand in terms of paying the money back.

Now, determine what your future spending goals are:

Future Spending Goals	
Retirement	$
College	$

Vacation	$
Emergency Fund	$
	TOTAL

By giving yourself the opportunity to take an in-depth look at your expenses versus your income — and future saving goals — you are on the right track toward financial freedom.

Ask Yourself Why You Overspend

There is a very simple formula to help you achieve your financial goals. It is simply the ability to spend less than you generate as income. Sounds easy, right? It is actually something that millions of Americans struggle with daily. If you are still in an overspending cycle, it is time to examine the real reasons why you overspend. Once you know what is driving your spending, you can make changes and start saving money so that you can actually spend less than you earn.

Too many credit cards

For most Americans, the reason why they find themselves overspending is because they have too much access to credit. Every day, Americans are overwhelmed with credit card offers, auto and student refinancing invitations, mortgage offers, and other mailed temptations. Often, just filling out an enclosed form or logging on to a Web site is all it takes to receive a new line of credit. Once the card is received with a generous credit limit, many people fall into the trap, thinking they have easy access to more money. The real problems start when items get charged that the individual does not have the funds to pay for. It is just too simple to think about the slight monthly payments rather than the total purchase price.

Not enough cash

It was not that long ago when people had to wait for paper bank checks from their employers, take a trip to the bank to deposit it, and keep cash handy or write checks. Those days, however, are gone, and most individuals enjoy access to their bank account around the clock.

When we had to keep the right amount of cash on hand or painstakingly balance our checkbooks each day, the act of spending money meant a little planning and some basic math. Now, all you have to do is run your card through the machine, and the funds are electronically taken from your account. When you are not actually handing someone cash or a check for a purchase, it is too easy to overspend.

Misusing credit cards

Credit cards are a great resource when used properly. When they were first introduced, credit cards typically obligated users to pay the balance in full each month. This was a valuable way to make purchases without using paper money, but still pay for those purchases in their entirety by the end of the month. When used correctly, it is actually like a short-term, interest-free loan.

The problem occurs when the balance starts to carry over each month. For example, if you make a $100 purchase on your card and realize at the month's end that you cannot repay the full amount, you have found yourself at the beginning of a slippery slope. Even the best intentions can get a responsible cardholder into trouble.

At this point, high interest rates begin to kick in. This is how credit card companies make their money. They essentially make the minimum payment due — a small amount. However, just continuing to pay the minimum means it can take years to pay off the original purchase, and you end up paying out more on interest than the initial cost of the item.

Emotional spending

Face it — it feels good to spend money on yourself. Maybe it is a small item, or maybe it is a trip; there is nothing wrong with treating yourself provided that you do not go overboard.

But do not throw away your potential for a future free of financial stress for a few guilty pleasures if it is not in your bank account. If you know you cannot afford an item, tell yourself to come back another time, and buy it when you can afford it.

Always be sure to set aside some extra cash so you have a little extra money. This way, you are not putting it on your credit card and do not feel deprived when a friend invites you out for drinks or when you want to catch a movie. Spending your money wisely and setting aside a mad cash fund of a limited amount will allow you to do this and still purchase some of the things you want.

How to Cut Living Expenses

You may have taken a close look at your budget and felt like there is little room to cut down on your living expenses. There likely is. Here are some tips to find more money to put toward bills and into your savings accounts:

- **Cut back on cable or satellite TV**: If you are paying for high-definition TV with DVR, consider switching to the basic package until you have saved more money.

- **Lose your landline and use your cell phone**: Cut down on your bills by cutting out the home line and using your cell for all your calls.

- **Save money on gas by combining trips**: Better yet, carpool with a neighbor when you run errands.

- **Eat at home and bring your lunch to work**: It is amazing at how quickly a pizza here, a fast food lunch there, or your daily coffee can add up. Start eating in more, and you will soon see how quickly you can save money.

- **Resist impulse buys**: Before picking up an item, ask yourself: "Do I really need this?" More often than not, the answer is no. If it is something you think you really want, promise yourself that you will think it over and come back a few days later.

- **Clip coupons**: It is amazing how much you can save just by clipping coupons or watching your grocery store circular for deals. You can plan your meals around what is on sale and stock up on great deals.

Sort through your bills

Assume that at this point, you have some income or cash on-hand. You have sent letters to the companies whose bills are piled on your kitchen table. How do you sort them out? As mentioned earlier, pay the bills that absolutely must be paid, if possible. Review your options and ask yourself what would happen if the bill was not paid.

If you do not pay your rent, you might be evicted. Is that acceptable? Can you move back home or in with a friend and save the money you would have spent on rent? If you do not pay your auto insurance, the state may revoke your registration or even your driver's license. Can you handle that? Can you give up your car and ride the bus or train to work? Do you have health insurance? What happens if you do not pay the premium and lose it? These are tough and even embarrassing decisions, but they must be made.

Increase your income

You may not think it is possible to increase your income, especially if you are working a full-time job already. However, it is achievable. If you have already made success in your career, consider finding a way to use your skills to pursue more opportunities. For example, if you are a teacher, look into tutoring on your summer breaks. If you are a graphic designer, find a local company that needs a brochure and offer to design it for them on your off hours. It is amazing at how easy it can be to put your talents to work for yourself. If you are not working in a field where you can pick up extra work on the side, consider taking the skills you already have and look for ways to qualify for better career opportunities. Here are some tips for making extra income:

- Go back to school to learn a new skill or increase your existing earning power.

- Take on a part-time job to earn extra money.

- Barter or trade your skills with local companies for discounts on each other's products and services.

- Ask your current employer for a promotion or pay raise.

Find money to pay your debts

If increasing your income is not an option, or if you still need to find more money to pay off your existing debts, do not worry — you still have other options:

- **Sell non-retirement investments**: If you have investments in taxable accounts, such as CDs, bonds, stocks, or mutual funds, you may want to sell some of those investments to put toward your debt. Though any gains on these investments will be taxed, when you compare the total amount of tax you are paying to the amount you will save by reducing the debt, it makes sense to sell.

- **Sell some personal items**: If you have items sitting around the house that are no longer being used, consider selling them. Although selling just a few items may not eliminate your debt, selling a larger number can help a great deal. Even making a few extra hundred dollars can make a difference.

- **Sell a major asset**: Whether it is a boat, motorcycle, or even a second home, selling a major asset may be the last thing you want to do. Look into how much the current market value of the item is, then compare that to your debt. If it is even half of what you need to pay off, it may be worthwhile. While major assets can bring pleasure or fun to your life, think about how worthwhile it will feel to use it to get rid of your current debt. Once it is paid off, you can always start saving for that major asset again.

Pay cash for everything

Paying cash may seem like the old way of doing things, and it may be a bit of a hassle. However, it can be one of the most significant ways that you can stay in control of your finances. Not only does it prevent you from spending money you do not have, but it allows lenders to see that you are responsible when it comes to handling your finances.

When you use credit cards, it is easy to spend money without thinking about the consequences. Cash helps get rid of that temptation because you only spend what you truly have. You literally can see the money leaving your pocket, and it is a great way to think carefully before you buy.

Smart Tips: Save Money Every Day

You already know that making small changes to your spending is important, but trimming your minor monthly expenses can actually lead to big savings. Here are some everyday tips to help you cut down on bills.

Change your cable television package

Cable and satellite TV subscriptions can cost you big bucks every month. Take a look at your current plan to see if there are any channels you do not watch very often. Downgrading your service to eliminate these channels may be wise. Also, be sure to contact your service provider and ask them about promotions or discounts. Let them know that you are shopping around — it may motivate them to offer you a discounted rate rather than having to lose you as a customer.

Cut out your subscriptions

Many of us subscribe to magazines that we barely have time to read. Take a look around you. Maybe you have signed up for a DVD rental subscription via mail, but only watch a few movies a month. What about your gym membership? You may not even realize that these subscriptions may be draining hundreds of dollars from your wallet every year. Take a close look at what you actually read, and get rid of the uneconomical subscriptions that are costing you.

Avoid banking fees

When you open a bank account, you may not be aware of the fees that your bank may be charging you. Whether it is monthly fees, overdraft charges, or fees for paper statements, these bank fees add up. Also, be sure to search for no-fee ATMs when you are away from your regular bank branch. Web sites like Money Pass®, at **www.moneypass.com**, will give you a list of no-fee ATMs nationwide — and will even provide driving directions to them.

Bring your lunch to work

Eating out on a daily basis can be costly. Though the last thing you may want to do when you are rushing off to work is pack a lunch, imagine how much spending just $6 each day on lunch during your break at work can add up — it can be more than $800 per year. To help cut back on lunch expenses, plan to bring your lunch to work at least a few days a week. This can save a few hundred dollars a year. To get started, take small steps like making specialty coffee at home or cutting down your restaurant meals to just once a week.

Play the grocery game

One of the easiest ways to save money is at the grocery store. However, for most people that is where they spend the most money. The key is to create a grocery budget and stick with it. Try these tips to help keep your grocery bill under control:

- **Plan your meals in advance**: One of the worst things you can do is roam through the store without any plan. You will walk aimlessly through the aisles trying to put meals together and will end up buying whatever you come across. This usually results in buying items you do not need — or buying things that go to waste. Spend some time before going to the store and plan out what you will need for that shopping trip. If you go to the store knowing the meals you want to make, it will help keep you from those extra purchases that are not necessary.

- **Do not shop hungry**: While this tips seems like common sense, it is one that can really cost you. Entering a grocery store while you are hungry actually does make you spend more money. If you must go grocery shopping when you are likely to be hungry — for example, after work — eat a snack before going. Just taking the edge off your hunger can help keep your impulse buying under control.

- **Try store brands**: Some people are wary of switching their favorite name brand items for generics. However, it is a great way to save on your food bill. In many cases, store brand products are just as good, and they cost less. Give them a try — you may find that they are well worth the money you save.

- **Scout for deals**: Almost all of the major grocery chains include their weekly ad in the newspaper or on their Web sites. Spend some time going through them to find the best sales before reaching the store. You will be pleasantly surprised at how this can help you find new recipe ideas and keep costs down.

- **Stock up**: When you come across a great bargain, be sure to stock up on it if your budget allows. This is a great tactic with regular necessities such as toilet paper, paper towels, and other items you go through on a regular basis. This trick works on food, too. You can freeze meats or buy other perishables that you will not eat right away, such as dry goods. Soon you will only be buying only what is on sale at the store and doing the rest of the shopping from your pantry.

- **Do not fall for multiple-sale scams**: Most grocery stores use marketing strategies to entice you to buy something by labeling a product "5 for $5." Before you buy the item, take the original cost of the product and multiply it by that the quantity you need to buy for the sale — you may find that it only saves you a few cents. If it is not something you do not need a large quantity of, you may end up spending more than you had intended. While sometimes these can be great deals, it is important to be careful that you are not buying more than you need. Also, with items that are being sold as 2 for $4, you can often still buy one for the $2 price — so do not buy more than you need just because you think you have to. It is always a good idea to read the sale fine print or check with the store clerk.

- **Make coupons your friend**: Now more than ever, coupons are essential shopping companions. They offer many opportunities to save money, and it does not take a lot of time to go through a local newspaper to see if there is anything you can use. In fact, just a couple of coupons can save you a few bucks each shopping trip. Also, be sure to check out coupon Web sites like **www.couponmom.com** and **www.couponcabin.com**. They can help you find local deals.

Look around the house

There are likely ways to save money right in your own home. For example, if you rent, ask yourself if you can get a roommate or find a less expensive place. If you are considering moving, weigh in the costs of reconnecting utilities, making new deposits, and transporting your belongings. You may also lose the deposit you placed on your old home. If you have a mortgage, a roommate may be the better option.

Also try setting your heating thermostat lower or your air-conditioning control higher; a few degrees will make more difference in your bill than in your comfort. Reset your water heater at a lower temperature as well. Turn off lights and appliances when not in use. Use the following tips for additional savings, based on the kilowatt hour (kwh) price of 12 cents:

- Clean or replace your heating and air conditioning filters at least once a month to lower your air conditioner's energy consumption by 5 to 15 percent (running the air for six hours each day can cost around $78 per month). *Savings: $4-12 per month.*

- Turn off your fans when you are not in the room. *Savings: $2.15 per month to keep a 42" ceiling fan on low all the time.*

- Only run your dishwasher when it is full, but do not worry about rinsing food off your dishes before loading the dishwasher. Most modern dishwashers will clean the food off, so pre-rinsing will only waste water. Depending on how many dishes you usually rinse, and how long you spend rinsing them, you can save a little cash. Most faucets run 2.5 gallons per minute, so if your water heater is 40 gallons, it will cost about $.80 to heat it. Thus, rinsing dishes for one minute will cost about $.05 in hot water. *Savings: About $1.50 or $2 per month.*

- Instead of using the drying feature on your dishwasher, let your dishes air-dry. Selecting the air-dry option for your dishes can save anywhere from 15 to 50 percent of the energy used by your dishwasher (most dishwashers use about $13 worth of energy per month but are cited as being more efficient than hand-washing). *Savings: $2-$6 per month.*

- Wash clothes in cold water and only when you have a full load. Washing one load per day with cold settings versus hot or warm settings will save about $.36 each load. *Savings: $10 per month.*

- Instead of using your dryer, try line drying your clothes. The average dryer runs for 45 minutes per load, which can add up, especially if you do one load per day. *Savings: $10+ per month.*

- If you have a cell phone, disconnect your landline telephone. *Savings: $30+ per month.*

- Increase the deductibles on your car and home insurance. *Savings: $10+ per month.*

- Use tap water instead of bottled water. *Savings: $10+ per month.*

- Instead of taking clothing to a dry cleaner, use one of the at-home cleaning products. *Savings: $10+ per month.*

- Replace your old fluorescent light bulbs with compact fluorescent light (CFL) bulbs. *Savings: $8 per month for five 75-watt bulbs that are on for 8 hours a day.*

- Turn off your computer when you are not using it. *Savings: $2 per month for turning your laptop off for 12 hours, and $6.72 per month for turning your desktop and LCD monitor off for 12 hours.*

More energy-saving statistics

- About 46 percent of your utility bill goes toward heating and cooling your house or apartment.

- A heat pump can trim the amount of electricity you use for heating by up to 40 percent.

- Electrostatic air filters trap about 88 percent of debris, including bacteria, mold, viruses, and pollen, making your air conditioning system more efficient (when ductwork gets clogged by these types of debris, the system has to run longer to heat or cool the same amount of space).

Slash your transportation costs

Another great way to save money is on transit. You can reduce your transportation costs while unemployed by using available public transportation, walking, or biking. If these options are not feasible (and they may not be while you are going on interviewing or visiting prospective employers), you can also reduce the costs associated with driving your personal car by following these tips:

- Do not let your car idle excessively. Warming up your car in the winter is actually best done by driving it slowly for a few miles, rather than letting it idle in the driveway.

- Drive within the speed limits, and avoid sudden starts and stops, which waste gas.

- Clean your car inside and out. If you have been carrying around boxes of personal items retrieved from your former office, the added weight can reduce your gas mileage.

- Check your tire pressure regularly to ensure that they are inflated properly. Also check your alignment and the tire tread to be sure you are getting optimum performance.

- Use the proper motor oil, as recommended for your car.

- Check fluid levels regularly, particularly engine coolant and transmission fluid.

- Change your car's air filter regularly.

- Combine trips to get the most out of your mileage when running errands or going shopping.

Have fun for free

Whether you live in a small town or a big city, there are free or affordable leisure options all around you. For example, you can save money on entertainment costs by taking advantage of local museums and galleries that offer free admission. Take your family to a park or area historic site. Borrow books and movies from the library (and be sure to return them on time to avoid late fees).

Make Saving Automatic

If you have a bank savings account but are not depositing money into it on a regular basis, now is the time to start. Generally, when you are paid money, it is deposited directly into your checking account, or you make a trip to the bank to make a deposit. In most cases, this money is put directly into a checking account, where it is available to pay what often seems like an endless list of bills.

Always save first

Most banks offer automatic savings programs. These allow you to save a certain amount on a regular basis without even thinking about it. Getting started with an automatic savings plan is simple: If your employer offers direct deposit, simply have a portion of your paycheck directly deposited into your account for savings. Whether it is $25 or $400, having this money put in automatically will help you ensure that you are saving every time you are paid.

If your employer does not offer direct deposit, your bank will also offer this service. They will typically link your savings and checking accounts together and set up automated transfers between the two.

Create an Emergency Fund

You are probably aware that in life, the unexpected will happen, which is the reason why you need an emergency fund. It is the most important way to take precautions for emergencies that would require additional money you may not usually have on hand.

Set aside three to six months

Most experts caution that you should set aside three to six months of your daily living expenses for your emergency fund. Of course, this depends on your specific situation — if you are still in the process of overcoming a financial obstacle, you should focus on that first and put aside just a little. That way, when more room frees up in your budget, you can set aside more. Accumulating just one month of expenses may take time. If you determine that your short-term goals are small, then you will have a better chance in achieving them. Three to six months is a good amount of time to create these savings, especially if you are planning for job loss. Be sure to prepare for worst-case scenarios, too, so that the minor emergencies can be easily covered.

Where to keep your emergency fund

The best place to keep your emergency fund is at a bank. If you do not currently have a savings account, open one. Get into the habit of making periodic deposits into this account. It is easier than you think to create a schedule and stick to it. Also, if you open your savings account at the bank that already have your checking account at, ask the teller if they offer a program that rounds up every purchase to the nearest dollar, then transfers it to your savings. For example, if you spend $5.60 on a sandwich for lunch, your bank will round the amount up to $6 and transfer the extra 40 cents into your savings account. It is a great way to save money without even thinking about it.

Although a savings account is easy and convenient, you may also want to consider accounts that earn a better interest rate — such as a money market account or certificate of deposit (CD). These mature after a certain amount of time, but once they do, you can access the funds quickly if there was ever an emergency. The benefit of these types of investments is that you have the potential to earn more money because the interest rates are higher. The longer you agree to have the funds frozen, the higher the rate. For example, a six-month CD can offer a rate of 1.29 percent, and a five-year CD offers a rate of 2.84 percent. However, one thing you do not want to do is have your emergency fund tied into investments like mutual funds or stocks. These rely on the market's performance, and the ups and downs of the market could result in your losing money in the short-term.

Remember, saving even just a little bit each month can be an easy way to build your emergency fund — and when the time comes to tap into it, you will be glad that you took steps to create one.

Summary

Taking control of your debt is the single most important way to eliminate your current debt and create a plan to stay debt-free in the future. From taking a close look at why you got into debt, to using a budgeting worksheet to stay informed on your expenses, money management can be easier than you think.

Chapter 9

How to Overcome the Social Stigma of Financial Misfortune

You may already be painfully aware of the social stigma associated with financial misfortune. Whether it is neighborhood gossip, your foreclosure appearing in the newspaper, or creditors refusing to give you loans for goods and service, the social stigma is yet one more aspect of a financial misfortune that you will need to cope with.

Financial Discrimination

Though other forms of discrimination are illegal, denying certain benefits to those who have poor credit histories is not. Such discrimination is why a low credit score will mean higher interest rates, denial of credit, denial of a lease on a residence, and possibly denial of employment. It is a fact of life, but one that can be managed.

The circumstances of your difficulty will have a major impact on how the financial world sees your credit history. Once you know what is contained in your credit report, you will be able to explain it. If you, like millions of others, were forced into bankruptcy by high medical expenses, be prepared to answer questions about your medical status. An employer may care more about your health and ability to perform your duties in the workplace than about the details of your finances.

Financial discrimination and bankruptcy

If you have a discharged bankruptcy, your financial outlook will actually improve because you no longer owe money — or at least you have dramatically lowered your level of debt. The bankruptcy may prevent you from obtaining a credit card with a $20,000 limit, but that is a good thing — it will keep you from running up big bills again. You will find that following discharge of a bankruptcy petition, you will receive credit card offers in the mail. These are sharks circling to take advantage of your new financial condition. Statistically, you are more likely to make payments after a bankruptcy than you were when you were drowning in debt.

Some of these offers may be for secured credit cards, meaning you back up your credit limit with your own cash by sending the card company a check for, say, $500. Then, you can enjoy a credit limit to that amount. If you fail to make your payments, they take the money out of your account. If you agree to such an arrangement, be sure the cash used to secure the account will build interest. Otherwise, you are just giving the bank or company free use of your money.

Some credit card companies may offer low-limit cards to test your credit worthiness for a year or two. If you have paid on time, they may increase your limit. Be aware that the interest rates in such offers are going to be very high, so, if you agree to these offers, pay off the balance every month. Avoid falling into the credit card trap again by closing out every card you can.

If you are attempting to purchase a vehicle and your credit rating is low, be prepared for high interest rates, possibly in the 20 percent range. You may face a car salesperson who will look at your credit report on his computer screen and shake his head. It is all part of the drama that is produced by serious credit problems. High interest rates will mean a high monthly payment on what may be a medium-quality vehicle. Do you really want to get back into this cycle? Remember, you are changing your spending habits. Stick with your budget. Buy an older car for cash, and put the money saved into a retirement account.

Financial discrimination and your job

When it comes to employment, some business owners use a person's credit history as a gauge of honesty and integrity, so negative items that are not your fault will not weigh as heavily as items that appear to cast doubt upon your character, like reckless spending. Your employer may not legally fire you solely because you have filed for bankruptcy. However, in terms of hiring, a person who has a truly awful financial history may not be the best candidate for a banking job, for instance.

CASE STUDY: IN OVER HIS HEAD

Allen Anderson

In August 2007, Allen Anderson purchased a new model home that he was not quite ready to move in to. He made an arrangement with the builder to lease back from them for a period of two to four years. The initial lease was for a year, and Anderson had to be given six months notice if they were not renewing. The builder had a great reputation in the community, as he had worked in this area for 18 years.

About six months later, Anderson discovered the builder was no longer using his home as a model, and it was basically just being used for storage.

As he was not ready to move in yet, Anderson decided he would try to sell the property. He had the home listed for sale for 14 months at the price that he paid for it. Every week, he also hosted an open house to try and sell it.

After more than a year of weekend open houses, he gave up and paid the mortgage without a tenant for the 14 months that he had listed the home for sale. The builder wound up going bankrupt, and the subdivision was left in disrepair with partially finished homes, empty lots, and mechanics liens. Even the subdivision gates were taken back by an unpaid vendor. As a result, the house value fell by 50 percent.

Ultimately, Anderson rented the property out for half of what the mortgage payment was and paid the balance out of his pocket monthly. He worked in the mortgage industry, which had been hit hard, and his income decreased by 40 percent. Anderson was unable to keep supplementing the mortgage and tried to work with his mortgage company.

The home was foreclosed on, and Anderson exhausted the equity in his current home to maintain the other home. Fortunately, his family lives within their means and not on credit. They have gotten past the foreclosure and are trying to rebuild some equity in their home to make up for the over $100,000 they lost trying to keep the other home.

Anderson felt the affects of the social stigma in his community, and even though his family was able to live within their means, they struggled with rebuilding their lives after going from a comfortable lifestyle to one of financial misfortune. Foreclosure put a black mark on Anderson's family, career, and financial future — but they remain positive looking ahead into the future.

How to Shuck the Social Stigma

If you have found yourself in one of these financial hardships, you have probably felt a sense of shame or embarrassment. Many people worry what people will think, and wonder if they will be treated differently or looked down upon. More importantly, they worry as to whether they have let their families down, and if their spouse or children will be emotionally affected. Other people wonder if their coworkers or boss will know their situation and treat them differently while on the job.

Here are some factors to remember to help you overcome the social stigma attached with bankruptcy, foreclose, eviction, and any of the other financial disasters in this book:

- **All families have "skeletons in their closet"**: Regardless of what these family secrets are, your financial disaster may be pretty mild when it is compared to those of other families.

- **Many families are not that much better off**: It is important to remember that disaster can strike anyone and everyone. If you have been a victim of foreclosure, many of your neighbors may never be more than just a few paychecks away from a similar situation.

- **Facing disaster can make you stronger**: Being faced with difficult issues and overcoming them does make you stronger than if you had never had to handle them at all.

- **Forget about everyone else**: Sure, it is not easy to forget that your financial disaster may be the talk of the town. But remember, it will be yesterday's news pretty quickly when something else comes up. Focus your energy on overcoming your disaster until then.

- **Time is a great healer**: This applies directly to your financial problems. You are most likely to face some form of discrimination at the depth of your crisis. As you begin the process of recovery, change your spending and budgeting habits, pay your bills, and resolve your financial issues. Then, fewer questions will be raised about your ability to pay back loans and meet other obligations.

Getting Support

How are you feeling? Angry? Embarrassed? Sad? There are many emotions people go through when they are faced with a financial disaster, and you may find yourself going through all of the above — and more. The key is to get support to help you cope. Look at the following options:

- **Therapy**: There are many counselors and therapists who are familiar with helping people in these situations. Look in your phone book, on the Internet, or even ask your family doctor for a referral.

- **Support groups**: Another good option is to look for help groups in your area. Your city or town may actually offer a support group, and it would be a valuable experience to meet with other people who know what you are going through and are willing to talk freely and openly about their experiences, too.

- **Online groups**: Another good resource is the Internet. There are Web sites, like **www.bkforum.com** and **www.all-foreclosure.com**, where people share stories, insight, tips, and support. You may even find lifelong friends you can bond with because of your similar hardships.

The emotional implications

You have probably heard about the seven stages of grief. They are:

1. Denial and shock
2. Guilt and pain
3. Bargaining and anger
4. Depression, loneliness, and reflection
5. The upward turn

6. Working through the situation and reconstruction
7. Hope and acceptance

Sound familiar? Going through a stressful situation can be much like grieving. Keep them in mind, and know that people have come through this before.

At this point, you probably already know that when you are upset, it is harder to make level-headed decisions, so try to stay calm. Maintain your composure, especially when you are dealing with lawyers, creditors, and the bank. Imagine if you were trying to negotiate with a creditor, and you treated him or her irately. It will be that much harder to get assistance if you sound irrational. Maintaining your composure is the best way to get things accomplished and get yourself out of the situation you are in.

Summary

From neighbors gossiping to employers and creditors discriminating against you, the social stigma of a financial misfortune is a reality for many Americans. Remember, no one knows why you are in the situation you are in better than you do. So, try to put the judgment of others behind you and move forward. Use support groups, online forums, or other ways to find others going through situations like yourself. In the long run, this too will pass, and you will be stronger for it.

 # Chapter 10

Striding Toward the Future

Now that you are armed with the knowledge to come out of any negative financial situation, it is time to look ahead to the future. You know what you have to do now to get back on track — and stay on track. However, it is also important to prepare a plan of action for what you want to do when this is all over.

Creating a Plan for Tomorrow

Whether you have spent a lot of time thinking about your future, or you have not even considered what you want to do when your current financial challenge is over, thinking about it is essential. Clearly, your financial obligations are your top priority, but there are important decisions you can make now to positively impact your life later.

Did you know that many financial experts believe that people will need close to 85 percent of their current income to live comfortably when you are retired? Because pension plans are slowly becoming things of the past, it is important to make sure you know what you want out of your future.

Determine your goals

Ask yourself what you want out of life. Maybe it is to travel, spend more time with family, start a new career, or even someday retire. Whatever your goals may be, knowing next steps is a good way to reach them. Sit down and make a list, or at least set aside time to think about what you want. When planning your short- and long-term goals for future, consider the financial expenses you may have in your life. These expenses include:

- Housing
- Health care
- Family
- Work
- Hobbies

College tuition planning

Another important consideration for the future is to prepare for your children's, or your grandchildren's, college educations. Because tuition costs are always on the rise, it is a good idea to help ensure higher education needs are met later by setting aside money for funding now. Here are some important ways to do this:

- **Coverdell education savings account**: This permits withdrawals that are tax-free for qualified education expenses for both K-12 and college.

- **529 plans**: These allow higher contribution limits and tax-free withdrawals for higher education expenses.

- **Mutual funds**: Because investing in mutual funds lets you rely on a professional to manage your savings, you do not have to watch the market every day.

Invest in Your Future

If you have access to a 401(k) or 403(b) plan with your employer, make sure you take advantage of it. It is an important way to help ensure that you are taking steps to afford the future you want. If you do not work for a company that offers one of these plans, consider an IRA. Putting away just a small amount now, even while you are taking care of your current financial misfortune, can make a huge difference later in your life.

401(k) & 403(b) plans

A 401(k) or 403(b) plan is a great way to use tax benefits in order to save for the future. These plans let you take money from your paycheck and place it directly into the plan before taxes are taken out. By doing this, you can help reduce the amount that your income is taxed. Also, you are not required to pay taxes on your earnings in the plan until you withdraw them. So, the money in your plan — both your contributions and your investment earnings — has the ability to grow unrestricted and earn additional income without taxes being taken out.

Employee-sponsored retirement programs often work just like variable annuities. It is up to you to decide the degree of risk you can tolerate with your investment and decide what percentage of funds you want in which risk class. Like IRAs and annuities, these retirement vessels have a minimum withdrawal age of 59 ½, at which you will not incur a penalty

Another important benefit of a 401(k) or 403(b) plan is that they may include a company match. This is simply money that your company contributes to your retirement savings plan account. For example, assume that your employer will match up to 5 percent of your paycheck. If you are paid $1,000 each pay cycle, you will want to contribute $50 so that the 5 percent threshold is met. In return, your employer will also contribute $50 for a total of $100 each payday. If you wish to contribute more than $50, the employer will not pay more, thus making extra payments into your retirement plan not quite as valuable.

If you do not contribute the full matched amount, it is almost like throwing away that 3 percent, which is like free money. Therefore, if your employer offers this benefit, be sure you contribute enough of your own money to get it.

Individual retirement arrangements (IRAs)

An IRA is another great way to help save for the future. There are two basic IRAs, a traditional and a Roth IRA (named after their main legislative sponsor, the late Senator William Roth). Both allow you to contribute a set amount of money each year that earns interest that grows upon itself over time — also known as compounded interest. IRAs are essentially investment accounts that allow you to invest in a wide range of products, such as stocks, bonds CDs and money markets. The biggest difference between these is the method used by the IRS when it comes to taxes.

- **Traditional IRA**: Offers immediate tax advantages by letting you make tax-deductible contributions.

- **Roth IRA**: Lets you withdraw the money tax-free when you retire, but does not offer tax-deductible contributions.

In 2009, the cap amount is $105,000 for single filers wishing to contribute the maximum amount to their Roth IRA. Only earned income can be placed in an Roth IRA — capital gains are ineligible. The age limit for penalties regarding early withdrawal is the same between traditional IRAs and annuities: 59 ½.

It is a little-known fact that you can actually convert your current IRA or Roth IRA into an annuity that functions as an IRA or Roth IRA tax-free. Some IRAs are annuities, some are not. Think of this as if the annuity were a vehicle and the IRA the driver. The driver is still subject to the laws that govern IRAs, while the annuity works like other products of its kind.

Both IRAs use the power of long-term compounding, which basically means your money is generating earnings upon itself to grow more quickly than an account that would be taxed. There are eligibility guidelines for each, but whichever IRA you decide to choose, there are tax advantages for your future.

Annuities

An annuity is a great way to invest in your future as well. An annuity is an agreement between an insurance company and yourself. You make a lump-sum payment, or a series of payments, and the insurer will agree to make payments directly to you right away or at some future date. The benefit of annuities is that they generally offer tax-deferred growth of earnings. They may also provide you with a death benefit, designed to pay your beneficiary a previously agreed-upon minimum amount.

Annuities have two phases: the accumulation phase, where money is put into the annuity and gains interest; and the annuitization (or payout) phase, where money is distributed out of the annuity to the annuitant. Annuities are funded by an investor over a course of time, tailored to his or her choosing. As mentioned before, this is called the accumulation phase. This can be done with a one-time premium (or payment) over the course of many years, or any time period deemed appropriate. Interest is earned in a compound fashion during the accumulation phase, meaning that the interest earned over a specific period will accumulate its own interest.

Once the accumulation period is over, the annuitization period begins. This is when the investor — the individual placing their money into an annuity — begins to see their money return to them. Annuities are taxed on a last-in, first-out basis, meaning that the principal amount is not taxed, but just the interest gained. This money is taxable first, leaving the principal amount, which is withdrawn in later installments, tax-free. This is due to the fact that annuities are usually purchased with post-tax dollars. Pre-tax, or qualified annuities, however, are treated a bit differently.

It may surprise you to learn that most annuitants do not go through with the annuitization of their contract. Instead, they make systematic draws from their accounts like they would from another retirement product. Though this gives investors easier access to their money, it may not be in their best interest. As you will see, annuities, if properly used, can have a profound impact on an investor's retirement. Features such as a guaranteed income for life are only available to those who annuitize their contract.

This is a cause of contention amongst investment experts. What is better: easy access to your money, or a guarantee that you will never run out of money? This is not a question that can be answered easily. The answer will vary from person to person, and it will even vary for the same person over a given period of time.

Generally, there are two categories of annuities — fixed and variable.

- **Fixed annuity**: This type of annuity offers a guaranteed minimum rate of return. The company also offers guaranteed periodic payments that may last for either a definite period, such as 20 years, or an unspecified period, such as your lifetime. The benefit of this type of annuity is that there are no contribution limits, and it helps add variety to your portfolio — also known as diversification. Plus, because it deals with a fixed amount, it is considered a low-risk investment.

- **Variable annuity**: This type of annuity will fluctuate with the stock market's performance, and it is generally placed in different investment options, such as mutual funds. The payments you receive in the future are periodic, and the rate of return on the purchase payments vary depending on the performance of your investment options. The benefit of a variable annuity is that it gives you the potential to take advantage of the market's appreciation and tax-deferral.

Though annuities are not FDIC-insured products (which stands for the Federal Deposit Insurance Corporation), they are guaranteed by the companies that sell them. If you are worried about the lack of a government guarantee, there are rating services that evaluate the fiscal strength of insurance companies. Moody's Investors Service, Standard & Poor's, and A.M. Best are three of the most popular rating agencies.

But there are many safeguards that exist in order to protect your investment. Strength ratings are one way in which consumers are protected. Another protection is the fact that each state has similar laws protecting the solvency of insurance companies. Most states have safeguards in place that protect investments up to $100,000, while other states, such as New York, go up to $500,000. This guarantee is made by each state's guaranty association. Although it is illegal for an insurance company to advertise that they belong to the guaranty association, in the majority of states, membership is a prerequisite for doing business in that state.

Most annuities offer rates superior to certificates of deposit or money market accounts. Because of this, annuities are growing in popularity amongst investors looking for safe returns, especially retirees, and those approaching retirement age who are not willing to take a risk with their money.

Annuities offer stability that the stock market cannot match, making them a valuable part of a retiree's portfolio. Even though the stock market may drop in value, most annuities are guaranteed products. True, an annuity may not see some of the dramatic increases that the stock market sees, but they are a way to avoid the natural fluctuations of the ever-changing market. This makes them the perfect choice for those who want stability in their portfolio. Annuities can do this because the insurance company acts as a middleman between the investment and the customer. In other words, the insurance company is the one managing the money, rather than the annuitant. The annuitant has a say in variable annuities as to which types of funds their money is put into, but it is ultimately the insurance company that oversees the funds.

There are a plethora of other advantages in owning annuities. Annuities offer professionally managed funds without the high commission charges that mutual funds carry. There are also ways to withdraw your money without added penalties or fees. Perhaps the characteristic that makes an annuity the most worthwhile investment for some is that they have a guaranteed death benefit to a beneficiary that avoids probate.

If the annuity that you are in is not performing well, there are always tax-free exchanges available to you, assuming that you are still in the accumulation phase. These exchanges are known as the industry as Section 1035 exchanges.

What type of investor is an annuity right for?

If you are getting near retirement age and want to preserve your assets and maximize your returns, an annuity is the perfect investment for you.

Annuities are much more predictable and stable than the stock market, yet they offer higher returns than the typical financial products offered by banks. An annuity, in conjunction with these products, can provide you with a fruitful retirement. If you are currently planning for your retirement, or if you will be at some point in the distant future, this option is for you. Annuities are flexible enough to serve the needs of almost anyone who wants a secure future.

Annuities are also beneficial to the younger population. Even if you do not have much in the way of savings, an annuity may be just what you are looking for. Variable annuities, when contributed to regularly over a long period of time, can be extremely beneficial to an investor.

Decide on Your Investment Style

After you have determined what your investment options are, it is important to decide on your investment style. You should also ask yourself how comfortable you are with fluctuations in the value of your investments, also known as your risk tolerance. To determine your risk tolerance, you need to determine your long-term goals and time horizon, as well as your comfort level with risk.

Some people thrive on risk, whereas others are a little more wary. When saving for your future, risk is something you need to potentially earn a return on your investment. All investments involved risk. For example, stock and bond investments rely on the market's performance, so your account balance may rise and fall as the market does, setting you up for the risk that comes with market performance. With stable-value investments, the risk is that your account may not keep up with the rising cost of inflation.

Stocks

Stocks are shares of ownership in a company. They historically have offered the greatest potential for higher returns over longer periods of time. However, because their values rise and fall, they also have the highest level of risk. Even if you are not that comfortable with risk, you may want to consider adding some amount of stock funds into your investment portfolio. This way, you will have the potential for greater returns.

The stock market offers huge returns on your investment — if you invest in the right companies. Stocks are a great investment if you can handle the emotional or financial risk associated with them. As people age and their investment goals change, the ratio of money kept in the stock market should also change. For a young professional just beginning his or her career, it is appropriate to invest in high-risk products such as stocks and funds that reflect stock growth because of the alluring returns. The market has historically offered a competitive rate of return over long periods of time, so if the market bottoms out and the investor loses a good portion of his or her savings, all is not lost. The career of a young professional is just beginning, meaning that the earning potential of that individual is still very high. It may take a few years to rebuild what has been lost, but he or she is still capable of recouping from the loss.

This is not the case with retirees, however, who are usually on fixed incomes. A dip in the stock market could result in the worst kind of disaster: An individual outliving their money. This is a fear that many senior citizens live with on a daily basis. While an annuity is not a catch-all solution to this, it can eliminate some of the financial stress associated with aging. Stability is a necessity for people living on fixed incomes; annuities can provide this.

This is not meant to dissuade you from investing in the stock market. The stock market is the backbone of our country's economic stability and is a valuable weapon in any investor's arsenal. However, you should invest in products that are going to fulfill the goals you have set forth for yourself. If a stable and consistent stream of income is important, stock market investments should be put on the backburner.

If you are interested in getting started with the stock market, here are some tips to keep in mind:

- **Decide how comfortable you are with risk:** If you are all right with taking a gamble, and potentially gaining higher returns with riskier investments, then individual stocks may be right for you. If you prefer more certainty, but still want to invest in stocks, then consider index or mutual funds.

- **Ask yourself how much time you really have to dedicate to playing the market:** Following the ups and downs of the stock market can literally be a full-time job. Therefore, ask yourself if you are willing to dedicate the time to develop the knowledge that you need. If not, stocks may not be right for you.

- **Start small:** Find a broker whom you trust and put a small amount of money into your stocks. This will give you the time to get comfortable with playing the market. To help reduce risk, take several months to invest in the market. As your experience — and, hopefully, earnings — grows, then you can add more stocks to your portfolio slowly.

Bonds

A bond is essentially an IOU between yourself and a company or the government. Basically, you lend them your money, and you earn an interest payment from the borrower. Once the bond matures, also known as the date that the issuer of the bond pays you back, you will receive your principal, which is your original investment, as well as the interest that you made on the investment. That is how you make money on a bond. It is important to consider that bonds do not offer a fixed price. However, they have historically provided higher returns than stable-value investments, like certificates of deposit (CDs). Therefore, their prices rise as interest rates fall, and vice versa.

Certificates of deposit

Certificates of deposits allow investors to put money into an account for a specified amount of time and offer a small rate of return that is guaranteed by the federal government. There is a penalty if you withdraw the money before the specified amount of time has passed. These time limits can range from a few months to a few years.

Generally, CDs are held for a time period of six months to five years. Keep in mind, however, that any gains made by CDs are subject to capital gains taxation rates each year, meaning that even though you make money, you will still have to pay in taxes.

Money market accounts

Money market accounts are higher-interest savings accounts that can typically also be used as in the same manner as a checking account. Banks usually require high balances for this type of account in order to avoid maintenance fees. They do offer more liquidity of your funds than an annuity typically will because you can debit your account with checks or a debit card at your own discretion. MMAs are great for keeping large amounts of money for a short-term period, but are not so good as a longer-term investment. In other words, if you are trying to plan for a retirement, an MMA alone will not suffice.

Mutual funds

Mutual funds are groups of pooled monies that can comprise stocks, bonds, indices, and other investment products. A fund manager who groups many investors' capital together in order to gain more equity closely oversees these funds.

Mutual funds are not guaranteed to make the investor money. In fact, mutual funds often lose money because they fluctuate with the stock market. When the market sours, so do the majority of mutual funds. There are also high commission charges and maintenance fees associated with mutual funds, but they can be cashed out whenever the investor deems necessary.

Exchange-traded funds

Exchange-traded funds (ETFs) are basket funds of like-minded companies that have soared in popularity over the last several years. A basket fund is simply a group of similar business stocks. For instance, a group of biotechnology companies might be included in the same ETF. Because they consist of smaller groups of companies, ETFs are oftentimes much more volatile than the overall market. All ETFs are included in the mutual fund family but, because these products are unstable, they are usually used by short-term traders rather than investors. Thus, if you are looking for a long-term investment, ETFs are not for you. Furthermore, ETFs are not actively managed by a fund manager. It is up to the trader to know when to enter or exit a position with ETFs. This is just another reason why long-term investors should steer clear of this type of product.

Choose Your Asset Allocation

Asset allocation is the mix of stocks, bonds, and stable-value funds you choose to invest in within your retirement portfolio. It uses the basic principle of diversification, which essentially puts your money into a wide range of investment types to help manage risk and gain rewards. When thinking about asset allocation, keep these factors in mind:

- **Be prepared for the market's peaks and valleys**: Market downturns, even the painful ones, are part of the investment circle of life; therefore, it is important to accept that they can, and will, happen. Consider the big picture. Also remember that these down markets may provide opportunities that you could not afford in good times. But never let your strategy be overly influenced by sudden market moves. Remember that what goes up, must come down.

- **Mix it up**: Remember the saying, "Don't put all your eggs in one basket." It is a good rule to live by when choosing an asset allocation strategy. The reason your plan offers so many different investments is so you can spread your money across several asset classes, including stocks (equities), bonds (fixed income), and cash (short term), which can reduce risk and possibly enhance return.

- **Ask for help**: A financial picture can be unclear for just about everyone. Do not forget that you have a wide range of tools and resources available to you. Find out what your plan offers in terms of guidance, and take advantage of those solutions — they can prove invaluable.

Experts agree that it is important to monitor the funds in your portfolio every year to make sure they are still meeting your needs. Make adjustments, if necessary. This is called rebalancing, and it is an important part of your retirement planning process.

Rely on the Power of Compounding

Tax-deferred compounding may sound confusing, but it is actually quite simple. Because your employer's retirement plan is tax-deferred, you do not pay taxes on your earnings until you withdraw them. So, all of the money in your plan, both your contributions and your investment earnings, can grow unrestricted and earn additional income without taxes being taken out. Your assets are generating earnings, which are reinvested to generate their own earnings, so your portfolio balance builds upon itself over time.

Think of it this way: If you invest $2,000 annually into your plan and earn a 10 percent return, your balance would be $2,200 after one year. The next year, your $2,200 also earns 10 percent, giving you $2,420, and so on. There are no annual taxes taken out, allowing your account balance the potential to grow quickly and ultimately putting you closer to reaching your future goals.

Keep Inflation in Mind

Inflation is simply the rise and fall in the price of goods and services. It can erode the buying power of your money and seriously impact the purchasing power of retirement investments. Therefore, it is an important factor to keep in mind when investing for the future. The best way to protect yourself from inflation is to make sure you pick some investments that offer more risk, such as stocks. This way, your portfolio has the best chance of keeping pace with inflation.

Based on the past, it is also important to remember that the cost of living may continue to rise, so you want to keep your investment portfolio ahead of the curve. For example, according to the Web site **www.dollartimes. com**, a $1 cup of coffee in 1989 cost $1.74 in 2009. That is a 2.82 percent inflation rise; thus, keeping inflation in mind is essential.

Plan Your Estate

Another important part of taking steps to safeguard your future is to plan your estate. Some reasons to plan your estate are to appoint a guardian for your children if they are minors, to minimize taxes and costs, to provide for your family, and to distribute your property according to your wishes.

Planning your estate can help you to accumulate wealth, preserve and protect that wealth, and eventually pass that wealth on to your heirs. To begin planning your estate, take inventory of your estate. This includes everything you own with the exception of your expenses, such as real estate, life insurance, cash investments, bank accounts, money markets, as well as taxable and nontaxable investments.

Establish a will

In regard to planning your estate, a will is an essential part of the equation. Many Americans are aware they need a will; however, many do not have one. It is a simple, legal way that you can specify where you want your assets to be distributed after your death.

Be aware that a will has some limitations. A will only designates ownership for assets whose distribution is not provided for in other ways. For example:

- Ownership registered as a joint account between two individuals
- Ownership by a trust
- A named beneficiary on a retirement account
- Investments registered as transfer on death (TOD) from the deceased to a named beneficiary

Drawing up a will is easy. You can contact an attorney to set up a will or use Web sites, like **www.doyourownwill.com**. For more information, you can contact AARP or visit the American Bar Association's Web site. The following will preparation checklist can also help:

Will Preparation Checklist	
1. Personal information concerning you and your spouse	
✓	Know full legal names
	Have a list of addresses and telephone numbers
	Name occupations
	Have list of dates and place of births
	Are the bank reconciliations mathematically accurate?
	Have a list of full names and dates of birth for all your children
	Know detailed information about your children: adopted, infirm, born out of wedlock, any children from a previous relationship
2. Information about your marital status	
✓	Know the date and place of current marriage
	Do you have a marriage license?
	List information about any previous marriages
	Any children from a previous marriage?
	Is prior spouse still alive?
	Are there any existing separation agreements?

3. Summary of your assets	
✓	Be able to list cash and bank accounts and where these are located, as well as account numbers
	Know details on life insurance policies: what company, the amount, and who is named beneficiary (for you and your estate)
	Be able to list securities, pension plans, and annuities: with whom, what amount, and if there is a designated beneficiary
	Have details on your principal residence (home); type of ownership: sole, joint tenants, or tenants-in-common; current market value and amount of your equity and mortgages
	Know similar information on any other real estate
	Have a list of information on businesses owned: proprietorships, partnerships, or private companies you have an interest in
	Be able to name any inheritance expected or other money or assets you are expecting
	Know your personal effects
	Have a list of household furnishings, cars, boats, jewelry, and personal belongings of sentimental value
	Be able to name the location of safety deposit box and important papers
4. Summary of your debts	
✓	Be able to list any debts, such as loans, mortgages, guarantees, promissory notes, and amount owed and to whom
5. Outline of beneficiaries	
✓	Know whom you want cash requests to go to and the amounts of each request (for example, spouse, children, former spouse, children by former spouse, family relatives, friends, business associates, charitable organizations, or educational or other institutions)
	In the event that you and your spouse are killed in a common disaster (for example, auto or plane crash), know how you want your estate to be distributed
	Know whom you want specific personal possessions to go to (be able to describe the asset in detail)
	Do you have alternative beneficiaries in case designated beneficiaries predecease you or cannot be located?
	Have you considered setting up a testamentary trust to have some or all of your assets in your estate managed on your death on behalf of your spouse or children?

	Do you have minor children or disabled children? At what age do you want your children to have access to their bequest?
	Do you want your executor or trustee to have the power to manage the investments to maximize returns, rather than immediately liquidating them and paying cash to the beneficiaries?
	Have you considered the benefits of a trust company to manage the trust?
6. Names of people in your will who will represent your interests	
✓	Know the names of your executor, trustee, lawyer, and guardian for infant children
	Have they agreed to do this job?
	Know what skills, attributes, or resources they have that makes them appropriate for the job
	Name their relationship to you
	Know their full names and addresses
	Do they know the location of your will?
	Do they know the location of your safety deposit box?
	Have you selected alternatives?
	Have you researched the benefits of using a trust company or lawyer?
	Have you completed the personal information record and put a copy in your safety deposit box?
7. Other information to obtain	
✓	Know other responsibilities
	Are you the executor or trustee of anyone's will? For whom?
	Do you hold any power of attorney or appointment? For whom?
	Know the names and addresses of financial, personal, or business advisors
	Know the names and addresses of your lawyer or trust company
	Know were you want to leave the original copy of your will (safety deposit box or with your lawyer or trust company)
	Previous will: Know when it was signed, where it is located, and when it was last reviewed
	If your spouse has a will, know when it was signed, where it is located, and when it was last reviewed
	Were both wills (of you and your spouse) reviewed in conjunction with each other?

	Have you had both wills (if applicable) recently reviewed by your lawyer and/or trust company (should be reviewed annually)?
	Have you discussed your will with a tax accountant and financial planner to make sure you have taken advantage of all the tax and estate planning strategies available?
	Do you or your spouse wish to change any provisions in your wills?
	Have you considered being an organ donor on your death, and have you discussed this wish with your spouse? Have you completed the appropriate forms? Contact your provincial organ donor registry for information or the national association dealing with specific organs (for example, heart, kidney, or eyes)
	Have you considered having a living will (not enforceable in many cases, but a reflection of your wishes in the case of a terminal or serious illness)?
	Have you considered giving an enduring power of attorney to someone over your affairs in certain situations (financial or health related)?
	Know details on burial wishes and funeral service instructions
	Know historical information for obituary purposes
	Know names and addresses of family, relatives, and friends for notification purposes

Consider a personal trust

Depending on your circumstances, you may also want to consider a personal trust when planning your estate. A trust is a legal agreement where a trustee holds the title to property or investments for another person, who is called a beneficiary. The trustee is expected to invest take care of the property wisely and make payments from the trust to meet the beneficiary's needs. A personal trust may help reduce or eliminate your federal estate tax, which ultimately means you pay less in taxes.

When you are alive a revocable trust can be created, revoked, or changed to take assets from your estate. With this kind of trust, your control is permanently and completely revoked, too. However, no changes can be made after your death. An irrevocable trust cannot be changed or revoked at any time. Also, if you decide to move the ownership of your assets into a trust, you do not give up control. You should also name a successor trustee to serve after you die. The person will close the trust and distribute the assets to your beneficiaries.

There are also additional types of trusts. These include:

- **Marital bypass trust**: People can transfer an estate of $1 million free of federal estate tax.

- **Special needs trust**: This type of trust offers support for individuals who are unable to take care of themselves.

- **QTIP (qualified terminable interest property trust)**: Used by couples who have children from previous marriages, it helps make sure that spouses' property goes to their children.

- **Charitable remainder trust**: An irrevocable trust that can offer a current income tax deduction.

The Facts About Life Insurance

Life insurance, as discussed in Chapter 1, is another important way to protect yourself and create a solid plan for your future. It is basically a form of insurance on the life of a person. If that person dies, the insurance policy provides a sum of money to the previously mentioned policyholder (generally someone in the person's family). There are a variety of types of life insurance, but the two that you will probably want to consider are term and permanent.

Term life insurance

This type of life insurance is usually less expensive and less complicated. It provides insurance protection for a limited time, which you specify when purchasing it, such as ten to 30 years. If you pass away within the term period and the policy is active, a benefit is paid to your previously mentioned beneficiary. If you are still alive at the conclusion of the term, the protection ends unless your policy can be renewed. There is no cash value, also known as an "accumulation" element, with term life insurance, which means you cannot borrow or cash out the money that you used to maintain the insurance.

Term life insurance is generally best for:

- Individuals who have a short-term need for insurance protection on their life

- People who require a large amount of security but have set budgets

- Individuals who have specific business needs (e.g., business owners who want to protect employees who have a definite number of years until retirement)

Initially, term life insurance provides protection for a low cost. Another benefit is that if your personal requirements change, most term policies let you to switch over to a permanent life insurance policy without being required to have a medical exam done or needing to report other information about your health. Overall, it is an important way to complement other coverage when new financial responsibilities come up, for a set period of time.

Permanent life insurance

Universal life insurance, whole life insurance, and variable universal life insurance are types of permanent insurance. They can provide protection for your entire life, or up to a specific age, at which the insurer pays the policy owner the value of cash. The difference between this type of life insurance and term life insurance is that permanent life insurance policies can often provide a cash value — which is essentially money that you can borrow, and possibly even cash out, to help achieve your financial goals.

Permanent life insurance also gets a favorable tax benefit, as the cash value can grow on an income-tax-deferred basis. This means you are not obligated to pay taxes on any earnings while the policy remains current. Withdrawals or loans against the cash value can be tax-free.

Permanent life insurance is good for:

- People who require the protection of life insurance for a long time

- Individuals who want to accumulate policy cash value to ensure they have funds for retirement, education, or other future goals

- People who want to benefit from the tax-favored treatment of these life insurance policies

Health Insurance Fundamentals

Health insurance is one of most important ways to protect yourself and your family. When you have it, you probably do not think about it. However, when you do not have it, it is like playing a risky game. If you are worried about money, health insurance may be low on your list of financial priorities. But not being covered by a health insurance plan could be a dangerous and costly decision.

If you find yourself sick or in an accident and do not have health insurance, it could lead to even more financial stress than you may be facing now. Whether your employer offers a health insurance plan, or you need to purchase your own, you can work with a health insurance agent who can assist you in finding the best plan for you and your family's needs. Remember, while it can be difficult to come up with the money for a health insurance plan, the alternative can be even more costly.

Summary

Remember, the person who is most concerned about your future is you. So while the sooner you begin saving, the better off you will be, it is also important to remember that your financial needs come first. Therefore, take strides to get your own finances in order before you start saving for a child's college education, wedding, or other financial needs. Your children and grandchildren will have more options for college funding than you will have for living in retirement.

Conclusion

Onward and Upward

As the saying goes, nothing worthwhile comes easily, and it holds true for traveling the financial path home. For some, it takes years to get out of a tumultuous financial situation. Regardless of how long your plan to get back on track may take, the key is to keep forging ahead. No one said getting back to where you want to be would be easy — but always remember that it will be worthwhile.

The Seven Steps of the Journey Ahead

Consider the following steps as your guidelines for getting back on track. They can help you stay focused, and also serve as checkpoints along your journey back to financial freedom.

1. **Learn from your past mistakes:** Always remember what got you into the financial mess you are in now. Whether it was divorce, unemployment, or a health problem that caused you to get financially off-track, it is important to regularly remind yourself what factors got you into that situation. Maybe it was a missed payment on a credit card that resulted in a high inter-

est rate, or maybe it was missed mortgage or rent payments that forced you into eviction and foreclosure. Whatever it was, remember your mistakes and vow not to make them again.

2. **Keep your eye on the prize:** Whether your ultimate goal is to purchase back your home, have a zero balance on all credit cards, or regain your possessions that were repossessed, you must always keep them in mind. They are your true motivation for success. Although it is important to always keep your past mistakes in the back of your mind, it is even more crucial to remember your goals. Having that ultimate reward will serve as inspiration when the journey is tough.

3. **Keep a clean credit record:** It cannot be stressed enough how important it is to keep your credit report clean so you can rebuild your credit score. Your credit record is the single most important factor in helping you get back on track financially. Remember that good credit is your key to the good things in life.

4. **Eliminate debt:** Though it can take years for you to rebuild your financial life, it can take mere seconds to get back into debt. One emergency, or even an impulsive purchase, can knock you off track quickly. Even if you are living paycheck to paycheck as you struggle to get your financial future in order, you should always continue to pay down your debt. It is the only way you can eventually achieve true financial freedom.

5. **Purchase a home:** Once you have gotten your credit record in good standing and have cleared out your remaining debt, you are on the verge of getting yourself back on track. At this point, begin the process of saving for a home, or if you choose

to rent, ensure that you have enough money saved to put down a security deposit. Once you have enough money in the bank, enjoy the feeling of securing a solid, reliable home for yourself and your family.

6. **Regain possessions:** If you have any possessions that were taken from you, and know that they are still available to be reclaimed, then now is the time. Maybe it is a piece of jewelry from a family member that you had to pawn, or a big-ticket item like a boat. Regardless of what the item is, you should now be back in the financial standing to reclaim it. One note of caution: Even if you have enough money saved to purchase these items back, remember that you have lived without them for a certain amount of time. Ask yourself if you truly still want the item. You may be surprised by the answer.

7. **Celebrate:** Now that you have your credit in good standing, have cleared your debts, and are living in your own home with your possessions reclaimed, there is one thing left to do: Enjoy the feeling of true success. No matter what got you into your negative financial situation, only one thing — your determination — got you out.

You Can Do It

Remember, regardless of the stage of your financial journey you are in right now, becoming financially secure is within your grasp. This is your life, and you deserve to turn your goals into a reality. Maybe the road ahead is long, or maybe it is short, but the only person who can take charge of your financial future is you.

Believe in yourself, check in on your progress, and feel confident that the hard work you put in right now will be for the best in the long run. Today is the first day of the rest of your life. Today is the day to overcome your past and survive and prosper.

Appendix A

Financial Freedom Checklist

Now that you have all of the information you need to overcome your financial obstacle, it is important to keep your action steps close to you. Make a copy of the following "financial freedom checklist" and keep it in a place where you can easily refer to it. It is a simple way to help keep you ahead of the game financially.

☐ **Spend less than you make:** It sounds basic, but this is one of the hardest steps for people to follow. No matter how much you earn, it is impossible to get ahead if you spend more than you take in. In a competitive job market, it can be easier to spend less than it is to earn more — therefore, a little cost-cutting can go a long when it comes to saving. Best of all, you do not have to make big sacrifices.

☐ **Stick to your budget:** As you now know from this book, budgeting does not have to be hard. Remember, it is impossible to know where your money is going if you do not follow a budget. No matter how much you earn, a budget is an easy, effective way to stay on track financially.

☐ **Eliminate credit card debt:** Credit card debt is the top obstacle to getting ahead financially. They are simply too easy to use, and even easier to forget that it is real money. Even if you are committed to paying off the balance quickly, the reality is that it is hard to do and getting into extensive debt can happen before you know it. Bottom line: use cash!

☐ **Contribute to a retirement plan:** If your employer has a 401(k) plan, it is in your best interest to contribute to it. A 401(k) or similar plan offers you benefits now for the tax advantages and later for the savings. If you are already contributing to a plan, try to increase your contributions. If your employer does not offer a retirement plan, consider an annuity or an IRA.

☐ **Pay yourself first:** Remember to save — even just a little each paycheck. The key is to save before you spend. If you wait until you have paid all your other financial obligations, chances are you will never put much away. Resolve to set aside a minimum of 5 percent of your salary — you can even have the money automatically deducted from your paycheck and deposited into a separate account. It is that easy.

☐ **Utilize other employer benefits:** Your employer may offer other great benefits in addition to a 401(k). Be sure you are enrolled in medical and dental insurance, as well as flexible spending accounts. They will be well worth the small fees now and can help you reduce your taxable income or out-of-pocket expenses.

☐ **Remember to stay insured:** Make sure that you have enough life insurance to protect your dependents, and make sure they have enough income death or disability. Whether you decide on whole or term, life insurance is critical.

☐ **Make a will:** Believe it or not, 70 percent of Americans do not have a will. Bottom line: If you have dependents, you need a will, regardless of how much you earn or what your assets are. You can either contact a lawyer for a small fee or, if your situation is simple enough, do your own with online software.

Appendix B

Bankruptcy Court Fee Schedule

Source: **www.paed.uscourts.gov/documents/fees/fees_m4.pdf**

The following are miscellaneous fees that are generally charged for services provided by the bankruptcy courts. No fees will be charged for services that are rendered on behalf of the United States, with the exception of those prescribed specific to items 1, 3, and 5, or to bankruptcy administrators that are appointed under Public Law No. 99-554, § 302(d)(3)(I).

It is also important to note that no fees under this schedule will be charged to federal agencies or programs that are funded from judiciary appropriations, such as, but not limited to: individuals, agencies, and organizations that provide services authorized by the Criminal Justice Act, 18 U.S.C. § 3006A.

Reproduction of any record or paper: 50 cents per page
This fee will apply to all paper copies made from either original documents or microfiche or microfilm reproductions of the original records. This fee will also apply to services that are rendered on behalf of the United States if the record or paper requested is electronically available.

Certification of any document or paper: $9

This is regardless of whether the certification is made directly on the document or by using a separate instrument. For exemplification of any paper or document or paper, the charge for certification is doubled.

Reproduction of recordings of proceedings: $26

This fee will apply to services that are rendered on behalf of the United States, if the reproduction of the recording is available electronically. This is regardless of the medium, and it also includes the cost of materials.

Amendments to a debtor's lists of creditors, matrix, schedules of creditors, or mailing lists: $26

This fee is for each amendment and is based on the fact that the bankruptcy judge may waive the charge in any case (for good cause). No fee is required when the purpose of the amendment is for an address change of a creditor or an attorney for a creditor listed on the schedules. No fee is required to add the name and address of an attorney for a listed creditor.

Search of the bankruptcy court records: $26

This is for each name or item search that is conducted by the clerk of the bankruptcy court or a deputy clerk. This fee will also apply to services rendered on behalf of the United States if the information requested is available through electronic access.

Filing a complaint: $250

If in the United States, other than a United States trustee acting as a trustee in a case under Title 11, or if a debtor is the plaintiff, no fee is required. If a trustee or debtor in possession is the plaintiff, the fee may be payable only by the estate and to the extent there is any estate realized. No fee is required if a child support creditor or its representative is the plaintiff, and if this plaintiff files the form required by § 304(g) of the Bankruptcy Reform Act of 1994, no fee is required.

Filing or indexing any document: $39

This pertains to documents that are not in a case or proceeding for which a filing fee has been paid.

Miscellaneous administrative fee: $39

In all cases filed under title 11, this is the fee that a clerk must collect from the debtor or the petitioner. This fee may be paid in installments in the same manner that the filing fee may be paid in installments, consistent with the procedure set forth in Federal Rule of Bankruptcy Procedure 1006.

Filing of a petition under Chapter 7: $15

When filing a Chapter 7 petition of the Bankruptcy Code, the petitioner must pay this amount to the clerk of the court for payment to trustees serving in cases as provided in 11 U.S.C. § 330(b)(2). An application to pay the fee in installments may be filed in the manner set forth in Federal Rule of Bankruptcy Procedure 1006(b).

Filing of a motion to convert a case to Chapter 7 of the Bankruptcy Code: $15

The movant (the person who makes the motion for application for a court order or judgment) must pay to the clerk of court for the payment to trustees serving in cases as provided in 11 U.S.C. § 330(b)(2). Upon the filing of a notice of conversion pursuant to Section 1208(a) or Section 1307(a) of the Code, this fee must be paid to the clerk of the court for payment to trustees serving in cases as provided in 11 U.S.C. § 330(b)(2). If the trustee serving in the case before the conversion is the movant, the fee shall be payable only from the estate that exists prior to conversion. When filing a motion to convert or a notice of conversion, a fee shall be charged in the amount of the difference between the current filing fee for the chapter under which the case was originally commenced and the current filing fee for the chapter to which the case is requested to be converted. If the filing fee for the chapter to which the case is requested to be converted is less than the fee paid at the commencement of the case, no refund shall be provided. A fee shall not be assessed under this item for converting a Chapter 7 or 13 case to a Chapter 11 case, as the fee for these actions is collected pursuant to statute under 28 U.S.C. § 1930(a).

Filing a motion to reopen a bankruptcy code case: $15

This fee must be collected in the same amount as the filing fee prescribed by 28 U.S.C. §1930(a) for commencing a new case on the date of reopening. The reopening fee should be charged when a case is closed without a discharge being entered. If the motion to reopen is made for a Chapter 7 case, an additional fee of $15 shall be paid to the clerk of the court for payment to trustees serving in cases as provided in 11 U.S.C. § 330(b)(2). For filing a motion to reopen a Chapter 15 case, a fee shall be charged in the same amount as the filing fee required under Item 16 of this schedule for commencing a new case on the date of reopening. The reopening fee will not be charged if the reopening is necessary: (1) to permit a party to file a complaint to obtain a determination under Rule 4007(b), or (2) when a creditor is violating the terms of the discharge under 11 U.S.C. § 524. The court may waive this fee under appropriate circumstances or may defer payment of the fee from trustees, pending discovery of additional assets. If payment is deferred, the fee shall be waived if no additional assets are discovered.

Sheet of microfiche film or microfilm jacket copy of any court record: $5 per sheet

Record retrieval $45

From a Federal Records Center, National Archives, or other storage location removed from the place of business of the court.

Returned checks: $45

For a check paid into the court that is returned due to lack of funds.

Docketing a proceeding: $250

This is when a proceeding is docketed on appeal or review from a final judgment of a bankruptcy judge pursuant to 28 U.S.C. § 158. A separate fee must be paid by each party filing a notice of appeal in the bankruptcy court, but parties filing a joint notice of appeal in the bankruptcy court are required to pay only one fee. If a trustee or debtor in possession is the appellant, the fee should be payable only from the estate and to the extent there is any estate realized. Upon notice from the court of appeals that a direct appeal from the bankruptcy court has been authorized, the appellant shall pay an additional $200.

Filing a Chapter 15 proceeding: TBD

The fee shall be the same amount as the fee for a case commenced under Chapter 11 of Title 11 as required by 28 U.S.C. § 1930(a)(3).

Cost of providing copies of the local court rules: TBD

The court may also distribute copies of the local rules without charge.

Charge for the handling of registry funds deposited with the court: TBD

This will be assessed by the clerk from interest earnings and in accordance with the detailed fee schedule issued by the Director of the Administrative Office of the United States Courts.

Joint case filing fee: TBD

When the debtor(s) request that a joint case filed under § 302 of Title 11 is divided into two separate cases, a fee shall be charged equal to the current filing fee for the chapter under which the joint case was commenced. If the motion to divide the case is made for a Chapter 7 case, an additional fee of $15 shall be paid to the clerk of the court for payment to trustees serving in cases as provided in 11 U.S.C. § 330(b)(2).

Motion to terminate, annul, modify, or condition the automatic stay: $150

Provided under § 362(a) of Title 11, a motion to compel abandonment of property of the estate pursuant to Rule 6007(b) of the Federal Rules of Bankruptcy Procedure, or a motion to withdraw the reference of a case or proceeding under 28 U.S.C. § 157(d). No fee is required for a motion for relief from the co-debtor stay or for a stipulation for court approval of an agreement for relief from a stay. If a child support creditor or its representative is the movant, and if such movant files the form required by § 304(g) of the Bankruptcy Reform Act of 1994, no fee is required.

Docketing a cross appeal from a bankruptcy court determination: $250

If a trustee or debtor in possession is the appellant, the fee must be payable only from the estate and to the extent there is any estate realized. Upon notice from the court of appeals that a direct cross from the bankruptcy court has been authorized, the cross appellant shall pay an additional $200.

Appendix C

Foreclosure Assessment Form

Source: Twin Cities Habitat for Humanity, **www.tchabitat.org/Document.Doc?id=78**

This form can help you if you are in financial distress and are concerned about going into foreclosure. As you know, the best way to avoid foreclosure is to pay your mortgage bills first each month — before any other bills. However, because this is not always possible, this worksheet can help you lay out all the required information before taking the next step.

I. YOUR INFORMATION

Date: _____

Name(s) _____

Address _____

Home Phone _____

Work Phone _____

Best Time to Reach _____

Marital Status _____

Spouse (if any) _____

Children (names and ages)_____

_____

_____

Others in Household _____

II. INFORMATION ABOUT PROPERTY BEING FORECLOSED ON

Address of Property (if different than above) _____

_____

Names of all Co-owners w/Address (if different) _____

_____

_____

Year Purchased _____

Original Purchase Price _____

Estimate of Current Value _____

Number of Rooms _____

Owner Occupant?

At Purchase? Yes ___ No ___

Now? Yes ___ No ___

Multi-Family Home? Yes ___ No ___

Name of Tenants _____

Rent Received _____

Condition: Exc ___ Good ___ Fair ___ Poor ___

Major Repairs Needed:
Describe:

_____

Number of Mortgages _____

Other Liens _____

III. YOUR MORTGAGE

Type of Mortgage Purchase Money _____

Refinance _____

Home Equity Loan _____

Debt Consolidation _____

Other _____

Year of Mortgage _____

Original Amount _____

Current Lender or Servicer _____

Address of Current Lender or Servicer _____

Phone: _____

Fax: _____

Contact Person _____

Loan Account Number _____

Investor/Insurer FHA Insured ____

VA ____

RHS ____

Fannie Mae ____

Freddie Mac ____

PMI _____

Other _____

Term of Mortgage (in months) _____

Interest Rate _____

Principal and Interest Payment (monthly) _____

Tax and Insurance Payment (monthly) _____

Total Monthly Payment _____

Months Behind _____

Total Arrears, Including Costs _____

Current Principal Balance _____

Payoff Amount _____

Are you in Default? Yes ____ No ____

Status/Amount of Monthly Payment _____

Reason for Default _____

Other Mortgages and Liens Yes ____ No ____

Describe:

_____

_____

Notes:

_____

_____

_____

_____

_____

_____

_____

_____

Appendix D

Sample Eviction Form

Source: Express Evictions, **www.expressevictions.com/forms/30DayNotice.pdf**

3-DAY NOTICE TO PAY OR QUIT

TO: _____

_____

_____

PLEASE TAKE NOTICE that your month-to-month tenancy of the described premises is terminated as of the date thirty (30) days after the service of this notice upon you.

You are required to quit and surrender possession thereof to the undersigned on or before the date thirty (30) days after service of this NOTICE upon you.

The Premises of which you are required to surrender possession are:

Address: Apartment or Suite No.: _____

_____

City: _____ State: _____ Zip: _____

County of: _____

THIS IS INTENDED AS A THIRTY (30)-DAY LEGAL NOTICE FOR THE PURPOSE OF TERMINATING YOUR TENANCY. THIS TERMINATION OF TENANCY IS IN ACCORDANCE WITH CALIFORNIA CIVIL CODE SECTION 789 AND/OR CALIFORNIA CIVIL CODE SECTION 1946.

Dated this _____ day of _____, _____

Signed _____
Landlord/agent

Proof of Service

I, the undersigned, being at least 18 years of age, declare under penalty of perjury that I served the above notice, of which this is a true copy, on the following tenant(s) in possession in the manner(s) indicated below:

☐ On _____, I handed the notice to the tenant(s) personally.

☐ On_____, after attempting personal service, I handed the notice to a person of suitable age and discretion at the residence/business of the tenant(s), AND I deposited a true copy in the U.S. Mail, in a sealed envelope with postage fully prepaid, addressed to the tenant(s) at his/her/their place of residence (date mailed, if different _____).

☐ On _____, after attempting service in both manners described above, I placed the notice in a conspicuous place at the residence of the tenant(s) AND I deposited a true copy in the U.S. mail in a sealed envelope with postage fully prepaid, addressed to the tenant(s) at his/her/their place of residence (date mailed if different).

Appendix E

Sample Statutory Will Form

Source: The State Bar of California, **www.calbar.ca.gov/calbar/pdfs/publications/Will-Form.pdf**

California Statutory Will

INSTRUCTIONS

1. READ THE WILL: If you do not understand something, ask a lawyer to explain it to you.

2. FILL IN THE BLANKS: Follow the instructions in the form carefully. Do not add any words to the Will (except for filling in blanks) or cross out any words.

3. DATE AND SIGN THE WILL, AND HAVE TWO WITNESSES SIGN IT: You and the witnesses should read and follow the Notice to Witnesses found at the end of this Will.

CALIFORNIA STATUTORY WILL OF

_____ (Print your full name)

1. *Will:* This is my Will. I revoke all prior Wills and codicils.

2. *Specific Gift of Personal Residence* (Optional — Use only if you want to give your personal residence to a different person or persons than you give the balance of your assets to under paragraph 5 below): I give my interest in my principal personal residence at the time of my death (subject to mortgages and liens) as follows:

(Select one choice only and sign in the box after your choice):

☐ *Choice One:* All to my spouse, if my spouse survives me; otherwise, to my descendants (my children and the descendants of my children) who survive me.

☐ *Choice Two:* Nothing to my spouse; all to my descendants (my children and the descendants of my children) who survive me.

☐ *Choice Three:* All to the following person if he or she survives me (Insert the name of the person): _____

_____

☐ *Choice Four:* Equally among the following persons who survive me (Insert the names of two or more persons): _____

3. *Specific Gift of Automobiles, Household, and Personal Effects* (Optional — Use only if you want to give automobiles and household and personal effects to a different person or persons than you give the balance of your assets to under paragraph 5 below): I give all of my automobiles (subject to loans), furniture, furnishings, household items, clothing, jewelry, and other tangible articles of a personal nature at the time of my death as follows:

   (Select one choice only and sign in the box after your choice).

   ☐ *Choice One:* All to my spouse, if my spouse survives me; otherwise, to my descendants (my children and the descendants of my children) who survive me.

   ☐ *Choice Two:* Nothing to my spouse; all to my descendants (my children and the descendants of my children) who survive me.

   ☐ *Choice Three:* All to the following person if he or she survives me (Insert the name of the person): _____

   _____

   ☐ *Choice Four:* Equally among the following persons who survive me (Insert the names of two or more persons): _____

   _____

4. *Specific Gifts of Cash* (Optional): I make the following cash gifts to the persons named below who survive me, or to the named charity, and I

sign my name in the box after each gift. If I do not sign in the box, I do not make a gift. (Sign in the box after each gift you make.)

Name of Person or Charity to receive gift (name one only — please print):

_____

Amount of Cash Gift: _____

Sign your name in this box to make this gift

Name of Person or Charity to receive gift (name one only — please print):

_____

Amount of Cash Gift: _____

Sign your name in this box to make this gift

Name of Person or Charity to receive gift (name one only — please print):

_____

Amount of Cash Gift: _____

Sign your name in this box to make this gift

Name of Person or Charity to receive gift (name one only — please print):

_____

Amount of Cash Gift: _____

Sign your name in this box to make this gift

5. *Balance of My Assets:* Except for the specific gifts made in paragraphs 2, 3, and 4 above, I give the balance of my assets as follows:

(Select one choice only and sign in the box after your choice. If I sign in more than one box or if I do not sign in any box, the court will distribute my assets as if I did not make a Will).

☐ *Choice One:* All to my spouse, if my spouse survives me; otherwise, to my descendants (my children and the descendants of my children) who survive me.:

☐ *Choice Two:* Nothing to my spouse; all to my descendants (my children and the descendants of my children) who survive me:

☐ *Choice Three:* All to the following person if he or she survives me: (Insert the name of the person): _____

_____

☐ *Choice Four:* Equally among the following persons who survive me: (Insert the names of two or more persons): _____

_____

6. *Guardian of the Child's Person:* If I have a child under age 18 and the child does not have a living parent at my death, I nominate the individual named below as First Choice as guardian of the person of such child (to raise the child). If the First Choice does not serve, then I nominate the Second Choice, and then the Third Choice to serve. Only an individual (not a bank or trust company) may serve.

Name of First Choice for Guardian of the Person: _____

_____

Name of Second Choice for Guardian of the Person: _____

_____

Name of Third Choice for Guardian of the Person: _____

_____

Appendix F

Sample Monthly Budget

Monthly Cash Flow	Income Amount	Expenses Amount
Your Monthly Income		
Wages and salary; include bonuses if standard for your line of work	$	
Investment income, such as interest, dividends, investment real estate income (rents)	$	
Maintenance or alimony and child support	$	
Any other income	$	
TOTAL MONTHLY INCOME	$	
Your Monthly Expenses		
Food		$
Transportation costs, such as car loan payments, lease payments, cost for running the car (gas, oil, etc.), monthly train or bus ticket, etc.		$
Clothing		$
Childcare		$
Pet care expenses, such as food, vet bills, etc.		$
Medical expenses not covered by insurance, including dental expenses and vision expenses		$
Flexible spending accounts and medical savings accounts		$

Contributions to retirement plans, such as a 401(k) or an IRA		$
Contributions to education plans, such as a pre-paid tuition plan, a state savings plan, or an IRA		$
Savings account		$
Loan payments		$
Credit card payments		$
Maintenance or alimony		$
Child support		$
Insurance payments, such as health, disability, and life insurance		$
Taxes, including income, social security, and self-employment taxes		$
Educational and sport expenses, such as tuition, books, equipment, and fees		$
Restaurants (meals)		$
Entertainment, such as theater tickets, sports events, concerts, hobbies, etc.		$
Charitable contributions and donations		$
Vacation expenses		$
Other expenses		$
Other expenses		$
Other expenses		$
TOTAL MONTHLY EXPENSES		$
TOTAL MONTHLY INCOME - TOTAL MONTHLY EXPENSES =	$	$
		= $

Appendix G

Letters Expressing Financial Hardship and Declaring Fault

Sample Hardship Letter

12 December 2007

Mrs. Judith Macrae
Anytown Savings and Loan
300 Banker Street
Boston, MA 02125

RE: 199 Main Street, Anytown, MA

Loan Number: 22332

Dear Mrs. Macrae,

This letter is in regard to the property listed above, owned by my husband Roger and myself. Though we have not missed any payments on this loan as of yet, we are very concerned that the recent changes in our financial situation could cause us to do so in the near future. I am writing today to request a meeting with a qualified loan officer to discuss options Anytown Savings and Loan might be able to offer us during this time to prevent our home from going into foreclosure.

Roger and I both feel very certain that our financial situation will resolve itself in the near future. Due to an on-the-job injury, Roger is out of work until June, at which point he will return to work. We are hoping that your bank will be able to help us by allowing for interest-only payments until the 25th of July 2008.

Please contact me at your earliest convenience. We are both eager to establish an agreement to keep our home from the risk of foreclosure. Thank you for your time and consideration.

Sincerely,

Mary. S. Merchant

cc: Margaret Stone, Bank President

Sample Letter Contesting Default

12 December 2007

Mrs. Judith Macrae
Anytown Savings and Loan
300 Banker Street
Boston, MA 02125

RE: 199 Main Street, Anytown, MA

Loan Number: 22332

Dear Mrs. Macrae,

This letter is in response to a notice of missed payment I received from your bank yesterday, 11 December 2007.

In the letter sent, it is noted that the mortgage payment of $1,230.45 due on 1 December 2007 was not made. Attached you will find a photocopy of the check received and cashed by your bank on the 28th of November for this exact amount.

I am requesting that you check your records carefully and credit my loan immediately. Additionally, I would like for you to be certain that the missed payment is not recorded on any of the three (3) credit reporting agency reports as a mark against my credit.

Thank you for your time and consideration. Should you have any further questions or concerns about this request, do not hesitate to contact me. I look forward to your prompt response.

Sincerely,

Mary. S. Merchant

cc: Margaret Stone, Bank President

Sample Notice of Default

LAW OFFICES OF HOWE AND NOT
5544 Beacon Hill
Boston, Massachusetts 02020
781-777-8846

Attorney for Plaintiff
Anytown Savings and Loan

COURT OF THE STATE OF MASSACHUSETTS
COUNTY OF SUFFOLK

ANYTOWN SAVINGS & LOAN : SUPERIOR COURT

Plaintiff,

VS.   : JUDICIAL DISTRICT OF BOSTON

ROGER ALLAN MERCHANT   : October 30, 2007

AND

MARY SAMANTHA MERCHANT   **COMPLAINT FOR**

JUDICIAL FORECLOSURE

Defendants,

_____

Plaintiff, Anytown Savings and Loan ("Lender"), complains and alleges
as follows:

VENUE

1. Venue in the Court of the County of Suffolk is proper under the laws of
   the State of Massachusetts because the property subject to this action is
   located within Suffolk County.

THE PARTIES

2. Bank is, and at all times mentioned herein was, a Massachusetts bank, chartered by the Federal Deposit Insurance Corporation, and doing business in the State of Massachusetts.

3. Bank is informed and believes, and thereon alleges that Defendants Roger Allan Merchant and Mary Samantha Merchant ("Borrowers" or "Defendants") are, and at all relevant times herein were, individuals residing in the State of Massachusetts.

THE LOAN DOCUMENTATION

4. On July 20, 1985, the defendants, Roger Allan Merchant and Mary Samantha Merchant, owed the Plaintiff two hundred thousand ($200,000) dollars as evidenced by his note dated on said date and payable to the order of the Plaintiff, together with an interest at the rate of six (6) percent per annum until July 20, 1990, being variable thereafter, and together with all costs of collection, including reasonable attorney's fees, in the event of foreclosure of the mortgage securing the note. Under the terms of the Note, Borrower agreed to make monthly payments of $1,020.00, comprised of principal and interest. The interest was calculated at a fixed rate of 8 percent per year, payable on the last day of each month. The Note provided upon default the holder could declare all monies payable thereunder immediately due, owing and payable. The Note also provided for a default interest rate of 3 percent plus the contracted rate.

5. On said date, by deed of that date, the defendants, Roger Allan Merchant and Mary Samantha Merchant, to secure said note, mortgages to the plaintiff the real estate described in Exhibit "A" attached hereto and made a part hereof. Said deed is conditioned upon the payment of said note according to its tenor and was recorded on 10 September 2007 in Volume 24, Page 204 of the Boston Registry of Deeds.

6. Said note and mortgage are still owned by the plaintiff, and the debt is due and partially unpaid.

7. Bank complied with all of its contractual obligations under the Note by disbursing monies as required.

LOAN DEFAULTS

8. The defendants, Roger Allan Merchant and Mary Samantha Merchant, have defaulted under the terms of the mortgage note and deed.

9. Although the note is in default and demand was made upon the defendant, said defendant has neglected and refused to make payment.

WHEREFORE, THE PLAINTIFF CLAIMS

1. Monetary damages and that the amount, legal interest or property in demand is greater than $95,000.00, exclusive of interest and costs.

2. Strict foreclosure of said mortgage, but in the event that the United States of America is a part defendant at the time of judgment, then a foreclosure by sale.

3. Possession of mortgaged premises.

4. A deficiency judgment.

5. Such other equitable relief as the Court may deem necessary.

6. Reasonable attorneys' fees as called for in the note.

Dated at Boston, Massachusetts, this 30th of October, 2007.

NOTICE

NOTICE: A person who is unemployed or underemployed and who (for a continuous period of at least two years to the commencement of this foreclosure action) owned and occupied the property being foreclosed as such person's principal residence, may be entitled to contain relief provisions under Massachusetts General Statute 32-67W, as amended. You should consult an attorney to determine your rights under this law.

THE PLAINTIFF

BY:

_____

Judith Macrae for
Anytown Savings and Loan

Sample Answer to Notice of Complaint

LAW OFFICES OF TRY AND MIGHT
200 Boylston Street
Boston, Massachusetts 02015
781-777-4546

Attorney for Defendants
Roger A. and Mary S. Merchant

COURT OF THE STATE OF MASSACHUSETTS
COUNTY OF SUFFOLK

ANYTOWN SAVINGS & LOAN : SUPERIOR COURT

Plaintiff,

VS.   : JUDICIAL DISTRICT OF BOSTON

ROGER ALLAN MERCHANT   : November 10, 2007

AND

MARY SAMANTHA MERCHANT   **COMPLAINT FOR**
                               JUDICIAL FORECLOSURE

Defendants,

Defendants, Roger Allan Merchant and Mary Samantha Merchant ("Borrowers") complain and allege as follows:

VENUE

1. It is agreed that the venue in the Court of the County of Suffolk is proper under the laws of the State of Massachusetts because the property subject to this action is located within Suffolk County.

THE PARTIES

2. It is agreed that the Bank is, and at all times mentioned herein was, a Massachusetts bank, chartered by the Federal Deposit Insurance Corporation, and doing business in the State of Massachusetts.

3. It is agreed that Defendants, Roger Allan Merchant and Mary Samantha Merchant ("Borrowers" or "Defendants"), are, and at all relevant times herein were, individuals residing in the State of Massachusetts.

THE LOAN DOCUMENTATION

4. It is agreed that on July 20, 1985, the defendants, Roger Allan Merchant and Mary Samantha Merchant, owed the Plaintiff $200,000 as evidenced by his note dated on said date and payable to the order of the Plaintiff, together with an interest at the rate of 6 percent per annum until July 20, 1990, being variable thereafter, and together with all costs of collection, including reasonable attorney's fees, in the event of foreclosure of the mortgage securing the note. Under the terms of the Note, Borrower agreed to make monthly payments of $1,020.00, comprised of principal and interest. The interest was calculated at a fixed rate of 8 percent per year, payable on the last day of each month. The Note provided upon default the holder could declare all monies payable thereunder immediately due, owing and payable. The Note also provided for a default interest rate of 3 percent plus the contracted rate.

5. It is agreed that on said date, by deed of that date, the defendants, Roger Allan Merchant and Mary Samantha Merchant, to secure said note, mortgages to the plaintiff the real estate described in Exhibit "A" attached hereto and made a part hereof. Said deed is conditioned upon the payment of said note according to its tenor and was recorded on 10 September 2007 in Volume 24, Page 204 of the Boston Registry of Deeds.

6. It is agreed that said note and mortgage are still owned by the plaintiff, and the debt is due and partially unpaid.

7. It is CONTESTED that Bank complied with all of its contractual obligations under the Note by disbursing monies as required.

LOAN DEFAULTS

8. It is CONTESTED that the defendants, Roger Allan Merchant and Mary Samantha Merchant, have defaulted under the terms of the mortgage note and deed.

9. It is CONTESTED that although the note is in default and demand was made upon the defendant, said defendant has neglected and refused to make payment.

WHEREFORE, THE PLAINTIFF CLAIMS

An enjoinment is made on this case brought before the court, until such time that

1. An audit of the account in question can be made by the defendants' accountant.

2. Such other equitable relief as the Court may deem necessary.

3. Reasonable attorneys' fees as a result of unlawful action are paid by the plaintiff.

Dated at Boston, Massachusetts, this 10th of November, 2007.

NOTICE

NOTICE: A person who is unemployed or underemployed and who (for a continuous period of at least two years to the commencement of this foreclosure action) owned and occupied the property being foreclosed as such person's principal residence, may be entitled to contain relief provisions under Massachusetts General Statute 32-67W, as amended. You should consult an attorney to determine your rights under this law.

THE DEFENDANTS

BY:

_____

Roger Allan Merchant and
Mary Samantha Merchant

Appendix H

Sample Small Claim's Court Fee Chart

Figure 3.3: Sample county clerk's office fee chart

June Aster, County Court Clerk

County of Haverson

101 Court House Square

McMureyville, XX XXXXX

Filing fees

Small claims court filing fee $100

Transfer to district court $250

Appeals $100

Counterclaim $50

Rent escrow $75

Debt collection escrow $65

Debtor examination $75

Request for disclosure (per defendant) $15

Request to show cause (per defendant) $15

Miscellaneous fees

Certified copies $10

Defendant service $25

DWI chemical dependency assessment $125

Exemption certificate (w/certified copy) $40

Executions $50

Fax filings (each 50 pages or part thereof) $25

Judgment search (per name) $5

Jury fee $175

Motions and responses to motions $50

Satisfaction of judgment $5

Subpoena $15

Transcript of judgment $30

Summary of judgment $20

Trust account filing $45

Uncertified copies $5

Writs $40

As established by the Honorable County Council for the county of Haverson on the 1st day of June 20XX, to become effective on the 1st of July 20XX, or until revised by action of the County Council in a regular public meeting in the future.

Helpful Web sites

BANKRUPTCY

Bankruptcy Management Solutions
A valuable Web site for anyone in a financial bind who is considering bankruptcy as a way out. Provides comprehensive information on all chapters of bankruptcy.
www.bankruptcy.com

HOUSING

Evictus

A helpful Web site that provides information on evictions, official forms, filing fee information, and more.

www.evictus.com

Rental Housing Online

The Internet's comprehensive rental property location.

www.rhol.com

Texas Low Income Housing Information Service

Organizes and empowers low-income people and communities to take the initiative to solve their community development problems.

www.texashousing.org

LEGAL

Legal Assistance Resource Center of Connecticut

A non-profit that advocates for policies that benefit low-income people.

www.larcc.org

Legal Definitions

An in-depth Web site for hundreds of definitions pertaining to legal matters.

www.legal-definitions.com

The 'LECTRIC LAW LIBRARY

A comprehensive online library of legal resources.

www.lectlaw.com

U.S. Foreclosure Laws

A comprehensive resource of detailed foreclosure laws for each state, as well as links to other foreclosure resources.

www.foreclosurelaw.org

MONEY MANAGEMENT

Credit.com

A comprehensive resource for all things credit-related, such as credit reports, credit cards, banking, loans, and debt help.

www.credit.com

Mind Your Finances

An online resource for personal finance advice, useful tools, and educational materials.

www.mindyourfinances.com

SavingAdvice.com

A personal finance Web site created specifically to show you different ways to save money.

www.savingadvice.com

U.S. GOVERNMENT

Federal Trade Commission

An independent agency of the U.S. federal government that encourages free enterprise and investigates unfair trade practices.

www.ftc.gov

The Federal Reserve Bank of Dallas

One of 12 regional Reserve Banks that, along with the Board of Governors in Washington, D.C., make up the nation's central bank.

www.dallasfed.org

The U.S. Department of Justice: Their mission is to enforce the law and defend the interests of the United States; to ensure public safety against threats foreign and domestic; to provide federal leadership in preventing and controlling crime; to seek just punishment for those guilty of unlawful behavior; and to ensure fair and impartial administration of justice for Americans.

www.usdoj.gov

 # Glossary

The following outlines one of the most comprehensive list of bankruptcy, foreclosure, and repossession terms that you will find anywhere. Be sure to refer to it at any stage in your financial misfortune process.

Adjustable Rate Mortgage: A loan for a real estate property with a set timeframe, where the interest rates increase, commonly between three to seven years, making mortgage payments more expensive.

Adversary Proceeding: A complaint filed with the court dealing with lawsuits affiliated with a case of bankruptcy.

Assignment of Deed of Trust: A legal statement that moves propitious interest in a deed of trust and note.

Assume: This refers to an agreement to continue to carry out specific duties under a contract or lease.

Authorization to Sign as Agent Agreement: The form that allows an agent to sign of document for a beneficiary.

Automatic Stay: A sanction that stops foreclosures, lawsuits, embellishments, and all motions of collection toward the debtor as soon a petition is filed for bankruptcy.

Bankruptcy: A legal option a person or business can file for if they are unable to repay their outstanding debts.

Bankruptcy Administrator: Comparable to the U.S. trustee, this is a judiciary officer that serves in Alabama and North Carolina's judicial districts who is responsible for administering bankruptcy cases; trustees and estates; monitoring disclosure statements and plans; reviewing overseeing application fees; creditors' committees; and fulfilling other statutory duties.

Bankruptcy Code: An unofficial reference to Title 11 of the United States Code (11 U.S.C. §§ 101-1330), the federal bankruptcy law.

Bankruptcy Court: A unit of the district court where a bankruptcy judgment is carried out in traditional effective service in every district.

Bankruptcy Estate: Refers to all equitable or legal interests of the person in debt that is in property when a debtor files for bankruptcy.

Bankruptcy Judge: A U.S. district court magistrate who is head of the court and holds the power to make decisions over a federal bankruptcy case.

Bankruptcy Petition: In free-willed cases, cases that are voluntary and that set the bankruptcy case in motion.

Beneficiary: The legal hearing that lets a debtor discharge certain obligations or debts without having to pay the full amount. Also refers to giving the debtor time to reorganize financial affairs in order to repay debts.

BID Authorization Letter: A written permission that instructs the trustee to open a bid at a foreclosure auction on the lender's behalf.

Breach: The failure to follow through on a promise that was originally made in a contract.

Calling Date: The date that your repossession case will be heard in court.

Calling Up Notice: A repossession notice that is sent to you if you have missed payments on your mortgage or secured loan. It lets you know that your lender is beginning the repossession proceedings.

Chapter 7: The type of bankruptcy that allows the bankruptcy court to sell all of a defaulter's property that is liable and have the profit paid to their creditors.

Chapter 9: The chapter of the bankruptcy code that allows the reorganization of municipalities (including cities, towns, counties, villages, municipal utilities, taxing districts, and school districts).

Chapter 11: The type of bankruptcy that applies to corporations that need to file for financial reorganizations.

Chapter 12: The type of bankruptcy that covers individuals in these job categories who are financially distressed but also have a regular annual income.

Chapter 13: The type of bankruptcy that requires you to pay a certain amount of your debts to creditors over a period of time.

Chapter 15: This is the bankruptcy code chapter that handles all cases of cross-border liquidation.

Claim: An assertion by a creditor to a debtor's repayment from assets or debtor.

Confirmation: This refers to the consent of a bankruptcy judges' plans of restructuring or eliminating in a Chapter 11 bankruptcy, or a payment plan in Chapter 12 or 13 bankruptcies.

Consumer Debtor: An individual who has debts related to products or services they have purchased.

Consumer Debts: Acquired debts from personal use rather than business use.

Contested Matter: Disputed matters that are not included in the definition of adversary process within

Rule 7001. This includes all matters excluding claim objections.

Contingent Claim: The type of claim a debtor may owe with certain factors present.

Credit Report: A report that lists a history of how well you have managed your credit in the past. It includes account balances, late or missed payments, and on-time payments.

Credit Score: An indication of how attractive you are as a borrower to lenders. Average credit scores range anywhere from 300 – 900.

Creditor: A person or an organization that a borrower is in debt with or claims to be owed money by that person.

Current Monthly Income: An average of the monthly income of the person in debt, starting six moths before the start of the bankruptcy case. This average includes earnings from the spouse of the debtor if the petition is joint, as well as regular contributions from non-debtors to household expenses.

Debtor: The individual who, under the bankruptcy code, has filed a petition for relief.

Declaration of Default: Written documentation that tells a trustee to legally record a default notice and sell a property that is secured to satisfy unpaid obligations.

Decree: This refers to the judge's decision as to who they are in favor of during repossession proceedings — the defender or the pursuer.

Decree of Removing: As known as "ejection." This means that you are no longer legally allowed to live in the property and must leave.

Deed of Trust: Written documentation of what the property is that is being offered as a security in order to repay an obligation.

Default: This is the failure to honor an agreement of a legal contract, such as a loan.

Defendant: The business or individual that a lawsuit is filed against.

Discharge: Letting the person(s) filing for bankruptcy not be held accountable for certain debts that are able to be discharged by the bankruptcy code. This also makes creditors not able to collect on debt or communicate about debt from the person(s) filling bankruptcy.

Dischargeable Debt: Money owed that is excused by the bankruptcy code.

Disclosure Statement: A statement prepared by the person filling for Chapter 11, with information to assess the plan of reorganization for Chapter 11.

Durable Power of Attorney: A person whom you appoint to make financial decisions for you in the event that you become unable to do so.

Ejection Order/Warrant of Ejection: This is a court order that states you must move out of your home so that it can be repossessed by the lender and sold.

Equity: The amount of money that you have in your home, or the profit you would make off it if you were to sell it.

Executory Contract or Lease: A lease or a contract where both sides still have tasks that need to be completed.

Exemptions, Exempt Property: Property that is allowed to be kept by person(s) filling for bankruptcy, under bankruptcy code or state law.

Extension Agreement: A written agreement that provides additional time to repay an obligation.

Family Farmer or Family Fisherman: An individual, married couple, partnership, or corporation that is employed in the agricultural or fishing operations and meets the standards to file for a Chapter 12 petition.

First Calling: This is the first time your case is heard in court.

Foreclosure: A situation in which a creditor, generally a mortgage company or bank, has to enforce repayment of a loan by selling a home at a public auction.

Fraudulent Transfer: When a person(s) filing for bankruptcy, property is moved with the purpose of fraud or receives less than the value of the property.

Fresh Start: A description of a person's situation after they have completed the bankruptcy process.

Heritable Property: Used in eviction cases, this term refers to property and land that cannot be moved.

Initial Writ: This is a document that lets you know that a county court application has been made. This is sent to an individual when their lender is applying for the right to repossess property or to order an individual to vacate the property.

Joint Administration: A court-approved mechanism that allows two cases to be conducted with each other.

Joint Petition: A petition filed by husband and wife for bankruptcy.

Judicial Foreclosure: A lawsuit against you for failure to pay your mortgage.

Junior Lien: A claim upon property that has been legally recorded following to another legal claim that is on the same property.

Lien: The right to use or sell a borrower's property for payment for money owed.

Limited Power of Attorney: A legal document that allows an individual to act as an attorney-in-fact for someone else, but with stated limitations.

Liquidation: This occurs when a debtor's property is sold to repay creditors or used for their advantage.

Liquidated Claim: A creditor's request for a certain amount of money after the debtor's property has been liquidated.

Living Trust: A kind of will that allows you to distribute and manage your assets while you are alive and then control the distribution of those assets after you die.

Living Will: A legal document that ensures your wishes regarding your health are known prior to an illness.

Means Test: A provision that determines if you qualify for Chapter 7 bankruptcy or must file for Chapter 13 bankruptcy. It is determined by whether your income falls below a certain level.

Modification Agreement: Written documentation that changes the terms of a note or deed of trust and is signed by both the beneficiary and the lender.

Mortgage: A legal and binding contract that pledges property as a security for a loan.

Motion to Lift the Automatic Stay: A claim a creditor uses to take action against a defaulter's property that would be protected by automatic stay.

No-asset Case: A Chapter 7 case where there are not any assets that meet the unsecured claims of creditors.

Nonjudicial Foreclosure: A process in which your lender does not have to go to court to take your home.

Nondischargeable Debt: Debt that is not able to be discharged under the bankruptcy code. This includes debts for alimony or child support, certain taxes, and a home mortgage, as well as debts that arise from death or personal injury that was due to intoxication and debts from a criminal fine.

Note: An IOU, or written promise, to pay a loan.

Notice of Default: A written notice of grantor's failure to meet agreement under a deed of trust.

Notice of Rescission: A document that stops the consequences associated with a notice of default. This only becomes valid once a default has become restored.

Notice of Trustee's Sale: A written document that characterizes the items being sold from a trustee's sale.

Party in Interest: A group of people the court has the ability to interview to help make judgment in a bankruptcy case.

Petition Preparer: A business that prepares bankruptcy petitions that is not authorized to practice law.

Plan: A detailed plan generated by the debtor on how they plan over a period of time to repay creditors.

Plaintiff: A business or individual that files a complaint formally with the court.

Postpetition Transfer: Transfer of person(s) filing bankruptcy made after the beginning of the bankruptcy.

Postponement: A verbal announcement made at the trustee's sale, which sets up for a new date and time for the sale. The original location cannot be changed.

Prebankruptcy Planning: The planning of the property of a person(s) filing bankruptcy, in order for them to have maximum time to use the exemptions to their benefit.

Preference or Preferential Debt Payment: A 90-day period before a the person in debt is able to file for bankruptcy (or, if the creditor was an insider, one year); this is a debt payment made to a creditor that gives them more than what they would generally receive in the debtor's Chapter 7 case.

Preliminary Injunction: A superior court judge-granted order that prevents the trustee from moving on with taking any more action on a foreclosure file until a settlement is reached or a trial.

Pre-Publication Period: A three-month waiting period that follows the recording of a note of default in a foreclosure. This term was formerly called the "reinstatement period" prior to 1986.

Proof of Claim: An official form that lists verifying documentation and a statement that is written and filed by a creditor that discusses the reason the debtor owes the creditor money.

Property of the Estate: All equitable or legal interests of the person(s) filing bankruptcy in property at the beginning of the case.

Publication Letter: A letter from a trustee to a creditor, allowing trustee to move on with sale of home, once the letter has been returned and completed.

Publication Period: A letter from a trustee to a creditor, allowing the trustee to move on with the sale of home, once the letter has been returned and completed.

Pursuer: The individual who began the legal action; for example, the lender in a repossession case.

Quit-claim Deed: A deed that conveys whatever ownership the grantor has and makes no guaranties about the title.

Reconveyance: This is a recorded document that provides notice that the loan was secured and has been paid in full.

Redemption Period: A set amount of time after a foreclosure sale where the original homeowners can purchase back their home.

Reinstatement: If past-due payments of a loan has been made, along with the fees and expenses incurred by the trustee, this refers to a settling of a default and restoring of the loan to the current status.

Reinstatement Period: A period of time from the recording of the notice of the default until five business days before the sale date. Any time during this process, the loan that is in default may be reinstated.

Reponing Note: This is a request that allows an individual to ask for the repossession case to be heard when you are able to attend. A good case for not having attended the original court case will be necessary.

Repossession: The seizing of collateral in the event that the loan on that collateral is in default.

Request for Notice: Recorded documentation that request a copy of a notice of default as well as the sale notice to be sent to the requestor.

Return and Account of Sale by Trustee: An itemization assembled by the trustee, which is sent to highest bidder at a foreclosure auction. This is showing a complete accounting of a successful bid.

Schedules: Official forms filed by a person in debt, with a petition that shows debtor's liabilities, assets, and other financial information.

Section 2 Order: This is a court order that can be used to stop repossession or at least delay it. This is only permissible for certain individuals.

Section 24 Notice: This notice is sent to individuals who have missed mortgage or secure loan payments. It lets them know that repossession proceedings will begin.

Secured Debt: Debt that is backed by some type of collateral (mortgage, pledge, other lien), which the lender can pursue if agreement is defaulted.

Secured Loan: A loan that has collateral attached to it. For example, a mortgage or car loan.

Short Sale: An agreement that is made between a borrower and lender, where the lender accepts less than the total amount due as total payment.

Small Business Case: A Chapter 11 case, where the debtor is able to have more oversight by the U.S. trustee than others filing for Chapter 11. This certain code is set up to cut the amount of time a small business debtor is in bankruptcy.

Statement/Invoice: A complete list of all of the fees and expenses incurred by the trustee at the end of a foreclosure proceeding.

Statement of Claim: A portion of the summons where the pursuer is able to outline the facts of why they are taking an individual to court.

Statement of Financial Affairs: A list of questions that must be in writing by the debtor on an official form that highlights the transfer of property, sources of income, and lawsuits by lenders.

Statement of Intention: A Chapter 7 declaration that discusses and outlines a debtor's plans for repaying debts.

Stayed: This means that a case is stopped to see how things will work out. During this time, a lender can recall the case if the terms of agreement are not met.

Substantive Consolidation: A method where assets and liabilities are placed in one category to pay lenders. Courts do not like to allow this type of debt consolidation because the consolidation itself must be explained, plus the pros and the cons that the creditors receive.

Substitution of Trustee: Where another beneficiary is appointed

trustee, must be signed by a public notary, and needs to be recorded with a county recorder.

Tax Lien: A claim placed upon a property that collects unpaid property taxes.

Term: The amount of time the debtor has to pay off a loan.

Toll: Refers to the ending during bankruptcy of any further foreclosure acts.

Transfer: When a person in debt leaves their property.

Trustee: The individual of the bankruptcy property who exercises statutory powers for an unsecured creditor, under the supervision of the court and the U.S. trustee or bankruptcy administrator. This is either a private individual or a corporation that is appointed in all Chapter 7, Chapter 12, and Chapter 13 cases, as well as some Chapter 11 cases.

Trustee's Deed Upon Sale: The written documentation by the trustee that legally transfers ownership at the foreclosure sale from the trustee to the bidder.

U.S. Trustee: This is an official elected by the attorney general who plays the administrative role in bankruptcy cases in over one or more federal judicial districts assigned to them.

Unsecured Loan: A loan that has no collateral attached to it; for example, medical bills or credit card debt.

Undersecured Claim: This refers to a debt that is secured by property and is estimated to be worth more than the total amount of debt owed.

Unliquidated Claim: A claim where a certain amount has not been decided on yet.

Unscheduled Debt: A debt that has not been filled in the original schedules, but should have been filed. Depending on the circumstances, the debt could or could not be charged.

Unsecured Claim: Credit that has been given by a lender based solely on a debtor's future ability to pay, such as an auto loan.

Voluntary Transfer: Consensual transfer of a debtor's property.

Will: A legal document that clears the path to the orderly distribution of your assets following your death.

Repossession Stoppers
www.repossession-stoppers.com

Saving Electricity
http://michaelbluejay.com/electricity

T.D. Service Company
www.tdsf.com/foregloss.htm

"The Foreclosure Survival Guide, Keep Your House or Walk Away with Money in Your Pocket," "Chapter 13 Bankruptcy, Keep Your Property & Repay Debts Over Time," 9th Edition, Stephen Elias, Nolo, September 2008

The Motley Fool
www.fool.com

"The New Bankruptcy: Will It Work for You?," Stephen Elias, Nolo, 2006

Typical Usage of Various Appliances
www.kwcityelectric.com/appliances.php

U.S. Courts
www.uscourts.gov

U.S. Department of Energy
www.energysavers.gov/your_home/space_heating_cooling/index.cfm/mytopic=12390

U.S. Energy Information Administration
www.eia.doe.gov/cneaf/electricity/epm/table5_6_a.html

Biography

About the Author

Born in the coastal community of Duxbury, Massachusetts, Tracy Carr discovered a love of writing at an early age. After completing her B.A. in journalism from the University of New Hampshire, she went on to get an M.S. in mass communications from Boston University. Tracy resides in the Raleigh, North Carolina, area with her husband and three daughters.

Index